Newman on development

NEWMAN ON DEVELOPMENT

The search for an explanation in history

Nicholas Lash

PATMOS PRESS
Shepherdstown, West Virginia
1975

Copyright © 1975 by Nicholas Lash. First published 1975. All rights
reserved. *Nihil obstat*: Francis J. Bartlett, Censor. *Imprimatur*: David
Norris, Vicar General, Westminster, 21 July 1975. This book is set in
11 on 12pt Baskerville and printed in Great Britain by The Bowering
Press Ltd, Plymouth

ISBN 0-915762-01-3   LC number 75-16649

Contents

Preface

In view of the interest aroused by Newman's *Essay on Development* in the first decade of this century, and of the renewed concentration on problems arising from an increased sensitivity to the historical nature of christian truth, it is surprising that a work, the pioneering status of which is widely acknowledged, should have been submitted to comparatively little detailed examination. My decision to attempt a methodological exploration of the *Essay* was dictated largely by the conviction that only when this prior task had been performed could further questions concerning the enduring significance of the *Essay* profitably be discussed. In chapters 1 and 7, therefore, I have indicated the wider context within which, I believe, the usefulness of this exploration is to be assessed. While I did not expect my long-suffering publishers to produce this thing in garish colours for less than the price of a packet of cigarettes, it is nevertheless my hope that it will be found to be of some interest and significance beyond the ranks of professional Newmanists.

I am grateful to my colleagues at St Edmund's House, Cambridge, for providing that context of scholarship and humanity which made the work of preparation not only tolerable but enjoyable. Amongst those whose advice, friendship and encouragement have meant a great deal to me, I would like to thank, first and foremost, Professor Peter Baelz, without whom this thing would never have seen the light of day, and also Professor Gordon Rupp and Dr J. Derek Holmes. In common with all recent students of Newman, I owe an immense debt of gratitude to Fr Stephen Dessain for the patience and kindness with which he unfailingly responded to even the most trivial request for advice and information, and to all the members of the Birmingham Oratory for their hospitality, and for permission to use unpublished material. I would also like to thank Canon R. Greenfield, of Portland, Oregon, and Dr Paul Misner, of Boston College, for permission to make use of their unpublished doctoral dissertations.

Finally I should like to thank Christine Brown for typing as faultlessly as she does rapidly, and Laurence Bright for his editorial help.

Nicholas Lash

Abbreviations

The Essay on Development

Dev	The third (revised) edition of 1878. References are to chapter, section and sub–section numbers : eg *Dev* 1.1.2; *Dev* 6.3.3.23; *Dev* 12.4. For the sake of consistency, this numbering has been retained even for those chapters, such as *Dev* 10, in which—in the standard editions—the sections are marked §1, §2, and so on, while the page-headings refer to 'sect 1' throughout the chapter.
	Where a chapter is introduced by one or more sub-sections before the first section-heading, such sub-sections are referred to as eg *Dev* 4.0.1; *Dev* 8.0.2.
	The sub-sections of the Introduction are referred to as eg *Dev* Int 5.
1845	The first edition
1846	The second edition.
1878	The revised edition when a general reference is made to it in the text in comparison with *1845* or *1846*.

Other Works by Newman

So far as possible, the abbreviations used are those listed in J. Rickaby, *Index to the Works of John Henry Cardinal Newman* (London 1914), with the additions recommended by C. S. Dessain, *Letters and Diaries of John Henry Newman*, xi (London 1961).

Apo	*Apologia pro Vita Sua.*
Ari	*The Arians of the Fourth Century.*
Ath i, ii	*Select Treatises of St Athanasius.*
AW	*John Henry Newman: Autobiographical Writings.*
Call	*Callista.*
Campaign	*My Campaign in Ireland.*
Cath Ser	*Catholic Sermons of Cardinal Newman.*

Consulting	*On Consulting the Faithful in Matters of Doctrine.* See Coulson [1961].
DA	*Discussions and Arguments.*
Diff I, II	*Certain Difficulties Felt by Anglicans in Catholic Teaching.*
Ess I,II	*Essays Critical and Historical.*
Flanagan	The Flanagan Paper. See de Achaval [1958].
GA	*An Essay in Aid of a Grammar of Assent.*
HS I, II, III	*Historical Sketches.*
Idea	*The Idea of a University.*
Insp	Essays on Inspiration. See Holmes [1967b].
Jfc	*Lectures on the Doctrine of Justification.*
KC	*Correspondence of John Henry Newman with John Keble and Others.*
L&D XI–	*The Letters and Diaries of John Henry Newman.*
LG	*Loss and Gain.*
MD	*Meditations and Devotions.*
Mir	*Two Essays on Biblical and on Ecclesiastical Miracles.*
Mix	*Discourses Addressed to Mixed Congregations.*
Moz I, II	*Letters and Correspondence of John Henry Newman.*
OP	Oratory Papers. See Murray, P. [1969].
OS	*Sermons Preached on Various Occasions.*
PN	*The Philosophical Notebook.* See Sillem [1970].
PS I–VIII	*Parochial and Plain Sermons.*
Perrone	The Perrone Paper. See Lynch [1935].
Prepos	*Present Position of Catholics.*
SD	*Sermons Bearing on Subjects of the Day.*
SE	*Stray Essays.*
SN	*Sermon Notes.*
Theses	*Theses de Fide.* See Tristram [1937].
TT	*Tracts Theological and Ecclesiastical.*
US	*Fifteen Sermons Preached before the University of Oxford.*
VM I, II	*The Via Media.*
VV	*Verses on Various Occasions.*

Other Abbreviations

BOA	Birmingham Oratory Archives.
CUL *Add* MSS	Cambridge University Library, Additional Manuscripts.

Dz   Denzinger, H. and Rahner, K., eds. *Enchiridion*
                Symbolorum. [31]Rome 1957.
Dei Verbum   Vatican ii. *Constitution on Divine Revelation.*
Lumen Gentium   Vatican ii. *Constitution on the Church.*

With the exception of those of Newman's works referred to by the
abbreviations listed above, the items in the bibliography are referred
to by author and date of publication : eg Dessain [1957b]. For
abbreviations used in the bibliography itself, see the note immediately
preceding it.

I

Introduction

'A people without history is not redeemed from time' (Eliot T. S.
[1944] p 43). The official response of the Roman catholic church
to the mounting pressures of historical consciousness, during the
past century and a half, has been to seek 'redemption from time',
not through the acceptance of its historicity,[1] with all the risks
that this entails, but by claiming, so far as possible, absolute status
for its past achievements, insights, affirmations and institutional
forms. It is as if the church were proud of its past, but fearful of
that dimension of time within which the past occurred, within
which the problems of the present have to be negotiated, and within which alone the future can be born.

In spite of the preference shown, in recent years, for images of
the church which take its historicity into account,[2] attempts to
submit the church's teaching and institutions to accepted canons of
exegetical and historical inquiry and evaluation still frequently
meet with hostility and suspicion. To the extent that the church's
understanding of its past is, in practice, sheltered from responsible hermeneutical and historical criticism, talk of God's 'pilgrim
people' is in danger of becoming mere rhetoric.

'It seems safe to estimate that more has been written about
development of doctrine since 1950 than was written between
Newman's *Essay* and the promulgation of the dogma of the assumption' (Pelikan [1969] pp 40–1). Yet even this increasing interest shown, during the past quarter of a century, in the problem
of doctrinal development, does not necessarily indicate that the
historicity of christian truth is being taken sufficiently seriously.
Though the constitution *Dei Verbum*, of the second Vatican Council, marked a step forward, it was not able adequately to confront
the central problem of criteriology (See Baum [1967d] pp 66–9;
Leuba [1968] pp 491–5; Ratzinger [1969] p 185; Van Leeuwen
[1967] p 9).

In this situation, a fresh examination of Newman's *Essay on the Development of Christian Doctrine* may prove fruitful, since Newman was one of the first catholic theologians seriously to attempt to hold in tension the demands of historical consciousness and the christian conviction that the gospel of Jesus Christ is irreplaceable and unchangeable.

Nearly every study of doctrinal development continues to acknowledge the seminal influence of the *Essay*. Thus Pelikan, who regards the *Essay* as 'the almost inevitable starting point for an investigation of development of doctrine' ([1969] p 3), recognises that 'the *Essay on Development* anticipated later generations of scholars by being the first to ask some of the questions about tradition, development, and continuity with which the history of doctrine must deal today' ([1971] p 58). He continues: 'Curiously, then, any student of historical theology is obliged by the facts of historical development—even though both of them would be shocked by the conjunction—to link the names of John Henry Newman and Adolf von Harnack'.[3]

But recognition of the historical significance of the *Essay* would be quite compatible with a judgement to the effect that shifts in method and perspective have, in recent decades, been so considerable that, although 'The study of doctrinal development is a study of importance . . . the debates of the eighteenth and nineteenth centuries must not be expected to throw any great light on the road we have to tread in pursuit of it at the present time' (Wiles [1967] p 2). So far as Newman's *Essay* is concerned, a judgement such as this rests on two principal components: firstly, an assessment of the aims, method and patterns of argument in the *Essay* itself; secondly, an assessment of the present climate of debate, and the extent to which it differs from that within which the *Essay* was written.

So far as the first of these components is concerned, there has always been, and continues to be, considerable disagreement concerning the nature of Newman's argument in the *Essay*, and concerning the nature of that 'theory of development' which Newman is supposed to have articulated in his writings. The range of disagreement is sufficiently wide to create a presumption that a detailed analysis of the argument of the *Essay* may be necessary before it is possible summarily to evaluate its relevance, or lack of relevance, to our contemporary debates. This presumption is strengthened when we observe that, in spite of the considerable quantity of literature that has been produced on Newman's 'theory of doctrinal development',[4] there have been very few studies devoted, in recent years, to a detailed examination of the *Essay* as a whole (cf Chadwick [1957]; Guitton [1933]; Walgrave [1957]), and none systematically devoted to an analysis of its methodological structure.

According to Maurice Nédoncelle, 'A commentary on the *Essay on Development* from the historical point of view is a task that cries out to be done', both tracing Newman's sources and assessing the use he made of them, and 'to compare the state of Newman's knowledge with the most established results of our own in order to distinguish what is living from what is dead in the general proof which the author believed he had discovered' ([1968] p 392). Although I am concerned, in this study, with making a contribution to the task outlined by Nédoncelle, I shall, for two reasons, only approach the goal that he describes partially, and tangentially.

In the first place, I am a theologian rather than a historian, and therefore am not competent directly to undertake the historical comparison requested by him.

In the second place, Newman's own stress on the hypothetical nature of his argument, and on the fact that he had not exhaustively tested his hypotheses against the historical data (*Dev* Int 21), together with the fact that it was issues of method, rather than content, which divided Newman from his contemporary critics, which underlay the debates at the time of the modernist crisis, and which lie behind Maurice Wiles' judgement that the *Essay* is now of merely historical interest, entitle us to suggest that a thematic and methodological analysis of the *Essay* may be of more fundamental importance than an (undoubtedly necessary) historical commentary.

The picture that emerges from any study of the *Essay* will depend partly upon the questions which the commentator puts to it : questions which express his own personal concern. The concern of the contemporary critics of the *Essay*—whether they were anglicans such as Milman and Mozley, or Roman catholics such as Brownson—was primarily defensive. Loisy was concerned with those features of the *Essay* which harmonised with the perspective on problems of doctrinal historicity that he was attempting to articulate. Chadwick took the *Essay* as an expression of that shift from static to dynamic conceptions of christianity which was characteristic of the period. Walgrave regarded the *Essay* as the key which would enable him to unlock the complexity of Newman's thought and to elaborate a synthesis of it. My own concern has been to understand, as fully as possible, the multiple themes and patterns of argument in the *Essay* so as to be able, without unfaithfulness to Newman's thought, to provide the materials on the basis of which theologians may tackle the further question : what light can the *Essay* cast on the significantly different situation in which christian theology today attempts to come to terms with the problem of change and continuity in christian doctrine ?

It may be that such a study as this is more likely to be of interest in Europe than in England. In this country, in which Newman has rarely been taken seriously precisely as a theologian, we are apt to overlook the considerable influence which interpretations of the *Essay* have had, and continue to have, on European debates on the development of doctrine.[5] Whether or not these interpretations have been accurate; whether the influence of the *Essay* has been beneficial or detrimental to theological progress; at least it is certain that Barter's prophecy, made in 1846, has not been fulfilled : 'His earlier publications "will follow him"', and retain a high place among the standard works of English divinity when his "Treatise on Development" has sunk into merited oblivion' ([1846] p 11).

The text of the *Essay* with which I have decided to work is that of the third, revised edition of 1878. This decision was dictated principally by the fact that it is this edition which has enjoyed by far the widest circulation and, therefore, the most considerable influence on subsequent theology. Moreover, although—as we shall see—not all the changes which Newman introduced enhanced the consistency of his argument, some of them do bear witness to developments in his thinking between 1845 and 1878. No critical comparative edition of the three editions of the *Essay* has ever been published (the variations between *1845* and *1846* are slight and, for the most part, insignificant. They are tabulated in the Appendix). I have been content to draw attention to those variations which in any way suggest a shift in the emphasis or form of an argument.

The task of analysing the *Essay* is not rendered easier by the fact that most of the themes and patterns of argument occur, in one form or another, in other places in Newman's writings, and have already attracted attention from his commentators. I have tried, so far as possible, to situate individual features of the *Essay* in the context of the rest of his published work and his correspondence. 'It would be impossible for any man living to go through all that has been written on Newman, or answer all the objections that have been raised, against works dealing with subjects so difficult, so complex and so numerous' (Williams, W. J. [1906] p 41). The flow of secondary material has shown no signs of drying up in the sixty-nine years since that was written. The use made of such material in this study is, therefore, necessarily selective.

Newman always held the persuasive force of cumulative, interlocking argumentation in higher regard than the relentless logic of linear deduction. For this reason, the structure of the *Essay* is so complex, and its components so interdependent, that any attempt such as this to isolate its principal patterns is unavoidably overschematic. The system that I have adopted of numbering the sections of each chapter is intended to show the relative importance of particular themes and methodological features, and also, by facilitating cross-referencing, to indicate the mutual interdependence of the constituent elements of the *Essay*. It may be said of many of the sections of this study, as Newman said in 1845 of the 'tests of a true development', that 'instances which have been arranged under one head might in some cases have been referred to another' (*1845* p 93).

Chapter 2 will be concerned with the question : what was Newman's personal aim and purpose in writing the *Essay*? Chapter 3 concentrates on some key features of Newman's general method of argument in 'concrete matters', and especially in regard to problems of christian historiography. In chapter 4 we shall examine those aspects of the *Essay* which are most closely connected with his claim that, 'from the nature of the human mind, time is necessary for the full comprehension and perfection of great ideas' (*Dev* Int 21). The following chapter discusses the hermeneutical counterpart to that claim : namely, the principle that later stages in the history of an idea may legitimately be used to interpret its comparatively obscure and ambiguous beginnings. In chapter 6, by discussing such questions as the meaning, in the

Essay, of a 'true development', the role of ecclesiastical authority in authenticating developments, and the relationship between the argument of the *Essay* and debates concerning the 'essence' of christianity, we shall try to cast some light on the problem of the normative standpoint adopted by Newman. The final chapter will outline the history of interpretations of the *Essay* since the turn of the century in order to suggest, in conclusion, the extent to which this study, by inviting a revision of certain received views of the *Essay*, might contribute to the discussion of further questions concerning its relevance and significance for the theological problems of our own day.

2

The aim and purpose of
the *Essay*

What was Newman's personal aim and purpose in writing the *Essay*? Too many accounts of his 'theory of development' proceed on the assumption that this 'theory' can be described and assessed more or less independently of the context provided by the answer to this question. In Newman's case, such a procedure is bound to fail, not only because he was a controversialist rather than a systematic theologian but also, and more fundamentally, because the individual strands in his web of argument are so tightly interwoven that it is only possible to do them justice in continual reference to the whole. In particular, while any formal distinction between 'aim' and 'method' in the *Essay* may not be pressed too far, throughout the work the elements of the latter are determined, shaped and qualified by their relationship to the former. Therefore, whereas the emphasis in the following four chapters will be on the methods of argument in the *Essay* : on its thematic components and their interrelationship, in this chapter we shall concentrate on the problem of why the *Essay* was written and what, in Newman's estimation, it was and was not intended to achieve. Our principal sources, apart from the Introduction to the *Essay* itself, will be Newman's references to the *Essay* in his correspondence and later writings.

After some introductory remarks concerning the change in ecclesiological perspectives which led up to the writing of the *Essay*, and to Newman's decision to become a Roman Catholic (*2.1*), we shall discuss its apologetic preoccupation and its relationship to that 'via media' which Newman was now partially abandoning (*2.2*), and the significance of his insistence that his 'theory' is an 'hypothesis to account for a difficulty' (*Dev* Int 21—*2.3*).

2.1 *The shift in Newman's ecclesiological viewpoint*
Before 1839, Newman had not doubted that the church of

England was a branch, or local embodiment, of the church of Christ. However defective and corrupt that English church which the participants in the Oxford Movement sought to restore to its former purity, independence from state control and evangelically single-minded commitment to 'Apostolical principles'[1], it was not in schism. That it was not was of vital importance to one who believed that the saving grace of God was communicated to man in and through the community of the visible church. The more convinced he became that the church of England *was* in schism, the more he believed his personal salvation to be imperilled[2] because, while 'all divines, ancient and modern, Roman as well as our own, grant even to a Church in schism . . . very large privileges . . . What they deny to such a Church is the power of *imparting* these gifts' (*Moz* II p 451).

This conviction only came slowly. The 'shadow of a hand upon the wall' (*Apo* p 118), which frightened him in the summer of 1839, temporarily receded. In July 1841, he could still write : 'we are neither accusing Rome of being idolatrous nor ourselves of being schismatical, we think neither charge tenable' (*Ess* II p 367, quoted *Apo* p 113 with slight variations). In the Advent of that year, his diminishing confidence in the anglican church's possession of the 'visible Notes' of a true church led him to emphasise, in four of his most poignant sermons, the 'inward' signs of holiness that nevertheless pointed to the presence of Christ within it (*SD* pp 308–80). He was by now on the defensive and, in November 1844, he could say that 'A clear conviction of the substantial identity of Christianity and the Roman system has now been on my mind for a full three years' (*Moz* II p 445).[3] In the previous month, he had written that he 'saw more in the early Church to convince me that separation from the See of Peter was the token of heresy and schism, than that the additions which that great body . . . has received upon the primitive faith were innovations' (*KC* p 21. He first wrote 'corruptions' for 'innovations'). Finally, two months after his change of allegiance he wrote : 'My book attempts to show that *so much* may be said for the *consistency*[4] of the Roman system, which is the outward token and test of its *infallibility*, that it is safest and best to submit to it' (*L&D* XI p 69).

What these extracts show is that Newman's ecclesiological shift during these years was not a matter of exchanging one theory for another, but rather of a gradual change in 'view' (see *3.22*). From within the perspective which he eventually acquired, it seemed to him obvious, not so much that Roman catholic doctrine corresponded most closely to the teaching of the apostolic church, but rather that the complex concrete reality of the Roman catholic church as he envisaged it (see the analysis of a 'real idea' in *4.1*) corresponded more closely than any other claimant to the concrete reality of the church of the fathers.

In other words, although the threat to his confidence in the anglican church was first experienced as a calling in question of its catholicity: 'securus judicat orbis terrarum' (Wiseman [1839] p 154; *Ess* II pp 1–111; *Apo* pp 114–17, 129), it was the question of apostolicity which continued to weigh most heavily with him.

It is easy, on a superficial reading of the *Apologia*, to obtain the opposite impression. In 1839, he believed that 'the cause lay thus, Apostolicity *versus* Catholicity . . . the special point or plea of Rome in the controversy was Catholicity, as the Anglican plea was Antiquity' (*Apo* pp 106–7; cf p 129). The church of England's apostolicity was unquestioned; its catholicity was problematic. The opposite was true of the church of Rome. If the simple obverse of this had been his frame of mind when he decided to become a Roman catholic, then he could perhaps have taken the catholic church's apostolicity on trust, and the *Essay* need never have been written. However: 'As to my *Essay* . . . it is not the argument from unity or Catholicity which immediately weighs with me (in it) but from Apostolicity. If that book is asked, why does its author join the Catholic Church? The answer is, because it is the Church of St Athanasius and St Ambrose' (*L&D* XIII p 78. Cf *Dev* 2.3.5; *L&D* XI p 110; XIII p 295; Ward, W. [1912] I p 237–8).

The outcome of a slow process of shifting perspective, or changing 'view', was the intuitive, imaginative conviction that 'the Roman Catholic Church' was the answer to 'the simple question . . . Where, what is this thing in this age, which in the first age was the Catholic Church?' (*Diff* I p 368). But the ground of his previous charge of corruption remained, as an obstinate 'difficulty.' Therefore the linguistic, argumentative expression of the new 'view' had to be, at the same time, the formulation of an 'hypothesis to account for a difficulty' (*Dev* Int 21). It is imperative, when analysing and assessing the arguments in the *Essay*, never to lose sight of the fact that they stand in that relationship of consequence and subordination to the conviction they seek to articulate which Newman habitually ascribed to 'logic', which is 'brought in to arrange and inculcate what no science was employed in gaining' (*Dev* 5.4.1). Because the 'view' which they attempt to justify had previously been judged, by Newman, to be untenable, their purpose is apologetic. Because 'the spontaneous process which goes on within the mind itself is higher and choicer than that which is logical' (*Dev* 5.4.2), they can only point to, persuade towards that 'view' which they abstractly and 'notionally' interpret : explicit, 'logical' argument 'being scientific, is common property, and can be taken and made use of by minds who are personally strangers, in any true sense, both to the ideas in question and to their development' (*ibid*). Because they seek, phenomenologically,[5] to express a total vision of historical christianity, the *Essay* 'does not pretend to be a *dogmatic* work' (*L&D* xii p 170), but an 'obscure philosophical work . . . to advertise people how things stood with me' (*KC* p 379).[6]

One of the early critics of the *Essay* claimed that Newman 'first decided that Romanism was true, and then looked out for evidence that it was plausible'[7]. The tone of voice is unfriendly, but the observation is perceptive. Newman's aim in writing the *Essay* was apologetic (*2.2*), but the apology does not claim to be a 'demonstration' (*2.3*). Indeed, 'the main object of the *Essay*' is to show that 'the grounds a person gives for his conversion cannot be expressed in a formula' (*L&D* xi p 109).

2.11   A test of 'certitude'

In order to ascertain the aim and purpose of the *Essay* as precisely as possible, it is important to notice the terms in which Newman later described his state of mind between September 1843 and October 1845. At the end of 1842, he was not yet 'near certitude' (*Apo* p 215). By September 1843 (when he resigned his living), at the latest, he had arrived at certain 'conclusions' (*Apo* p 214). From then on : 'I had nothing more to learn; what still remained . . . was, not further change of opinion, but to change opinion itself into the clearness and firmness of intellectual conviction' (*Apo* p 200). The 'conviction' for which he waited, and which came to him when the *Essay* was 'partly printed'[8], was that 'certitude' which he described as 'a reflex action; it is to know that one knows' (*Apo* pp 215–16). The 'clearness' could only be attained 'when the argumentative views, which were actuating me, had been distinctly brought out before me in writing' (*L&D* XIII p 328). The 'firmness' demanded the passage of time: the 'views' had to be given 'a fair trial of their enduring' (*L&D* XVIII p 102. See *2.1*, note 4 above).

It is therefore misleading to say that, 'before he had finished' the *Essay*, 'he yielded to the *evidence*' (Walgrave [1957] p 37, my stress. Cf Bouyer [1958] p 243). It was not the 'evidence' which he was watching, but his own state of mind in regard to that evidence. There is a measure of truth in Newsome's judgement that 'The Oxford movement had been primarily a movement of the heart. Newman's conversion was too' ([1970] p 87), but he confuses the issue by saying that 'It is . . . something of a paradox that, while Newman rejected Evangelicalism because it made feeling a test of growth in grace, he appears in the end to have accepted Romanism because he made feeling, above all else, the crucial test for discerning the identity of the one true Church' (*ibid*). Newsome seems here to identify all forms of personal conviction, indiscriminately, with 'feeling'. Geoffrey Faber, whose account of Newman's change of mind was similarly imprecise, said that 'His intellect justified him; but it took its direction from feeling' (Faber, G. [1933] p 416. For a devastating critique of Faber, see Dawson [1933] pp viii–ix). Certainly it is true that, for Newman, 'certitudes about matters of fact are always personal' (Sillem [1969] p 84). But to describe a certitude that was undoubtedly 'personal' as 'an essentially subjective judgement' (Newsome [1970] p 87) is to lead us back into that morass of misunderstanding for which Bremond, above all, is responsible; which 'originated here, in England, and [which] looks as if it will die here long after it has died everywhere else'.[9] Newman's 'certitude' concerning his duty to join the Roman catholic church was a matter of 'intellectual conviction': directly as a 'view' of christian history, reflexively through the elaboration of those arguments which expressed this conviction in explicit, argumentative form.

Stern correctly observes that the 'theory of development' 'ne fut jamais le fondement ultime de sa conversion' ([1967] p 177). But he wrongly takes issue with Chadwick for contending, also correctly, that 'If the infallible Church . . . had condemned the theory of development . . . Newman's *argumentative* reasons for becoming a Roman Catholic would have perished' ([1957] p 138, my stress).

The account of certitude cited above was to occupy a key place in the *Grammar of Assent*, together with the claim that certitude, thus conceived, was 'indefectible' or 'infallible' (cf *GA* pp 197, 224–58; *AW* p 150; Pailin [1969] pp 179–82; Sillem [1969] p 140). It is interesting to notice that, if von Hügel's memory is to be trusted, Newman confessed in 1876 that 'I cannot see my way to any absolute tests of false certainty and true. I quite see that this is the weak point of "the Grammar" ' (Brown, R. K. [1961] p 28).

2.2 *An apologetic for the new 'view'*

Throughout the *Essay*, Newman assumes that christianity is 'a revelation which comes to us as a revelation, as a whole, objectively' (*Dev* 2.2.5), the maintained public availability of which in history is assured by divine providence. The *Essay* is not aimed at those who do not share this assumption (cf *Dev* Int 2–3). Nor is it aimed at those who, while sharing the general assumption, 'give reasons from history for their refusing to appeal to history' (*Dev* Int 4), 'despair' of 'historical Christianity' (*Dev* Int 5)[10] because of the complexity and ambiguity of historical evidence, and 'fall back upon the Bible as the sole source of Revelation' (*Dev* Int 4).[11]

In spite of this cavalier dismissal of positions with which he does not propose to do battle, Newman does 'concede to the opponents of historical Christianity' that the 'idea' of christianity cannot simply be read off its long and turbulent history. There have been 'certain apparent inconsistencies and alterations in its doctrine and its worship' (*Dev* Int 7), and therefore, confronted by the 'problem of finding a point of view from which minds born under the gracious shelter of Revelation may approximate to an external and general survey of it' (*1845* p 4), 'a theory is necessary' (*Dev* Int 21), if it is plausibly to be maintained that there exists in the world today an authentic, adequate and authoritative embodiment and expression of the original revelation.

Of the four such theories, or interpretative 'hypotheses', which he considers, two are given short shrift : the view that 'Christianity has even changed from the first and ever accommodates itself to the circumstances of times and seasons' (*Dev* Int 7), and the theory of the 'Disciplina Arcani' which, though it 'goes some way to account for that apparent variation and growth of doctrine, which embarrasses us when we would consult history for the true idea of Christianity; yet . . . is no key to the whole difficulty' (*Dev* Int 20). Both these positions abandon the tension between historicity and unchanging revelation which is at the heart of Newman's theological concern. Having dismissed them, the decks are cleared for doing battle with the one adversary with which, as a work of apologetic, the *Essay* is seriously concerned : namely, the theory of the *Via Media* as elaborated by Newman himself between 1833 and 1839 (cf *VM* I p xxxvii; Stern [1967] p 205).

Newman's writings in general, and the *Essay* in particular, eloquently illustrate the truth of the principle that 'The public statements of Victorian critics and essayists . . . are often best regarded as refutation, qualification, or approval' (De Laura [1969] p xi) of some view other than that which they express. Any account of Newman's 'theory of development' which fails to take this feature of his method into consideration cannot hope to do justice to his thought. In 1945, Nédoncelle charged the majority of French Newmanists with overlooking the fact that, as a controversialist, Newman regularly accepted his opponent's choice of weapons ([1945] p 72).

From a personal point of view, the over-riding apologetic preoccupation of the *Essay* is not surprising. A new 'view' of the relationship between contemporary christianity and 'the Church of the Fathers' demanded a new 'theory' to account for the differences between past and present. And the new theory could not simply ignore, but rather had to be elaborated in opposition to, that which it superseded. Nevertheless, by casting the constituent arguments of the *Essay* into an apologetic mould, he inevitably weakened his case. The charge of Roman 'corruption' was levelled especially at such distinctively Roman doctrines and practices as those of the papal 'supremacy', the veneration of our Lady and the saints, the sacramental forgiveness of post-baptismal sin, monasticism, communion in one kind, and so on. Newman therefore takes these areas and argues, with varying cogency, that they may be seen as instances not of 'corruption', but of 'true development'. As with all inter-denominational apologetic, the impression is unavoidably given that precisely those things which differentiate one denomination from another are central to its specific character

and concern. It is hardly surprising that the anglican critics of
the *Essay* should have been puzzled, hurt and angry, especially
when Newman simply took over his former arguments and used
them to reach an opposite conclusion.

An illustration of this is the use made, in the *Essay*, of a passage from the *Lectures on the Prophetical Office* concerning the
early history of the doctrine of purgatory (cf *1845*, pp 417–21;
Dev 9.4.4–6; *VM* I pp 174–80. The textual variations between
the 1837 and 1877 editions of the *Lectures* are insignificant. There
are also small discrepancies between the text of the *Lectures* and
that of their citation in the *Essay*.) In 1837, the conclusion drawn
from the historical evidence was that 'Nothing can be clearer'
than that the doctrine of purgatory 'was the result of private
judgement, exerted, in defect of Tradition, upon the text of
Scripture' (*VM* I, p 177); 'there was no definite Catholic Tradition for Purgatory in early times . . . instead of it, certain texts of
Scripture, in the first instance interpreted by individuals, were
put forward as the proof of the doctrine' (*VM* I p 180). The latter
passage was quoted in neither edition of the *Essay*. The former,
included in *1845* (p 420), was omitted in *1878*. In both editions of
the *Essay*, the conclusion drawn from the evidence is that the
doctrine of purgatory may be regarded as a 'true development'
standing in a relationship of 'logical sequence' to primitive beliefs
concerning post-baptismal sin. In *1878* there was added, immediately after the quotation : 'When an answer had to be made to the
question, how is post-baptismal sin to be remitted, there was an
abundance of passages in Scripture to make easy to the faith of
the inquirer the definitive decision of the Church' (*Dev* 9.4.7; cf
notes of 1877 to *VM* I pp 174, 177). We shall discuss, in the
following chapter, the historiographical principles which enabled
Newman so drastically to reinterpret historical evidence.

By continually defining his present position in reaction against
his former views, Newman was also led to underestimate those
features of the *Via Media* which he might otherwise have shown
to be of enduring validity. This was not, however, a deliberate
strategy. When he wrote, in the *Apologia*, that by Augustine's
words ' "Securus judicat orbis terrarum !" . . . the theory of the
Via Media was absolutely pulverised' (*Apo* p 117), he palpably
exaggerated. In fact, in the Introduction to the *Essay*, he takes
care not to over-react against his former position. Thus he does not

reject 'the dictum of Vincentius', the motto of the *Via Media*, out of hand, but merely observes that 'The solution it offers is as difficult as the original problem' (*Dev* Int 19). It would be left to others to suggest that the same may be true of the 'theory' which now replaces it.

We shall consider, in a later chapter, the extent to which the *Essay* is weakened by the apparent abandonment of that doctrine of the 'fundamentals' which played so central a part in the *Via Media* (see *6.21*). So far as this general introductory description of the aim of the *Essay* is concerned, it is sufficient to notice the unfortunate influence of the apologetic stress on the 'unreality' of 'middle views', so far as Newman's conception of the unity of the church is concerned.

After 1845, one of Newman's most characteristic claims was that 'there was no medium, in true philosophy, between Atheism and Catholicity' (*Apo* p 198. Cf *GA* 495–501, note of 1880; *L&D* xi pp 86, 110; xiii pp 78, 319; xiv p 38). In 1836 Froude, in an article 'corrected' (see Froude, R. H. [1839] p 346; Houghton, E. R. [1963] p 125) by Newman, noted—and rejected —Blanco White's contention that 'Between . . . absolute latitudinarianism on the one hand, and on the other unreserved submission to all the dogmata of Trent . . . no middle ground is open to protestants' (Froude, R. H. [1836] p 219). In 1837, Newman admitted that 'the *Via Media*, viewed as an integral system, has never had existence except on paper' (*VM* i p 16). In those years, it was the ecclesiological programme of the movement. But 'The proof of reality in a doctrine is its holding together when actually attempted' (*VM* i p 16). By 1845, the attempt is judged by Newman to have failed and, as a result, the doctrine is dismissed, quite gently (cf *Dev* 2.3.4), as 'perspicuous and plausible on paper, yet in fact unreal, impractical, and hopeless' (*Dev* 6.3.3.18; cf 5.3.4. In both passages the judgement is made indirectly through the filter of historical typology).

Whereas one of the achievements of the *Essay* is the recognition, however tentative, that not even the creed is immune from that historicity to which all human grasp of truth is subject,[12] one of its weaknesses is the espousal of a concept of the *unity* of the church which cannot acknowledge 'ecclesial reality' in any denomination other than the Roman catholic church. In 1837, he recognised that 'the duty of unity admits of fuller or scantier fulfilment' (*VM* i p 202). In 1877, he glossed this text : 'Visible unity surely does not admit of degrees. Christians are either one polity or they are not. We cannot talk of a little unity' (*ibid*; cf *L&D* xv pp 58, 152).

It would be unrealistic to expect Newman not to have shared, as a Roman catholic, a concept of church unity which was, at that time (and which remained until the second Vatican Council), a dominant feature of Roman catholic ecclesiology. Nevertheless, we can regret that he was so easily able to do so. The judgement that, unlike the theory of the *Via Media*, the view expressed in the *Essay* is a 'real' one, is facilitated by his ability to see, in a monolithically conceived Roman catholic 'system' (cf *Dev* 2.3; 3.1.1), the fulfilment of those biblical prophecies of the 'kingdom' which he had long tended to interpret with disturbing literalness (see *3.23*).

The stress, in the *Essay*, on the structural unity of Catholicism, and the mutual interdependence of its doctrines and practices, is partly due to the fact that his 'object' was 'to put before the mind a straightforward argument for joining the Church of Rome, leaving difficulties to shift for themselves' (*L&D* xi p 55). As we shall see in more detail later on (*3.22*), the conviction that 'to *begin* with particular cases is to begin at the wrong end' (*L&D* xi p 69; cf xiv p 349), is a characteristic feature of the *Essay*'s methodology.

The most important consequence of this aspect of Newman's method is that the *Essay* was not written to 'prove' the Roman catholic doctrine of the papal primacy; nor was it the result of approval of the practice of Roman 'supremacy'. However incomprehensible it may have been to Newman's anglican critics, for whom the papacy, at least in its contemporary form, was the symbol of all that they most feared and disliked in Roman catholicism, he insists, again and again, that he did not join the Roman catholic church because he came to believe in the papacy but accepted the papacy because he came to believe that Roman catholicism represented the one 'real', living embodiment of the christian 'idea' : 'If the Roman (*Catholic*) Church be the Church, I take it (and submit to it) whatever it is (monarchical, aristocratic, or democratic)—and if I find that Papal Supremacy is a point of faith in it, this point of faith (though not capable of proof on its own merits) is not to my imagination so strange, to my reason so incredible, to my historical knowledge so utterly without evidence, as to warrant me in saying "I *cannot* take it on faith" ' (*L&D* XI p 190).

The words in brackets were added in 1876, when Newman described this as 'The *argument* . . . on which my *Essay on Doctrinal Development* is founded' (cf *L&D* XI pp 174–5, 238, 239; XIII p 301; XIV pp 354, 360–1, 365–8, 369–72; XV pp 19, 39, 41–2; XX pp 304–9; XXIII pp 275, 288; XXIV p 253; XXV, pp 4–5, 203, 308–9).

In 1876 he wrote to Bloxam : '*I* was not converted by the "claims of the Pope", but by the claims of the Church—and the question seems to me to be, has the Catholic Church a claim upon us? has the Church of England any claim to be considered that body which the Apostles set up at Pentecost?' (*L&D* XXVIII p 17).

2.3 'An hypothesis to account for a difficulty'

In 1848, Newman insisted that 'my Essay on Development of doctrine . . . *is not written to prove the truth* of Catholicism, as it distinctly observes (eg in the first 4 pages) but to answer an *objection against* Catholicism' (*L&D* XII p 332). Newman inherited from his undergraduate days a tendency to employ 'the terms "Mathematical proof" and "Scientific proof" as synonyms'.[13] In theoretical matters, quasi-mathematical, deductive 'demonstration' may be the appropriate method of reaching a conclusion. But in the *Essay*, as in all his controversial writings, Newman is concerned with the concrete, rather than the abstract; with the 'real', rather than the 'notional'. He feared the 'Liberalism' which held that 'there is no legitimate or possible way of attaining a knowledge of the truth save by "demonstration" or by formally reasoned argumentation' (Sillem [1969] p 62. See *3.21*). If he is reluctant to describe the arguments in the *Essay* as constitutive of a 'proof', it is because the judgement towards which he persuades his reader is not the conclusion of an abstract syllogism, but the fruit of a complex, personally acquired appreciation of the concrete facts of christian history.

In so far as the process of arriving, cumulatively and inductively, at judgements concerning the concrete may also be described as 'proof', Newman habitually refers to it as 'moral' proof : 'Moral proofs are grown into, not learnt by heart' (*L&D* XI p 110). The 'main instrument of proof in matters of life' is not linear, deductive argumentation, but the cumulative use of arguments from 'antecedent probability' (*L&D* xii p 5. See *3.21*).

It follows from Newman's insistence on the persuasive, non-demonstrative function of the arguments in the *Essay* that the sense in which these arguments may be said to constitute 'a theory' of development is heavily qualified. Neither Newman's use of the term, nor the widespread habit of referring to 'Newman's theory of doctrinal development', may allow us to lose sight of the fact that the claim which such a use embodies is both weaker and more tentative than, on the basis of contemporary scientific usage, for instance, we might have expected. We shall have occasion to return to this point several times in the course of this study. For the moment, it is sufficient to point out that to line up the arguments in the *Essay* beside 'Bossuet's theory of clearer explanation and the scholastic theory of logical explication', as a 'third force in Catholic theology' (Chadwick [1957] p 149), is to invite misunderstanding. The Anglican critics of the *Essay* were, I believe, mistaken in claiming 'that there was no real difficulty at all' (Nicholls [1965] p 394). However, they were not so clearly wrong in rejecting 'the theory of development as not being a theory at all' (*ibid*).

In 1851, Newman wrote that his 'primary view' of the 'theory of development' in the *Essay* was that it provided a 'method of *answering objections*'. However, having invoked it to perform this function, 'it becomes an *evidence*, when you see it proceeds on a *law*' (*L&D* xiv p 378). This account of his successive appreciation of the twofold status of the 'theory' was repeated in the *Apologia* (*Apo* p 198, quoted in *Dev* 7.1.5) and, finally, in a *Note* added in 1880 to the *Grammar of Assent* (p 498). To describe the 'theory of development' as embodying the recognition of a 'law' of doctrinal history does not, however, mean that the admission that the achievement of the *Essay* is largely *negative* has been abandoned. In 1848 he described the 'very subject of the book' as being 'an attempt to give the *laws* under which implicit faith becomes explicit' (*L&D* xii p 171. Cf *Diff* i pp 394–6; ii p 314). But, in the following year, he still regretfully admitted that 'What I *want* to do and can't . . . is to construct a *positive* argument for Catholicism. The negative is most powerful—"Since there must be one true religion, it can *be none other* than this" ' (*L&D* xiii p 319). Although the passage of time, and such events as the definition of the dogma of the Immaculate Conception (*L&D* xvi pp 435, 526, 536), confirmed him in the 'availableness' of his 'view' (*Dev* p viii), it does not seem that, when he came to rewrite the *Essay* in 1878, he had significantly revised his estimate of the status of its constituent arguments. The force of these arguments is still seen to be primarily negative, even though he now claims that indirectly, or '*ultimately*' they furnish a positive argument in its behalf' (*Dev* p vii, my stress; the phrase is a curious one). An exhaustive examination of the significance to be attributed to the shift in emphasis between the two editions would have to ask: to what extent is it simply expressive of a general tendency, during the second half of the nineteenth century, to ascribe to theories of development, progress, or evolution a descriptive or 'scientific', rather than an 'optative' status?

In other words, the argument of the *Essay* remains 'an hypothesis to account for a difficulty'. It '*starts* with assuming the historical identity of the present and the past Church' (*L&D* xii p 333; cf xi p 214), and does not set out to establish that identity. Not only does it not seek to 'demonstrate' where demonstration is impossible, but also it does not claim to provide a systematically elaborated explanation of variations in church teaching and practice. Newman himself described the method of the *Essay* as 'a way of inquiry of my own, which I state without defending (*Apo* pp 79–80). Although a recognition of the qualifications with which Newman surrounded the claims which he made for the *Essay*'s achievement may considerably restrict the amount of light which it can be expected to cast on our contemporary problems, nevertheless the very modesty of Newman's claims is evidence of an appreciation of the complexity and obduracy of historical facts that is rather more sensitive than that shown by many subsequent purveyors of more confidently presented 'theories' of doctrinal development.

3

Newman's method of argument in 'concrete matters'

What Newman needed, and what he sought to provide in the *Essay*, was a 'view' of christian history (see *2.2*, *3.22*). In this chapter we shall concentrate on those features of his method which account for the fact that the elaboration of the viewpoint (*Dev* 2) precedes the rather cursory examination of evidence (*Dev* 4), and for the fact that the chapter devoted to 'The Historical argument in behalf of existing Developments' (*Dev* 3) is not so much an 'argument from history' as a defence of his method. We shall see that, in general, Newman's conception of historical method corresponds to the following description : 'The historian brings a projected conception of history as a whole to the texts; the documentary evidence speaks for or against this conception and precisely in so doing is historically cognized. Thus the historian's preconception of history as a whole makes specific research possible; and specific research verifies, modifies, or disqualifies the historian's preconception' (Jenson [1969] p 220; a summary of the final section of Pannenberg [1970b]).

An examination of the ways in which Newman justifies his method (*3.1*) will show that his conception of historiography is only a special case of his view of the only appropriate method of argument in all 'concrete matters'. In such a method, the 'presumptions' influencing the interpreter 'antecedently' to his detailed examination of the 'facts' (cf *GA* p 383), acquire particular importance. We shall therefore examine the relationship between 'antecedent probability' and evidence (*3.2*), and the range of data regarded as relevant to the inquiry (*3.3*).

3.1 Hypothesis and evidence

'Some hypothesis . . . all historians must adopt, if they would treat of Christianity at all' (*Dev* 2.2.14). The general appeal to history is thus further specified by the claim that any such appeal inevitably entails the use of an historical method formally similar to that defended in the *Essay*. The 'rule of historical interpretation . . . professed in the English school of divines . . . lays down a simple rule by which to measure the value of every historical fact' (*Dev* Int 8), and even 'infidelity has its views and conjectures, on which it arranges the facts of ecclesiastical history' (*Dev* Int 21). In other words, Newman's chosen method is that employed by other historians (*3.11*). Although it is distinct from the methods of the positive sciences, it has affinities with them (*3.12*). Theologically, the justification for studying christianity in this way (and thus exposing it to criticism from secular historiography) is the fact that christianity differs from 'other religions and philosophies . . . not in kind, but in origin' (*Dev* 2.1.2). Nevertheless, an historical study of christianity that prescinds from the claims of christian belief is dangerously reductionist (*3.13*).

3.11 The interpretation of history

According to Chadwick, although Newman 'repudiated the historical methods and principles which he . . . found in the Germans and the liberal Anglicans . . . [he] could not help learning from them'.[1] This is misleading. It was not, fundamentally, the method in question which Newman 'repudiated', but the use of that method by some historians, and 'the spirit in which it is too often conducted' (*Diff* i p 156). This is clear from the long passage, omitted in *1878*, in which he compared the method of the *Essay* with that of historians such as Gieseler, Gibbon,[2] Thirlwall and Mosheim (*1845* pp 182–202). The method in question 'is no peculiarity of Catholic and orthodox reasoning, but is equally found in infidel and heretic, and in history or ethics as well as in theology' (*1845* p 183). There is no need of Chadwick's hypothesis that Newman only criticised Thirlwall 'gently' because 'he was the historian of Greece and not of the Church, perhaps because he was now a bishop of the Church of England' ([1957] pp 99–100). The simpler explanation is that Newman approved both of Thirlwall's method and of his use of it : he 'uses hypothesis as well as fact, and presumption as well as evidence, but is properly careful to discriminate between them' (*1845* pp 193–4).

Chadwick further maintains that the omission, from *1878*, of the discussion of these other historians 'illustrates a marked feature of that revision—the partial restatement or removal of the appeal to history, and the consequent weakening of the basis and structure of the argument' ([1957] p 149; cf pp 189, 190, 247–8). The opening pages of the section in question (*1845* pp 179–82) were concerned to defend methodological pluralism and to plead for the autonomy of historical method. These pages, which contain the essential argument, were retained in *1878* (*Dev* 3.2.1–4. cf *3.12*). The omission of the lengthy extracts and summaries from the writings of other historians can hardly be held significantly to weaken the structure of an argument on which Newman continues to lay considerable emphasis. As Maurice had said, in 1846 : 'All Mr Newman's doctrine about the nature of evidence may be granted. It is, as he says, common to him with those who are most at variance with him. Were more than sixty octavo pages required to prove points which seem not to advance the argument one step?' (Maurice [1846] p xlviii. For a recent discussion of the possible influence of Maurice on *1878*, see Prickett [1973].)

When, in the Preface to *1878*, Newman concedes that 'Perhaps his confidence in the truth and availableness of this view has sometimes led the author to be careless and over-liberal in his concessions to Protestants of historical fact' (*Dev* p viii), he seems to have in mind statements such as 'I have called the doctrine of Infallibility an hypothesis . . . let it be so considered for the sake of argument, that is, let it be considered to be a mere position, supported by no direct evidence' (*Dev* 2.2.14). In other words, throughout the *Essay* Newman the controversialist is trying 'to clear as large a range for the *principle* of doctrinal Development (waiving the question of historical *fact*) as was consistent with the strict Apostolicity and identity of the Catholic Creed' (*Apo* pp 79–80). It seems an over-simplification to say that, in 1878, Newman was 'removing' many of 'the historical admissions' (Chadwick [1957] p 190). With few exceptions, the same historical facts are conceded in both editions. This is not to deny the importance of those shifts in terminology to which Chadwick calls attention (cf *1845* p 167; *Dev* 4.3.4; Chadwick [1957] p 246. See Appendix), but to suggest that their interpretation is more complex than his comments indicate (see *5.41*). The clue to the passage in the Preface to *1878* lies in the recognition of that ambiguity in the notion of an 'appeal to history' with which this section (*3.1*) is concerned. For Newman, an 'appeal to history' is not simply an appeal to the 'facts', but rather to those facts as seen in the light of that interpretative hypothesis which seems most satisfactorily, and economically, to account for them (see *Dev* 2.2.14).

The chronicler plays a safe game; the historian (as Newman understands his task) a dangerous one. His method is 'very frequently difficult and dangerous . . . delicate and doubtful' (*1845* p 202), and Newman's consciousness of the fact is illustrated by a paragraph on the 'Homoousion', consisting mostly of a critical description of Bull's method of interpreting the ante-nicene Fathers.[3] Bull's title 'shows that he is not investigating what is true and what false, but explaining and justifying a foregone conclusion . . . he begins with a presumption, and shows how naturally facts close round it and fall in with it, if we will but let them. He does this triumphantly, yet he has an arduous work' (*Dev* 4.1.11. In *1845*, p 158, for 'shows . . . conclusion', read 'shows that he is not seeking a conclusion, but imposing a view'). That this perceptively critical description of his own method (for this is what it amounts to) was no temporary failure of nerve is indicated by the fact that he not only retained it in *1878*, but heightened the critical tone. In 1871 he included, as Note IV to the third edition of *Arians* (pp 432–44), an abbreviated version of an article originally published in *Atlantis* in 1858. To this he added (without indicating that it did not form part of the original text) a final paragraph (see *Ari* p 444), equally critical of both Bull and Pétau. If this may be regarded as his mature view of the problem it suggests, even more explicitly than *Dev* 4.1.11, an awareness of the fragility of many of the arguments in the *Essay*.

3.12 The *'way of history and the way of science'*

One of the reasons for Newman's insistence that he was 'no theologian' (*L&D* XVII p 433, cf XXIII pp 10–11, 369; XXIV pp 212–13, 226, 363; XXV pp 32, 66, 100) and that the *Essay* was not a work of theology (cf *KC* p 379; *L&D* XII pp 170–1, XVI p 526), was that, for much of his life, he accepted the view that deduction was the only appropriate method of proof and argument in theology. Late in life he came to modify this view, and there are traces of this shift in viewpoint in *1878*.

He 'accepted Bacon's distinction between physics and natural theology, according to which physics is fundamentally an inductive science and theology a deductive science' (Sillem [1969] p 189). Yet his attitude towards theology, thus conceived, was ambivalent. On the one hand, his lifelong preoccupation with 'the *personal* conquest of truth' (cf Boekraad [1955]), his acute sensitivity to the limitation of all human discourse about God, and his preference for inductive, cumulative methods of argument, all conspired to make him suspicious of a 'science' the 'very perfection [of which] . . . causes theologians to be somewhat wanting in tenderness to concrete humanity' (*Insp* p 144; cf VM I p xlviii). On the other hand, his desire—especially in his early years as a Roman catholic—to bring his thinking into line with the 'ethos' of the Roman schools of the period,[4] his suspicion of 'private judgement', and his concern for the integrity of doctrinal tradition, enabled him positively to assess a conception of theological method which was otherwise alien to his whole mentality. In the Dublin lectures, this concern underlies his judgement that the introduction of 'the method of research and of induction into the study of Theology' has been a 'huge mistake' (*Idea*, p 447; cf Culler [1955] p 246), and his insistence that exegetical and historical inquiry in theological matters should be subordinated 'to the magisterial sovereignty of the Theological Tradition and the voice of the Church' (*Idea* p 452). This conception of the immunity of the 'Theological Tradition' from the corrosive influence of history is an aspect of that form in which the concept of 'Episcopal Tradition' was carried over into his catholic writings (cf *Dev* 2.2.3; see *6.21*).

His Dublin experience and the rise of conservative ultramontanism taught Newman to appreciate the need for theological creativity and freedom of research. The resulting shift in emphasis in his writings[5] accounts for several of the changes introduced into *1878*. By 1870, he could group together 'experimental science, historical research, or theology' as classes of 'concrete reasoning' (*GA* p 359) and, in the same year he wrote to Robert Dale: 'You have truly said that we need a *Novum Organon* for theology' (*L&D* xxv p 56. Cf *GA* p 271). By the time that he came to revise the *Essay*, the shift in his conception of theological method allowed him to use the term 'theology' in contexts where he had previously been unwilling to do so.[6] A striking instance of this is his replacement of 'controversial method' by 'theological method' in the following passage: 'It is very evident, what a special influence a view such as this must have on the controversial method of those who hold it. Arguments will come to be considered rather as representatives and persuasives than as logical proofs; and developments as the spontaneous, gradual and ethical growth, not as intentional and arbitrary deductions, of existing opinions' (*1845* p 337; cf *Dev* 7.2.10, and *Dev* 7.3.1–3, new material for *1878*, with its emphasis on theology as 'investigation', rather than merely deductive proof. See *6.22*).

In 1851, Newman declared that there were two 'legitimate instruments for deciding on the truth of a religion . . . the way of history and the way of science' (*Prepos* p 57). By 'science', in this context, he meant the deductive method employed by theologians who 'carry out' the 'great system' of catholic doctrine 'into its fulness, and define [it] in its details, by patient processes of reason' (*Prepos* p 57). If the method of the *Essay* was not that of 'theology', in terms of the Baconian distinction, neither was it that of the physical sciences : it proceeds 'by way of history'. Newman therefore finds it necessary to defend the autonomy of historical method, as he conceives it, for 'Bacon is celebrated for destroying the credit of a method of reasoning much resembling that which it has been the object of this Chapter to recommend' (*Dev* 3.2.1).

In the Introduction, he had pointed out that the use of 'hypothesis' or 'theory' to account for and to interpret data was an 'expedient' that was as necessary for the natural scientist as it was for the christian apologist (*Dev* Int 21). While it may be true, however, that both historians and natural scientists are concerned with the accumulation of data, and the formulation and testing of hypotheses, this general description obscures the crucial difference between historical and scientific method. Newman examines this difference in an important passage, pleading for the autonomy of historical (and 'ethical') method (*Dev* 3.2.1–4; the only part of the section on 'parallel instances' to survive into *1878*). Bacon's criticisms were directed at the application of a method such as that which Newman is recommending 'to what should be strict investigation, and that in the province of physics' (*Dev* 3.2.1). In the natural sciences, 'with the senses we begin . . . we do not begin with surmise and conjecture, much less do we look to the tradition of past ages, or the decree of foreign teachers, to determine matters which are in our hands and under our eyes. But it is otherwise with history, the facts of which are not present' (*Dev* 3.2.1;

cf Collingwood [1966] p 170; Bloch [1954] p 48). '. . . if we proceed on the hypothesis that a merciful Providence has supplied us
with means of gaining such truth as concerns us, in different
subject-matters, though with different instruments, then the simple
question is, what those instruments are which are proper to a
particular case . . . He may bless antecedent probabilities in ethical
inquiries, who blesses experience and induction in the art of medi-
cine' (Dev 3.2.2; cf Idea p 442, Apo p 199; Butler, J. [1896] ii,
p 51).

At one level, Newman is saying that the historian or the
christian apologist is justified in starting with 'the opinions of
others, the traditions of ages . . . analogies, parallel cases' (Dev
3.2.1; cf 3.2.4), and so on, because these are, as it were, the 'facts'
of his discipline, and must be handled 'like the evidence from the
senses' (Dev 3.2.1). More basically, what is at stake is that 'ethic'
of historical and religious inquiry which Newman defended,
throughout most of his life,[7] against a temper of mind which insisted that nothing should be accepted as true by an individual
until he had himself demonstrated its truth.[8] Newman's defence
of his method does not simply rest on the fact that it is the method
employed by other contemporary historians (see 3.11); he is also
concerned to justify that method by the nature of his subject-
matter : 'if the formal basis on which He has rested His revelations be, as it is, of an historical and philosophical character, then
antecedent probabilities, subsequently corroborated by facts, will
be sufficient, as in the parallel case of other history, to bring us
safely to the matter, or at least to the organ, of those revelations'
(Dev 3.2.2; cf US p 61, note of 1871).

Although Newman is concerned to defend methodological
pluralism in general, and the autonomy of historical and 'ethical'
method in particular, he does not posit an absolute disjunction
between historical and scientific method. Bacon had claimed that
'our method of discovering the sciences does not much depend
upon subtlety and strength of genius, but lies level to almost every
capacity and understanding' (Dev 3.2.3). Newman, with his acute
awareness of the role of personal skill in the conquest of truth, is
unhappy with this : 'surely sciences there are, in which genius is
everything, and rules all but nothing'.[9] That remark shows an insight into the nature of scientific discovery which has perhaps been
generally appropriated only in our own day.

The one other passage in the *Essay* in which Newman draws an explicit analogy between his method and that of the natural scientist indicates a problem which we shall later consider in detail. According to Wood's *Mechanics*, the 'laws of motion', provisionally perceived and formulated by the scientist, are modified by further experiment so that 'the more accurately the experiments are made . . . the more nearly do the experiments coincide with these laws'.[10] Newman comments: 'In such a method of proof there is, first, an imperfect, secondly, a growing evidence, thirdly, in consequence a delayed inference and judgement, fourthly, reasons producible to account for the delay'. (*Dev* 4.0.2. The terminology here is influenced by the *Grammar*. In *1845*, the passage ended with the previous sentence which, in turn, was significantly reworked in *1878* : see *1845*, p 142). This analogy between the 'laws of motion' and 'certain doctrines' rests upon the assumption that the doctrines in question were 'really held' from the beginning of christianity. Thus, for example, scattered and imprecise references in the early Fathers to the divinity of Christ or the papal primacy are regarded as 'imperfect' and 'growing evidence' of the 'presence' in the church, in some sense, of doctrinal positions fully elaborated at a later date. This puzzling conception of doctrinal history will be discussed in *5.4*.

3.13 'Historically human and doctrinally divine'
Newman's preoccupation with the role of 'antecedent probability' in historical inquiry is due, not simply to his conception of historical method in general (*3.11*) and of the historian's relationship to the data with which he deals (*3.12*), but also to more explicitly theological considerations.[11]

'Christianity has been long enough in the world to justify us in dealing with it as a fact in the world's history' (*Dev* Int 1). But if it is simply a fact in the world's history, then the history of christianity can be adequately interpreted without appeal being made to the transcendent or the 'other-worldly'. The spectre of the erosion of christian belief by rationalist philosophy and 'liberal' criticism haunted Newman throughout his life (eg *Idea* pp 381–404). 'What tenet of Christianity will escape proscription, if the principle is once admitted, that a sufficient account is given of an opinion, and a sufficient ground for making light of it, as soon as it is historically referred to some human origin' (*Ess* II p 241.

The crucial word is 'sufficient' : 'The evidence of History, I say, is invaluable in its place; but if it assumes to be the sole means of gaining Religious Truth, it goes beyond its place' *Idea* p 95; cf *GA* p 488).

In order to appreciate the acute form in which the problem of a 'theological' interpretation of history arises in the *Essay*, the article from which that passage is taken may be used to illustrate Newman's general approach to the problem.

In spite of the 'stringency' (cf Chadwick [1957] p 100) of Newman's review of Milman's *History of Christianity* (*British Critic* 1841; *Ess* II pp 186–248), 'la méthode de M. Milman, en elle-même, ne l'effarouche nullement' (Guitton [1933] p 49). Newman's charge against Milman is that, by attempting to view christianity 'as a secular fact, to the exclusion of all theological truth' (*Ess* II p 188), he has in fact, though not in intention, adopted a perilously reductionist viewpoint. Unlike those christians who would claim that the history of belief and practice has its own laws, and is therefore in some way immune from the critical gaze of the secular historian,[12] Newman admits that christianity, since 'It consists of men . . . has developed according to the laws under which combinations of men develop' (*Ess* II p 196, cf p 194, *SD* pp 98–9). Yet he regards Milman's book as dangerous because : 'viewing Christianity as an external political fact, [he] has gone very far indeed towards viewing it as nothing more' (*Ess* II p 213).

According to Newman, 'The Christian history is "an outward visible sign of an inward spiritual grace :" whether the sign can be satisfactorily treated separate from the thing signified is another matter' (*Ess* II p 188). His claim, in other words, is not that the history of the church may not legitimately be seen as a 'fact in the world's history', but that 'what is historically human can be doctrinally divine',[13] and that the only theory or interpretative viewpoint which adequately accounts for the historical phenomena is one that takes into consideration not only the 'outside' but also the 'inside' of the events in question.[14] His fear that Milman's use of his method may encourage a reductionism such as would render the perception of the divine meaning in human history impossible is thus expressed in characteristically 'sacramental' terminology. (See *Ess* II p 193; *Dev* 7.1.4; 7.4; 8.2; *Apo* p 27). Sillem regards the Milman article as 'of capital importance for Newman's Sacramental idea of matter' ([1969] p 172), which he inherited from Butler and the Alexandrian Fathers (cf p 181).

It seems, says Newman, that Milman's original intention was merely to state 'the *facts* of Christianity, without notice, good or bad, of the *principles* which are their life. But such an adherence was impossible . . . He does make a *theory* of the facts which he records'.[15] Here he seems to be saying that when the historian's interpretative viewpoint (or 'theory') is not that of christian belief, although he may attempt a 'neutral' stance, prescinding from issues of belief or unbelief, he will in fact inexorably tend to adopt the interpretative viewpoint of unbelief, or at least will too easily be understood to do so.[16] Milman was undoubtedly a better historian than Newman, but Newman was perhaps more sensitive to those problems which confront the christian who wishes to treat both history and the claims of christian belief with equal seriousness, and who is not prepared to relax the resulting tension by opting for a fideistic dualism.

'The relation between the historical and the theological components of Newman's position on doctrinal development is not easy to determine'. (Pelikan [1969] p 34). Chadwick's suggestion that this is due to the 'interweaving' of 'two distinct but interdependent lines of thought—the one historical, the other doctrinal' (Chadwick [1957] p 139), perhaps implies a sharper prior differentiation of disciplines and methods than Newman, in the *Essay*, would have wished to sustain. The argument of the *Essay* hinges upon the assertion that 'Unless . . . some special ground of exception can be assigned, it is as evident that Christianity, as a doctrine and worship, will develop in the minds of recipients, as that it conforms in other respects, in its external propagation or its political framework, to the general methods by which the course of things is carried forward'.[17] Here the frank recognition that the history of christianity follows the general 'laws' of historical process is combined with the doctrinal claim that therefore this process is 'proved to have been in the contemplation of its Divine Author' (*Dev* 2.1.8). The propriety of such a claim will call for frequent examination in the course of this study. The aim of the present section has simply been to situate it within the general problem of Newman's view of the historical method appropriate to the christian study of history.

3.2 Antecedent probability

In order to bring the description of the method of the *Essay* into sharper focus, it is necessary to examine more closely the concept of 'antecedent probability', and the relationship between the interpreter's hypothesis and the data (*3.21*). The stress laid in the *Essay* on arguments from antecedent probability is both an expression of Newman's lifelong espousal of a particular 'ethic of assent' (cf Harvey [1967] p 33), and an indication of the pastoral and apologetic nature of the *Essay* (*3.22*). Finally, the fragility of many of the apparently positive theological arguments in the *Essay* will be discussed in the context of those passages in which a case is made for the 'antecedent probability' of the emergence of a particular form of church order (*3.23*).

3.21 Antecedent probability and patterns of persuasion

'. . . if I have brought out one truth in any thing I have written, I consider it to be the *importance of antecedent probability* in conviction. It is how you convert factory girls as well as philosophers . . . This has been my feeling both when I wrote of Development of doctrine and of University Education' (*L&D* xv p 381). The re-ordering of the material made the dominant role played by arguments from 'antecedent probability' even clearer in *1878* than it had been in *1845*. Chapter 2 of *1878* argues that it is antecedently probable that doctrine will develop, and that there will be, in the church, an 'infallible developing authority'. Chapter 3 is a defence of the method which has thus been put to use. Chapter 4 tries to show what the early evidence looks like if the argument of the preceding chapters is accepted (*Dev* 4.0.1).

For Newman, the term 'probability' refers to propositions; to conclusions reached by methods of argument other than 'demonstration' (see *2.3*): 'he never uses it of a state of mind'.[18] Although one of those from whom he inherited the distinction between 'probability' and 'demonstration' was Butler,[19] he 'transformed Butler's problem by distinguishing, both in the *Apologia* and the *Grammar*, between "certitude", which is a property, or state, of mind, and "certainty", which is a quality of propositions' (Sillem [1969] p 177). Thus it is possible to possess 'certitude' concerning matters the proof of which only amounts to 'probability' or 'moral certainty'. Cf Stewart [1814] II p 242. One of Newman's favourite examples is his 'certitude' that 'I am living in an island'

(*GA* p 212). Even in later works, Newman's use of the terms 'certitude' and 'certainty' is not completely consistent (see Pailin [1969] pp 177–85; Pailin's attempt to clarify the situation is only partially successful) and, in earlier writings, 'certainty' is sometimes used when, on the basis of the later distinction, 'certitude' would be more appropriate : cf, eg *L&D* xi pp 289, 293.

The phrase 'antecedent probability' does not occur in Butler. According to Willam, its origin is to be traced, through Whately,[20] to the Stoic *prolepsis* and the Ciceronian *praesumptio*.[21] A state of affairs is said to be 'antecedently probable' when, prior to an examination of the direct evidence for it, the conclusion that this is the likely state of affairs has been reached on the basis of other considerations, such as : 'the opinions of others, the traditions of ages, the prescriptions of authority, antecedent auguries, analogies, parallel cases . . . and the like, not indeed taken at random, but, like the evidence from the senses, sifted and scrutinised' (*Dev* 3.2.1; cf Whately [1849] p 32). Thus Willam claims that the notion of 'antecedent probability' plays a similar role in Newman's thought to that played by the *Horizont des Verständnisses* for Husserl, or *Vorverständnis* for Bultmann (see Willam [1969] p 39).

At least in principle, an argument from antecedent probability is not the imposition of a 'preconceived theory' upon the evidence (as Wiles seems to think; see Wiles [1967] p 15), but a more or less well-founded claim that it is reasonable to expect that, in a particular case, the data bear witness to one state of affairs rather than another.[22] Indeed, unless the data are examined in the light of that heuristic anticipation set up by the judgement of antecedent probability, they are unlikely to be recognised *as* evidence : 'whereas mere probability proves nothing, mere facts persuade no one . . . probability is to fact, as the soul to the body' (*US* p 200; cf p 226).

There is nothing particularly startling in Newman's claim that 'antecedent probability is even found to triumph over contrary evidence' (*Dev* 3.2.5), and that 'antecedent probabilities . . . go very far towards dispensing with' the need 'for positive evidence' (*Dev* 3.2.11), especially when we bear in mind that Newman is primarily concerned with the rationality of the beliefs and judgements of the ordinary man.[23] It is, of course, of crucial importance that the 'antecedent probabilities' should be continually open to re-examination,[24] and that any argument from antecedent probability can be overthrown by a sufficient body of contrary fact. Newman is well aware that 'Facts cannot be proved by presumptions' (*GA* p 383) although, in his early years as a catholic, he did tend, at least rhetorically, to understate the indispensability of historical evidence for religious belief : see *OS* p 69; *Prepos* p 302. Not the least of the reasons for the emphasis on arguments from antecedent probability in a work whose aim is the removal of 'objections', rather than the furnishing of positive proof (see *2.3*), is Newman's recognition that it is when 'negative' that 'Antecedent reasoning' is most 'safe' (*GA* p 381).

The clue to appreciating the role which arguments from antecedent probability play in Newman's writings is the realisation that his model for the pattern of argument in 'concrete matters', where 'demonstration is impossible',[25] is fundamentally jurisprudential :[26] like Cicero, whom he admired as 'the only master of style I have ever had' (*L&D* xxiv p 242), he is a 'pleader' (*HS* i pp 263, 272, 279). 'Brilliant as the argument is, it is advocacy, not science. Catholicism is on trial, and we are listening to counsel for the defence' (Fawkes [1903] p 54).

The section entitled 'Developments of Doctrine to be Expected' (*Dev* 2.1), for instance, brings to the bar of judgement a variety of witnesses : a summary of the argument of chapter 1, that the history of christianity is that of a 'living idea' (*Dev* 2.1.1); the fact that 'great questions exist in the subject-matter of which Scripture treats, which Scripture does not solve' (*Dev* 2.1.5; cf examples in 2.1.4–7); a series of arguments by analogy with the history of prophetic fulfilment (*Dev* 2.1.8–13). Counsel's speech at the end is confident in tone (*Dev* 2.1.17), but the danger is that the jury may be seduced by forensic brilliance into confidently making a judgement when a verdict of 'not proven' would often be more appropriate (cf Mozley, J. B. [1846a] p 173. On authorship see *L&D* xi p 87). Nevertheless, the reader is not being invited simply to accept Newman's conclusions without a prior intellectual effort at least comparable to his own : 'People shall not say, "We have now got his reasons . . ." No, you have not got them, you cannot get them, except at the cost of some portion of the trouble I have been at myself . . . You must consent to *think* . . . Moral proofs are grown into, not learnt by heart' (*L&D* xi p 110; cf *US* p 275, Ward, W. [1912] ii p 357).

A method of argument such as Newman's may be compared to the action of a pair of scissors.[27] The upper blade is the complex of assumptions that ground the claim that X is 'antecedently probable'. The lower blade is the description of X that emerges from a detailed examination and evaluation of the historical data. The attempt to 'close the scissors' consists, on the one hand, in the permanent task of critically testing and revising the assumptions and, on the other hand, in an increasingly sophisticated and critical use of techniques available for the handling of the data. As he said, in 1877 : 'two things were necessary for the defence of the Anglican Church, a broad, intellectual, intelligible theory, and a logical and historical foundation for that theory' (*VM* i, p xxiii).

In the course of this study we shall be concerned to examine a number of the historical, philosophical, psychological and theological assumptions that form the 'upper blade' of the argument of the *Essay*. But what of the 'lower blade'? What are the criteria for deciding that a particular fact or set of facts constitutes the rock (to change the metaphor) on which even the strongest of antecedent presumptions must founder? This question may be illustrated from the article which Newman added, in *1878*, to conclude the section on the 'State of the Evidence'.

As with many of the substantial additions in *1878*, the language is less subtle, less nuanced, than in *1845*. Newman wishes to meet the objection that 'the difficulty of admitting these developments of doctrine lies, not merely in the absence of early testimony for them, but in the actual existence of distinct testimony against them—or, as Chillingworth says, in "Popes against Popes, Councils against Councils" ' (*Dev* 3.2.12). He reduces the objection to a mere matter of 'differences in individual writers'; and these, he says, 'are consistent with, or rather are involved in the very idea of doctrinal development' (*ibid*). If this were all that the objection amounted to, Newman would be right because, as we shall see, his description of doctrinal history takes into account its dialectical nature. He then claims that 'the one essential question is whether the recognised organ of teaching, the Church herself, acting through Pope or Council as the oracle of heaven, has ever contradicted her own enunciations. If so, the hypothesis which I am advocating is at once shattered' (*Dev* 3.2.12; cf *L&D* xi p 69).

At first sight, this admission is striking evidence of Newman's submission of his hypotheses to the bar of historical fact.[28] There is no doubt (as his correspondence during the Vatican Council shows) that this is his intention. But the matter is not so simple. Are not some of the assumptions on which the *Essay* rests such as to prevent, in the event, any proffered fact or set of facts from having this devastating effect? Newman is one of a long line of catholic theologians whose commitment to the antecedent improbability of the church's ever having radically 'changed its mind' is so powerful that even the most uncomfortable facts are fitted into the framework of a cumulative, irreversible 'view' of doctrinal history. Total interpretations of doctrinal history are often so constructed as to be, in fact though not in intention, unfalsifiable. The interpretative claims of the *Essay* tend to be, in the sense in which the term is currently used by philosophers hostile to transcendental claims, 'metaphysical'.[29] As such, they may perhaps appropriately be used by an individual to structure and organise the pattern of his own historical experience. Whether they may legitimately be used as a significant element in the justification, before the event, of dogmatic definitions which will be held to be binding, in principle, upon the faith of all christians, is another matter. 'Evidence which may be strong enough to make it safer to believe, may yet be insufficient to enable us to preach and impose what it attests' (*VM* i, p 247). The danger of using a particular form of argument from antecedent probability, originally designed to show, negatively, that there is 'nothing in history to contradict' modern doctrine, in a different context, is seen in the way in which Newman reacted to the plans for defining the dogma of the immaculate conception : see *L&D* xiii p 82; xvi pp 435, 526.

3.22 Taking a 'view'

According to Newman, there are two ways of looking at history : 'piecemeal and as a whole' (*OP* p 256). The latter approach is described as 'realising' the person or situation which is the object of study and, 'while I freely and distinctly acknowledge the benefit of what may be called the dogmatic, or documentary, I think it is perfected, not thwarted, by the historical . . . I wish to be in possession of that living view of him, which shall be a living key of all . . . which has been committed to tradition or writing concerning him' (*ibid*, cf GA p 79). Many of the key concepts with which we shall be concerned in this study are combined in that passage : the notion of 'realising' a past event; the hint that an idea, when thus 'realised', becomes 'living'; the notion of interpreting the past from a synthetic standpoint in the present, and so on. Only by employing a synthetic, imaginative, 'historical' method, in which the flair of the interpreter is as important as the data he attempts to interpret and coordinate, can the historian hope to get a 'view' of his subject. Newman's attitude towards the historian's task is, at this point, strikingly consistent : see, in 1836, his comments on Burton in Newman [1836c], p 214 and, in 1872, his criticism of Döllinger for failing to 'throw himself into the state of things which he reads about' (Cross [1933a] p 172).

According to Butler, the 'kind of proof' appropriate to the 'evidence' of christianity 'may be compared to what they call *the effect* in architecture or other works of art; a result from a great number of things so and so disposed, and taken into one view'.[30] For Newman, the term 'view' refers to that synthetic, personal grasp of concrete reality which was his educational and intellectual ideal.[31] The only 'method by which we are enabled to become certain of what is concrete' is by 'the cumulation of probabilities' (*GA* p 288). Thus, the cumulative patterns of argument which abound in the *Essay*, and which Newman once compared with 'a *cable* which is made up of a number of separate threads, each feeble, yet together as sufficient as an iron rod' (*L&D* xxi p 146; cf xv p 457, *Mir* p 8), are the instruments by which alone such a 'view' may be sought.

Just as Newman's defence of the use of 'assumptions' in interpreting data is not a defence of *any* assumption (see *3.21*), so his stress on the importance of 'taking a view' is not a recommendation to neglect the detailed examination of the data in favour of speculative and over-hasty synthesis. The latter Newman described as 'viewiness' : 'Viewiness . . . is the opposite extreme from "mere learning". As mere learning was fact without system, so viewiness is system without fact' (Culler [1955] p 197). Especially in his attitude towards hagiographical tradition, Newman sometimes tends towards 'viewiness', as in the famous passage in which he goes so far as to say : 'If the alleged facts did not occur, they ought to have occurred' (*US* p 343; cf Egner [1969] pp 45–9; Holmes [1966b] p 530).

A true 'view' incorporates and synthesises data laboriously

gained while, at the same time, it 'breaks through' the techniques of 'technical history and historical research'.[32] At least as an ideal, it represents the 'closing of the scissors' (see *3.21*). The *Essay* is not an exercise in academic history but, even if it were, the historian would not be excused the obligation of attempting to have a 'view'. Although Newman valued Fleury's work, it was a mere collection of facts (*L&D* xvi p 244). His criticism of Schlegel's work was that 'it has no *view*—only a number of detached remarks' (*ibid*; cf Pailin [1969] p 63). And, as we saw in *3.11*, his criticism of historians such as Gibbon was not that they interpreted their data from a coordinating philosophical viewpoint, but that the viewpoint adopted was incorrect, or the use made of it illegitimate. For the academic historian, the attempt to take a 'view' may be a slow and leisurely affair. When urgent practical decisions are at stake, however, Newman insists that the attempt must be made, even though particular details and difficulties remain unexamined and unaccounted for. Indeed, he sometimes suggests that if all the difficulties and exceptions were accounted for, one would have good reason to suspect the 'reality' of the 'view' : cf *L&D* xi pp 55, 69; xv, pp 497–8.

'It is difficult for me to take a step without what I should call *a view*' (*L&D* xix p 26). Christianity, for Newman, is essentially a 'practical' matter and, in practical ('ethical') matters, if we waited, before adopting a course of action, until we had subjected the evidence, on the basis of which we are to act, to exhaustive personal examination, we would 'blunt the practical energy of the mind' (*US* p 188; cf *DA* p 201) if, indeed, we ever got started at all. In order to adopt, and to execute, a policy of action, we have to risk 'taking a view',[33] the basis of which is an interlocking structure of moral certainties or 'probabilities'. 'Nor is it in slight matters only or unimportant that we thus act. Our dearest interests, our personal welfare, our property, our health, our reputation, we freely hazard, not on proof, but on a simple probability, which is sufficient for our conviction, because prudence dictates to us so to take it. We must be content to follow the law of our being in religious matters as well as in secular' (*Dev* 3.2.5; cf 2.2.1, 3.1.2, 3.2.1–2; 7.2).

The dominant role played by 'the cumulation of probabilities' in the *Essay* thus discloses an 'ethic of assent' that seems to correspond to that 'orthodox belief' which, according to Harvey, 'corrodes the delicate machinery of sound historical judgement'.[34] In order to appreciate the force of Newman's lifelong methodological preference for 'faith', rather than 'reason',[35] however, it is necessary to recognise that it is not exclusively, or even primarily, religious 'faith' that is under discussion.[36] Newman is recommending his readers to adopt the same attitude to the 'developments' of christianity as they are accustomed to do when confronted with 'other alleged facts and truths and the evidence for them, such as come to us with a fair presumption in their favour' (*Dev* 3.1.2). The grounds of the 'presumption' in question are described in the previous article, which is a cumulative summary of seven arguments employed in the first two chapters. In offering this as a 'true view', which we are urged initially to 'meet . . . with a frank confidence', Newman's primary aim would seem to be the negative one of undercutting the barriers of 'suspicion and criticism' (*Dev* 3.1.2) with which these 'developments' were regarded by the majority of his fellow anglicans. As a positive 'proof' of the 'truth' of the Roman catholic 'system', the arguments in question are, to say the least, inadequate. In describing the 'developments' as 'alleged *facts and truths*', he seems to be echoing the Tractarian critique of Hampden's 'distinction between the "Divine facts" of revelation, and all human interpretations of them' (Church [1891] p 136, cf p 142).

If Newman's 'fiduciary' rather than 'analytic' attitude towards language and evidence[37] runs the risk of encouraging an uncritical credulity or, as he would say, 'superstition', it may also be true that the highly developed critical sensitivities of, for example, the scientific historian, carry the opposite risk of reducing the chances of what today would be referred to as 'commitment' in human affairs. It cannot be taken for granted that the notion of what would count as 'sound historical judgement', where the historical component in the ground of christian belief is concerned, is beyond discussion. There are prior questions to be asked, concerning the propriety of taking those practical risks which love may demand, and which reason does not forbid, even though it cannot adequately justify them.[38]

The urgency of Newman's recommendation to his readers to risk attempting to 'take a view' is also due to his fear of the scepticism which inevitably results from an excessive preoccupation with individual detailed problems: 'When we have lost our way, we mount up to some eminence to look about us', we do not plunge 'into the nearest thicket to find out [our] bearings' (*L&D* XI p 69). Ignatius Ryder, he once wrote, 'is ever deep in Devonshire lanes—you never know the lie of the country from him—he never takes his reader up to an eminence, whence he could make a map of it' (*L&D* XXIII p 227). In order to prevent the enquirer from arriving at a 'view', the sceptic or unbeliever so conducts the enquiry 'as to make it appear that, if the divided arguments be inconclusive one by one, we have a series of exceptions to the truths of religion instead of a train of favourable presumptions, growing stronger at every step. The disciple of Scepticism is taught that he cannot fully rely on this or that motive of belief, that each of them is insecure, and the conclusion is put upon him that they ought to be discarded one after another, instead of being connected and combined' (*Dev* 3.1.9 quoting Davison [1861] p 19, in a different edition).

Newman himself has often been accused of scepticism.[39] He was not unaware of the element of truth in the charge,[40] yet his was 'the sort of scepticism which must beset any thinker who takes history seriously' (MacKinnon [1968] p 170, referring to Collingwood; cf House [1966b] pp 159–60). The vigour of his opposition to 'liberalism', 'rationalism', and 'latitudinarianism' was generated not by insensitivity, but by appreciation of the strength of the sceptic's case. If, as a result, he tended to over-react, it is nevertheless necessary to bear in mind the persuasive, apologetic mood of the arguments in the *Essay* (see *2.3*). It would be anachronistic to describe him as an 'existentialist',[41] and yet it is his conception of christianity as a 'practical' matter that accounts for his obsession with the inevitability of risking fundamental concrete decisions without waiting upon the resolution of the intractable theoretical and historical problems that underlie them.[42]

3.23 The negative force of arguments from antecedent probability
The primarily negative purpose of arguments from 'antecedent probability' (see *2.3*) is often not immediately apparent. The arguments for the 'antecedent probability' that a highly centralised, monarchical model of papal primacy is a 'true development', that is, a development 'contemplated by its Divine Author' (*Dev* 2.1.17), are a good illustration of this feature of the *Essay*.

According to Guizot, 'Religion has no sooner arisen in the

human mind than a religious society appears; and immediately a religious society is formed, it produces a government'.[43] To describe such a process as an 'ethical' (*Dev* 1.2.6 from 1881 on; *1845* and *1878*, 'moral') development, is to say that, although the historian may regard the institutionalisation of any religion, and the emergence of some system of government within it, as more or less inevitable, the realisation that this is the case can only be expressed in terms of what is likely, 'desirable . . . appropriate'; it is not a matter 'for strictly logical inference' (*Dev* 1.2.6). It is antecedently probable not only that such a process will take place, but that it will, at least in principle, be authorised by God : 'the social principle, which is innate in us, gives a divine sanction to society and to civil government' (*Dev* 1.2.7).

The second part of chapter 2 moves the argument from this high level of generalisation to embody more particular claims. A cluster of arguments is brought forward to show that 'an infallible authority' is 'antecedently probable', of which the most important is that revelation needs to be authoritatively interpreted at every stage in the church's history : 'the very idea of revelation implies a present informant and guide, and that an infallible one; not a mere abstract declaration of truths unknown before to man . . . but a message and a lesson speaking to this man or that' (*Dev* 2.2.12). Since Newman is concerned to create a broad presumption in favour of Roman catholic theory and practice, he does not enter into a detailed discussion of the nature of this 'guide' : the relationship between pope and church, for instance, remains highly ambiguous. Although phrases such as 'As creation argues continual governance, so are Apostles harbingers of Popes' (*Dev* 2.2.10) are merely rhetorical, the general drift of the argument is clear : 'If Christianity be a social religion . . . what power will suffice . . . but a supreme authority'; 'The only general persuasive in matters of conduct is authority'; 'By the Church of England a hollow uniformity is preferred to an infallible chair; and by the sects of England, an interminable division' (*Dev* 2.2.13).

The argument is further specified in chapter 4, where, after suggesting various reasons for the fact that the papacy only gradually emerged in the course of history, and before examining some of the early evidence for the primacy, he summarises the hypothetical component in the argument : 'It is the absolute need of a monarchical power in the Church which is our ground for anticipating it. A political body cannot exist without government, and the larger is the body the more concentrated must the government be. If the whole of Christendom is to form one Kingdom, one head is essential' (*Dev* 4.3.8; cf 2.3.2, 6.2.13).

At first sight such a passage, which echoes sentiments frequently found in Newman's writings,[44] is an argument for the antecedent probability that the emergence of the nineteenth-century form of papal government is just what any reasonable christian would have expected to take place. The grounds of this expectation are a questionable analogy between the nature and exercise of authority in the church and in secular society, described by Nédoncelle as central to the argument ([1962] p 142), a preference for a particular form of political structure (monarchical),[45] a particular conception of the notion of unity appropriate in ecclesiology (see 2.2), and a misunderstanding of the relationship between the kingdom of God and the church in history.[46]

But the form of the argument is misleading. Newman's fundamental concern is not to make positive claims for the antecedent probability that the papacy of Pius ix represents the ideal form of church government but, negatively, to show that the existing doctrine and practice of the Roman catholic church is not necessarily a 'corruption' (cf *Dev* 4.3.7; 2.2).

Undoubtedly, once he had begun to see a way through the 'difficulty' presented by the Roman 'developments', and to regard the Roman catholic church as the authentic heir of primitive christianity, his conception of 'prophetic fulfilment' and his particular brand of toryism facilitated the elaboration of the arguments in question. But the rhetorical power with which he constructs his case, 'comme un bon avocat' (Nédoncelle [1962] p 146), masks the extent to which he here, as always, sits lightly on the applicability, in 'concrete matters', of a priori, theoretical argumentation—see the long note he added, in 1871, to his article on 'The Catholicity of the Anglican Church' : *Ess* ii pp 74–109, esp p 108. Were it otherwise, the implied ecclesiology would be difficult to reconcile with the tripolar, dialectical description found in the 1877 preface to the *Via Media*, and with a non-monarchical conception of church government. Yet Newman was able to introduce, in *1878*, phrases which echo the former[47] and, in 1871, to envisage with equanimity a future situation in which the church would cease, once again, to be a 'monarchy'.

As an anglican he had asked : 'Why should it not be the intention of Divine Providence, as on the one hand, still to recognise His Church when contracted into a monarchy, so also not to forsake her when relaxed and dissolved again into a number of aristocratic fragments?' (*Ess* II p 44). The year following the Vatican Council, he added a note : ' "Why not?" because, in fact, it is *not* so dissolved; doubtless, *were* it so dissolved, were the Pope, as indistinct a power as he was in the first centuries, and the Bishops as practically independent, the Church would still be the Church' (*Ess* II p 44). In the same direction, compare the interpolations made in 1876 to his copy of a letter written in 1846 (*L&D* XI p 190, quoted above, *2.2*). However, the ambivalence implied in the term 'indistinct', in the passage just quoted, is clearly seen in two important letters written to Pusey in 1867 : *L&D* XXIII pp 98–100, 104–7.

In other words, Newman's fundamental concern is with the negative force of the arguments from 'antecedent probability' in the *Essay*, although the form in which these arguments are presented is often misleadingly positive. In his view, the former sufficed to 'account for' the 'difficulty', to justify his own move into Roman catholicism, and his recommendation of a similar move to others (see *3.21*). 'He does not indeed claim, formally and in words, for his theory, more than, if fairly supported, it is entitled to; but . . . he has succeeded, to some extent, in conveying an impression that he has achieved more than, even if his theory were admitted, he could be fairly held to have accomplished' Cunningham [1846] p 427. Cuningham was one of the few contemporary critics of the *Essay* to have seen the importance of the point with which we have been concerned in this section. He went on to say that 'The theory of development, if established and conceded, merely removes a general preliminary objection against Romanism' (*ibid* p 432).

3.3 Newman's field of data

In the study of doctrinal history, the criteria according to which the field of relevant data is delimited are as important as the interpreter's assumptions and hypotheses. The components of the 'lower blade' are as important as those of the 'upper'.

Pelikan, observing that 'The historical study of the development of doctrine is largely the creation of German Protestant scholarship during the eighteenth and nineteenth centuries' ([1969] p 46), regrets the fact that '*Dogmengeschichte* has concentrated not on the history of what the Church believed, taught and confessed, but on the history of erudite theology'. There was, until quite recently, a similar tendency, in Roman catholic studies, to restrict the field of data to propositions of scripture, ecclesiastical authority, and 'erudite theology'.

The field of data to which Newman appeals in the *Essay* includes, in principle, all aspects of the church's life and experience (*3.31*). In practice, however, both the apologetic nature of the *Essay*, and Newman's own competence and interests, seriously reduce the effective range of the data (*3.32*).

3.31 Unrestricted in principle

If the 'development of doctrine' consists simply in the clarificatory translation of propositions, or in the designation of propositions inferred from scriptural or conciliar statements as 'revealed truth' (prior to the *Essay*, at least, these were the 'two traditional ways of explaining dogmatic history'—Chadwick [1957] p 189), it is more or less inevitable that the only data regarded as relevant to an inquiry into doctrinal history will be the propositional articulation of christian belief.[48]

However, the truth or adequacy of doctrinal statements depends not only, or even primarily, on the extent to which they have been correctly argued to from previous statements, but also on the use to which they are put in the life, worship and witness of the church; a principle more likely to be appreciated by historians than by logicians. Newman, the historian, recognised that the history of the church's doctrine was the history of the *church*, of a 'fact in the world's history' (*Dev* Int 1), and not simply the history of talk about the fact. If the collapse of the 'Via Media' was due to the fact that, as a system, it only existed 'on paper' (*VM* I p 16; cf *Apo* pp 68–72; *Diff* I p 55), the new 'view' must be that of a 'living system' (*Apo* p 106; cf *Diff* I p 18). As a 'theory', the Via Media 'broke down under *facts*, historical facts' (*L&D* XIV p 182).

The field of data to which Newman appeals excludes, in principle, no dimension of the church's life.[49] Perhaps the most striking illustration of this is the emphasis placed (amongst the five 'kinds of development' regarded as relevant to the inquiry) on 'political' developments (*Dev* 1.2.10; cf 1.2.1–3, 2.1.13 etc). The passages at the end of each section of the long chapter on the 'first note' are brilliantly drawn descriptive parallels between the church of the Fathers and nineteenth-century Roman catholicism as Newman envisaged it in 1845 (*Dev* 6.1.30, 6.2.17—cf *OS* p 129, 6.3.3.23, also 2.3.5). They are phenomenological sketches in which 'doctrine' in the narrow sense plays a very small part. In *1878*, Newman added a note in which, using the terminology of the 1877 Preface to the *Via Media*, this is explicitly acknowledged : 'I have confined myself for the most part to her political aspect; but a parallel illustration might be drawn simply from her doctrinal, or from her devotional' (*Dev* 6.3.3.23). The influence of *VM* I is clear from Newman's first draft of this sentence, in which he admitted having 'confined' himself 'to her regal aspect, but a parallel illustration might be drawn from her prophetic or from her sacerdotal' (*BOA* D.7.6). This is an interesting admission concerning a chapter which occupies nearly a quarter of a study of the 'development of Christian *doctrine*'.

Again, the use which Newman makes of his distinction between 'principle' and 'doctrine' (see esp *Dev* 5.2, 7; *5.42*) enables him to appeal beyond what is said by christians about their beliefs, to the deep principles structuring the church's dynamic orientation, principles that are manifested in its style of life, attitudes and organisation : 'Principle is a better test of heresy than doctrine' (*Dev* 5.2.3). Similarly, by making use of the concept of 'prophetic tradition', he is able to appeal, not simply to the doctrinal *consensus fidelium*, but beyond it to 'a certain body of Truth, pervading the Church like an atmosphere, irregular in its shape from its very profusion and exuberance . . . poured to and fro in closets and upon the housetops, in liturgies, in controversial works, in obscure fragments, in sermons, in popular prejudices, in local customs' (*Dev* 2.2.2, quoting *VM* I p 250).

In thus appealing to the whole of the church's history, he was undoubtedly helped by his use of organic analogies, and by an epistemological perspective in which the whole life of the church, and not merely its theoretical component, could be described as the history of a 'living idea' : 'The grant of permanency was made in the beginning, not to the mere doctrine of the Gospel, but to the Association itself built upon the doctrine'[50] (*Ari* p 258).

Whether the search for a 'view' of history, such as that for which Newman sought, is not doomed to failure once one has admitted the principle that 'if one appeals to history, one must appeal to the whole of history' (Kent [1970] p 87) may, at this stage, be left as an open question. My purpose in this section has simply been to draw attention to the fact that, unlike many others who have written on the development of doctrine, Newman took the risk, in principle, of not arbitrarily restricting the field of data.

3.32 Restrictions in practice

If, in principle, the field of data for Newman's inquiry is as wide as the whole of christian history, in practice it is severely restricted both by the apologetic nature of the Essay and by the limitations of his competence and interest.

So far as the latter are concerned, Newman knew little or nothing of post-patristic Orthodoxy,[51] or of medieval christianity; the reformation is hardly discussed (cf Chadwick [1960] p 54), and post-reformation Roman catholic thought is represented by a handful of extracts, some of them taken at second-hand (cf Dev 7.2.6–9, 7.4.3–5).

Newman's preoccupation with his fundamental assumption, that contemporary Roman catholicism is the nearest approximation to, and as such the authentic heir of primitive christianity, explains his comparative lack of interest in the history of the church between those poles on which he concentrates. Moreover, the effect of the presumption that the 'true development' of primitive christianity is to be identified with one denomination 'taken as a whole' (see 5.3), is virtually to restrict the relevant evidence to the characteristics of the Roman catholic church: 'Mr Newman's ultimate conclusion is, that Christianity is Romanism, and Romanism is Christianity' (Irons [1846] p 40). Thus, although the anglicanism of the Via Media is at least treated as a serious adversary, all forms of protestantism are dismissed in a cavalier fashion. Cf Dev Int 5–6, 5.4.4—the 'whimsical theory . . . that Strauss and Kant are the "logical" development of Luther's thought', Chadwick [1957] p 248—7.1.2.

The field of data to which appeal is made in the Essay is restricted, not formally (on the assumption that certain aspects of the life of the church are irrelevant to an inquiry into the history of 'doctrine'), but materially because, from the ecclesiological standpoint that dictated the inquiry, he could hardly admit that 'it is quite as just to conceive a development of *all* Christianity as a development of the Roman Church' (Butler, W. A. [1850] p 175).

Any 'scientific' study of doctrinal development, the aim of which was not restricted to interdenominational apologetic, would be unable to exclude the evidence of medieval and post-reformation catholicism, or of the Orthodox and protestant churches. The danger is that methodological restrictions of the field of data, perhaps acceptable in pursuance of a very limited goal such as Newman's in the *Essay*, might remain in operation, almost unrecognised, even when the focus of inquiry had considerably shifted. Newman himself was to some extent caught in this trap in the debates that surrounded the Vatican Council. To say that nineteenth-century catholicism is not a 'corruption' is one thing; to say that it is therefore normative for the future development of the church and papacy is quite another (see *3.21*).

4

The development of an 'idea'

Accounts of Newman's 'theory of development' usually concentrate, not on the *Essay* as a whole, but on some particular feature or constitutive theme of its complex argument. As a result the aim, argument and method of the *Essay* have often been oversimplified or misunderstood. Debates on doctrinal development, from the modernist crisis until quite recently, were more concerned with the search for a 'theory' of development that would meet the aparently stringent demands of orthdox belief than with the prior task of *understanding* the complex patterns of doctrinal history. Misunderstanding was perhaps inevitable when theologians thus preoccupied with the search for a 'theory' found Newman saying, in the Introduction to the *Essay*: 'from the nature of the human mind, time is necessary for the full comprehension and perfection of great ideas . . . This may be called the *Theory of Development of Doctrine*' (*Dev* Int 21). That quotation indicates those aspects of the argument of the *Essay* which we shall examine in this chapter, in order to clarify the sense in which Newman may or may not be said to have had a 'theory of development'.

An examination of Newman's treatment of the notion of the 'idea' in the *Essay* (and especially in the first half of chapter 1) raises a number of important issues concerning the aim and method of the *Essay*, and the philosophical and theological perspectives within which it is written (*4.1*). In particular, it will be necessary to discuss some implications of Newman's use of the analogy between the history of ideas in the mind of an individual, and in a society (*4.2*), and the extent to which the argument of the *Essay* rests upon an assumption that the history of an 'idea' is an homogeneous, expanding and irreversible process (*4.3*).[1]

4.1 A 'real and living idea'

In order to indicate the most important features of Newman's treatment, in the *Essay*, of the notion of an 'idea' and its 'development', we shall concentrate on the first section of chapter 1 : 'On the Process of Development in Ideas'.[2] The difficulty of this important section is due partly to Newman's less than consistent use of the term 'idea',[3] and partly to the fact that, as so often in reading Newman, it is insufficient to rest 'on the surface' of the text : one has to try to enter into the perspective of his very personal 'phenomenological investigation of experience' (Sillem [1969] p 19).

The elements of the argument with which we shall be concerned are : the classification of some 'ideas' as 'real and living'; the relationship between the concepts of 'idea', 'view' and 'aspect'; the relationship between cognitional process in the individual and the appropriation of an 'idea' by a society; and the problem of identifying that 'idea' of christianity the 'development' of which Newman has in mind in this introductory description (which raises the question of the theological dimension of the argument). Finally, we shall ask how, on the account given in these pages, the process of the 'development' of an 'idea' reaches a term.

'Living' and 'real ideas'. In *1845*, the concept of the 'idea' gradually shifts in the course of the argument. In the opening passages 'ideas' are described as those 'habitual judgements' which are 'exercised' on the 'things which come before' the mind (p 30). By the end of the section, the term seems to refer to an objective entity, existing independently of and influencing the minds of men. In *1878*, this shift in meaning is less marked and, throughout the section, the term refers principally to some objective fact or reality, apprehended as a whole. The term is still occasionally used to refer to those 'judgements' or 'mere opinions' that are 'nothing more than ideas, which we mistake for things'.[4] Culler says that, for Newman, 'unreal . . . means partly that a set of opinions has no consistency within itself and partly that it has no relation to reality' ([1955] p 197). In this section, it is the latter use which is dominant.

In both editions, 'mere' ideas are distinguished from those which correspond to objective reality. In *1845* the latter are said to be 'real, that is, represent facts existing' (p 30, cf p 32). In *1878*, while this terminology is sometimes retained, there is an increased use of the term 'objective' (*Dev* 1.1.1; 1.1.2). There is one similar use in *1845* : 'The number of persons holding an idea is no warrant for its objective character, else the many never could be wrong' (p 31—on the significance of this notion of 'objectivity', see *4.12*). Newman is able to regard 'bodily substances' as analogous to 'real' or 'objective' ideas (*Dev* 1.1.2) because his notion of 'things' or 'facts existing' is wide enough to include theoretical systems: thus 'the Platonic philosophy' is referred to as an 'intellectual fact' (*Dev* 1.1.3; cf *Ari* p 134; *Diff* I p 276; *Ess* I pp 35, 68–9; *L&D* xvi p 297). The applicability of the argument of this section to the problem of doctrinal development depends upon the 'Platonic' assumption that a 'real idea' ontologically pre-exists the minds into which it enters.

In using the term 'Platonic' of Newman's thought, I intend it to refer not 'to the platonism of Plato, but to the christian platonism of the Alexandrian Fathers' (Boekraad [1961] p 24; cf Artz [1968] p 99; Bouyer [1936] p 290; Guitton [1933] pp 5, 10; Sillem [1969] pp 92, 171–2; Stern [1967] p 24 and refs). 'The Fathers, especially the Alexandrians, form the background of all his theological thinking' (Tristram [1945d] p 236), but although 'His writings show a certain slight acquaintance with Platonic doctrine . . . we have it on tradition from his own lips that he had never read the works of Plato' (Tristram [1945a] p 275). As Willam has shown, the influence on Newman of Aristotle or, to be more exact, of Whately's Aristoteleanism, was both lasting and profound, but 'there is no reason for holding, as Dr Willam does, that Newman is a pure Aristotelean' (Sillem [1969] p 163; cf Boekraad [1958] pp 141–2). For instance, Willam asserts that 'Eines ist klar: bekennt sich Newman nicht zu ihr [the link with Aristotle's Metaphysics], so bleibt er eine Art Locke-Jünger, und jene haben recht, die seine Theorie der Dogmenentwicklung unvereinbar mit der Tradition halten' (Willam [1964] p 194). Fundamental options are rarely so stark in the interpretation of Newman.

'When an idea, whether real or not, is of a nature to arrest and possess the mind, it may be said to have life, that is, to live in the mind which is its recipient'.[5] The category of the 'living' idea is introduced at that point in the description at which, in *1845*, the move is most strongly made from the notion of the idea as a 'judgement' by the individual mind to that of it as a pre-existing reality 'received . . . in this or that form into many minds' (*Dev* 1.1.4).

Whereas the characterisation of an 'idea' as 'real' clearly embodies a truth-claim (there is that of which the idea is the 'representative'), its characterisation as 'living' at first sight appears simply to rest upon its observed influence on the mind of an individual or a society, though it will be seen (*4.31*) that this is misleading. If christianity may legitimately be described as an 'idea', then whether or not it is a 'real' idea (and this, in the *Essay*, Newman takes for granted), its turbulent history undoubtedly entitles one to classify it as 'living' (cf *US* p 316).

From the point of view of method, we have seen how Newman justifies the historiographical method of the *Essay* on the grounds that it is a special case of a generally valid approach to the study of history (see *3.1*). Similarly, the explicit level at which the argument of this section moves is that of a description of 'real' and/or 'living ideas' in general (this was a principal reason for the charge, by Newman's contemporary Anglican critics, that the argument of the *Essay* was 'rationalistic' : see Nicholls [1965] p 383). The specification of the description in its application to christianity is almost entirely implicit (nevertheless, the reference to christianity is present to Newman's mind in every phrase : notice the careful addition 'and their leaders and guides' in *Dev* 1.1.5; cf *1845* p 37). In the following section, he excludes certain types of development as irrelevant to the study of christianity (cf *Dev* 1.2.1, 1.2.10). It is of particular interest that he excludes 'mathematical' developments 'because they are conducted on strict demonstration' (*Dev* 1.2.1), and 'physical', i.e. organic developments (*ibid*; see *4.31*).

'Views' and 'aspects' of an 'idea'. Newman's preference for visual analogies of cognitional process is partly accounted for by his existentialist or personalist approach to epistemological problems. An individual's grasp of an 'objective' or 'real idea' is perspectival : it represents that idea as seen from a particular point of view (cf *Dev* 1.1.1, 1.1.2, 1.1.4; *3.22*). If this were the end of the matter, then the resolution of disputes between those who saw things differently would be impossible. This is, of course, in practice often the case.[6] But were Newman to admit that it had to be so in principle, he would be trapped into one form of that 'liberalism' which he so feared. The creative tension at the heart of the present section arises from the fact that the description of the 'development of an idea' is an attempt to reconcile the 'situated-

ness' of the individual in his grasp of the truth with the possibility of an eventual state of affairs in which 'the idea . . . will be to each mind separately what at first it was only to all together'. (*Dev* 1.1.4. A similar phrase, in *US* p 291, has strong overtones of the Pauline doctrine of the body: cf *4.2* and *Ess* I pp 40–1, 209; GA p 464; and the defence of his terminology against Brownson in *L&D* XII p 98).

Whereas an 'idea' is the potentially or actually apprehended representative of the whole object, an 'aspect' is any partial knowledge of the idea (and so of the object) from a particular point of view: 'The idea which represents an object or supposed object is commensurate with the sum total of its possible aspects'.[7] Here, Newman's analogy with 'bodily substances . . . which admit of being walked round, and surveyed on opposite sides, and in different perspectives . . . in evidence of their reality' (*Dev* 1.1.2; cf *Jfc* p 121), enables him to bring off a controversialist's tour de force. The *Essay* is concerned to explain the 'embarrassing' fact that christianity has known considerable variation in teaching and practice in the course of its history. Here this rich multiplicity of 'aspects' is proposed as an 'argument for its reality' (*Dev* 1.1.2, but no longer as 'proof', *1845* p 32). Like so many of Newman's arguments, this one, if taken in isolation from the rest of the strands in the 'cable' (*L&D* XXI p 146; see *3.22*) and pushed to extremes, would be nonsense: the more disagreement there has been amongst christians, the greater the evidence for the truth of christianity (contrast the peremptory assertion, in 1830, that 'the multitude of men are wrong, so far as they differ', *PS* VIII p 185). Yet Newman is surely correct: it is the deep truths concerning man and his history that elicit the richest variety of insight and affirmation, that provoke the widest disagreement, and that most successfully elude man's attempts to comprehend and linguistically to exhaust his experience: 'There is no one aspect deep enough to exhaust the contents of a real idea, no one term or proposition which will serve to define it' (*Dev* 1.1.3; cf *HS* III p 194; *Idea* p 45).

The process described in this section is that of the 'warfare of ideas under their various aspects',[8] as men struggle, under the pressure of events and of the tension between different 'aspects' of truth, less inadequately to express and to embody the truth which has grasped them. (One could have said: the truth which they have grasped, but this would not sufficiently indicate that independence and sovereignty of the 'living idea' which is so marked a feature of the closing paragraphs of the section.)[9] The 'development' of an idea is thus defined as the 'process . . . by which the aspects of an idea are brought into consistency and form' (*Dev* 1.1.5).

'. . . when an idea is very complex, it is allowable, for the sake of convenience, to consider its distinct aspects as if separate ideas' (*Dev* 1.1.3). In *1845*, that apparently harmless admission was followed by a firm rejection of the possibility of isolating the 'leading idea' of christianity (pp 34–5). In *1878*, while still insisting that he is only doing so 'for convenience', he is prepared to 'call the Incarnation the central aspect of Christianity' (*Dev* 1.1.3; cf 7.1.3). The extent to which this shift marks a significant weakening of the argument will be discussed in *6.31*.

The individual and society. In the course of the argument, in *1845*, attention shifts from the individual mind to the society in which the process of the development of an idea is described. (This move corresponds to the shift, already mentioned, in the concept of the 'idea'). The link is the discussion (in a passage on pp 31–2, omitted from *1878*) of the extent to which the fact that many people hold an idea is a 'warrant for its objective character'. In principle, this cannot be so 'else the many never could be wrong . . . But when one and the same idea is held by persons who are independent of each other, and are variously circumstanced . . . then it seems to have a claim to be considered the representative of an objective truth'. In *1878*, the shift is less marked, attention being concentrated throughout on the idea as such.

So far as the general method of the *Essay* is concerned, the important point to notice is that Newman's account of the process of the development of an idea in society is explicitly grounded upon his strongly 'Platonic' conception of the independence and sovereignty of a 'real' and 'living' idea, rather than upon the latent analogy between the movement of thought in an individual and in society.

The 'idea' of christianity. Although the application of the argument to christianity remains, in this section, largely implicit, it is clearly important to ask : what is that 'idea' the development of which Newman has in mind? According to *Dev* 1.1.3, the answer is 'Christianity', or 'Revelation' (in this article, these seem to be identical). Christianity is an 'idea' inasmuch as it is the human apprehension of that 'fact' which is christianity considered as God's word, or self-disclosure of his will and purposes for man. The 'idea' is one because the 'fact' is one : because God is one and his word is one. The 'idea' is 'real' because God's revelation is an 'objective fact', and not an illusion of man (cf *US* p 328). The 'idea' is 'living' because it is God's living word. This theological dimension of Newman's argument is not spelt out in this section, and will be discussed more fully later on (*4.31*).

When Newman says, therefore, that christianity is a 'fact in the world's history' (*Dev* Int 1), or that it is a 'fact, and impresses an idea of itself on our minds' (*Dev* 2.1.1), he is not only observing that there are certain social or historical phenomena to which we give the name 'christianity', but also affirming that objectivity of God's word, and its priority over the response of man, which is at the heart of his theological concern and is the ground of the 'dogmatic principle'.

The final article of this section is perhaps the most frequently quoted passage in the *Essay*; it has given delight to those who would adopt a 'strong' theory of doctrinal change, and horrified those who see in it Newman's abandonment of any sense of the primacy of scripture. It undoubtedly contains a 'progressive' view of the history of christianity and, as such, it is untypical. It must be borne in mind that, throughout the *Essay*, Newman is reacting against his earlier suspicion of the degree of change, and of that confidence in the authenticity of its self-understanding, which seemed to him to mark the Roman catholic church. While we may reasonably regard this passage as an over-reaction, it represents a mood rather than a 'theory' of doctrinal development. The use of the 'stream' image, in particular, if seen against the background of Rose's diametrically opposed use of it,[10] amounts to little more than an affirmation of that relationship between church and scripture which Newman believed that he had learnt from Hawkins.[11] This interpretation of the passage does not necessarily conflict with that offered by Nédoncelle, who sees its origin in a debate between Newman and Burton ([1958] p 211; cf Biemer [1967] p 75).

The mood which the passage represents is that of unswerving confidence in the providential guidance of the church (cf *Diff* II pp 355-6). As such, its language is rhetorical, rather than descriptive. Moreover, this confidence is given specific form in the christological motifs the presence of which account for the fact that the 'idea' is, in this article, not merely hypostatised, but personalised. (For a discussion of the christological imagery that, in this and other passages in the *Essay*, counterpoints the phenomenological analysis, see *4.31*.)

Finally, although the 'idea' changes *quoad nos* during the course of its realisation in human history (see *4.12*), Newman can regard this process of change with equanimity because he believes the 'idea' (as also the 'object' of which it is the idea) to be *quoad se* 'immutable' (*Dev* 2.1.1): 'It changes . . . in order to remain the same' (*Dev* 1.1.7). The extent to which it is possible coherently to justify this conviction is another matter (see *4.3*), but at least it is clear that, even in this passage, Newman does not intend to abandon the tension between immutability and change, between the transcendent and the historical.

The term of the process of development. Newman defines 'development' as the 'process . . . by which the aspects of an idea are brought into consistency and form' (*Dev* 1.1.5). But how does this process reach a term, and how is it known to have done so? This question will be discussed in *4.32*; so far as this opening section is concerned, two points may be made.

In the first place, it is uncertain whether the situation described in the middle of *Dev* 1.1.4, in which the 'idea' has become 'to each mind separately what at first it was only to all together', is intended to refer to the term of the process (in which case the second part of the article would be a recapitulation of the first, from the point of view of the relationship of the idea to other 'doctrines or facts'), or (which is more probable) to that stage in the process which is marked, for example, by the articulation of the creed.

In the second place, it seems clear that the final sentence of the article does refer to the term of the process, which is described as the emergence of that 'body of thought' which is 'little more than the proper representative of one idea . . . its complete image'.[12]

A comparison of these brief notes with other descriptions of Newman's notion of the 'idea' in the *Essay* shows, for example, that Walgrave's classification gives insufficient weight to the 'Platonism' of these pages ([1957] p 95, esp the over-hasty judgement 'not that subsistence is attributed to it'), and that Sillem's sensitive description of Newman's account of cognitional process concentrates, even when he explicitly refers to this section of the *Essay*, on that process in the mind of the individual ([1969] pp 110–23). Because the concern of both authors is philosophical, they miss those theological overtones the presence of which must be recognised if an adequate account is to be given of these pages.

4.11 Newman's preoccupation with comparing the 'terms' of the 'process'

According to Acton, Newman's *Essay* 'did more than any other book of his time to make his countrymen think historically, and watch the process as well as the result' (cul *Add* mss 4987.60). It is undoubtedly the case that the central insight of the *Essay*, the 'hypothesis' that the history of christianity can be viewed as the 'development' of an 'idea', powerfully expresses an awareness of the significance of the process of history. Nevertheless, if the method and structure of the *Essay* are to be faithfully described, it must be insisted that, as was the case with the *Lectures on the Prophetical Office*, the central interpretative hypothesis is methodologically subordinated to the attempt to set up a comparison beween primitive christianity and the contemporary church. In both instances the aim was defensive : in the former case, to provide 'for the defence of the Anglican Church', that 'broad, intellectual, intelligible theory' (*VM* I p xxiii) which was the theory of the *Via Media*; in the latter case, to provide for the defence of Roman catholicism that 'hypothesis' which is the 'Theory of Development of Doctrine' (*Dev* Int 21). 'The fact of the operation from first to last of that principle of development in the truths of Revelation, is an argument in favour of the identity of Roman and Primitive Christianity' (*Apo* p 199; cf *VM* I p xxxvii).

Thus it is that the first 'Note' of a 'Genuine Development', 'Preservation of Type', is not concerned with the process itself, but with the comparability of its terms. This is less clear in *1878*, where the greater part of the summary description of this note consists of material which, in *1845*, formed a general introduction to all seven 'tests' (pp 58–63, cf *Dev* 5.1.4–9. Nevertheless, it is still evident from chapter 6, the whole argument of which is directed to the famous concluding paragraphs of each section (*Dev* 6.1.30; 6.2.17; 6.3.3.23). In reading the *Essay*, Newman's own warning needs to be borne in mind: the word 'development . . . is used here . . . on the one hand for the process of development, on the other for the result' (*Dev* 1.2.1).

Newman came to regard it as more or less self-evident that 'of all existing systems, the present communion of Rome is the nearest approximation in fact to the Church of the Fathers, possible though some may think it, to be nearer still to that Church on paper. Did St Ambrose or St Athanasius come suddenly to life, it cannot be doubted what communion he would take to be his own'.[13] There remained the 'difficulty' of the 'apparent' differences between the church of St Athanasius and that of Pius IX. To account for this difficulty a hypothesis was necessary: 'The Essay on Development aimed at testing whether late expressions of the original idea or impression expressed in Scripture were true to that original idea' (Davis [1964] p 173). It was those particular, concrete, 'later expressions', the doctrine and practice of the Roman catholic church, which Newman 'aimed at testing', rather than any theoretical argument concerning them.

Newman claimed to have a 'theory of development': 'from the nature of the human mind, time is necessary for the full comprehension and perfection of great ideas' (*Dev* Int 21). When he passes, however, from the general phenomenological description in *Dev* 1.1 to an account of the 'kinds of development in ideas' (*Dev* 1.2), he presents us with five types of historical process so different from each other that it is difficult to see how they could be related within a systematically unified 'theory' of doctrinal development. Even Walgrave, usually so uncritical of Newman's achievement, is puzzled: 'we are left wondering how these five types can find a place in a single process which is nothing but the unfolding of an original idea in all its aspects and relations—a formula which seems to Newman to sum up the whole process of development' ([1957] p 300). Acton, too, was irritated by the rudimentary state of the 'theory' in the *Essay*: 'The idea, the view was enough for him. He took the rest for granted . . . therefore he did not carry out the argument'.[14] Thus Irons was not too far wide of the mark when he admitted that 'we are compelled to the conclusion, that the theory has no ideal unity whatever, if regarded apart from its subject-matter, which is the Roman Church. It is rather, a number of theories, more or less analogous, kept together by an ingenious writer for a definite purpose—but having no internal oneness—and therefore not capable of being submitted to any "test" ' (Irons [1846] p 44).

The apologetic nature of the *Essay* dictates Newman's 'point of vision' (*Dev* 1.1.2), and both accounts for and determines his attempt, on the one hand, to compare the 'Church of the Fathers' with English christianity in the nineteenth century and, on the other hand, to vindicate the claims of Roman catholicism in comparison with other claimants to the title of heir to the primitive church.

In our own day, the fact that christianity has in some sense 'evolved', 'developed' or 'changed' in the course of its history is an assumption that we simply take for granted, whether we consider the process to have been one of improvement, or 'progress', or whether our evaluation of it is more guarded and more tentative. Therefore, when a theologian today offers a 'theory of doctrinal development', we have come to expect from him a systematic and unified interpretation of doctrinal history. Those who read the *Essay* with such an expectation are puzzled and disappointed. But Newman did not share the assumption to which I have referred. To him, as a pioneer, it was the *fact* of 'development' which he offered as a 'hypothesis', as an alternative to 'immutability', on the one hand, and 'corruption' on the other. He took into consideration many widely differing types of 'development', both because the complexity of the historical evidence demanded this, and because his heuristic conception of 'development' as the key to the problem was not further implemented in the form of any single 'theory of development', in the modern sense, at all.

The *Essay* undoubtedly contains, in rudimentary form, the seeds of a number of such theories, the systematic elaboration of which might show that they are not mutually compatible. Thus, as we shall see, there are traces of that analogy between the psychological history of an individual and the 'mind' of a society which figures largely in the fifteenth *University Sermon*, and in the *Perrone Paper* (*4.2*); there is the analogy between the history of christian belief and practice and the process of organic growth (*4.31*); there are many passages which explain why commentators have attributed to Newman a 'homogeneous', 'cumulative' view of the history of doctrine (*4.3*); there are suggestions of a less linear, more episodic view of the history of the 'idea' (*4.12*); and there are hints of that tripolar dialectic between theology, church order and the worshipping life of the local community which Newman described in the preface to the third (1877) edition of the *Via Media*, and which represents his most mature view of some important aspects of the problem.

Newman's critics were irritated by the fact that 'Mr Newman has no consistent theory whatever'.[15] We are today perhaps closer in spirit to Newman than to those thinkers, in the intervening century, who believed that it was possible to construct single 'theories' or 'philosophies' of doctrinal history which would be applicable to all ages and all cultures. In fact, such theories are usually either cast at so high a level of generalisation as to be incapable of falsification, or else they are so narrowly conceived as to be manifestly inadequate as an interpretation of the concrete life of the church in history.

4.12 *Two views of the process: 'linear' and 'episodic'*

In the previous section (*4.11*) it was suggested that, in so far as a 'theory of development' is taken to mean a systematically elaborated theoretical interpretation of christian history, the *Essay* offers us, at most, a 'view' of the history of christian belief and practice which contains within it a number of such theories in rudimentary form. Before examining, in *4.2* and *4.3*, two of the major presuppositions which underly Newman's argument that, 'from the nature of the human mind, time is necessary for the full comprehension and perfection of great ideas' (*Dev* Int 21), it may be useful briefly to indicate two rather different conceptions of doctrinal development which are to be found in the *Essay*, and which are neither fully elaborated nor systematically unified. In doing so, we shall touch upon a number of topics (such as Newman's concept of revelation, and his attitude towards dogmatic formulas) which will receive more detailed treatment later in this study.

In a letter protesting about W. G. Ward's proposed degradation by the University of Oxford, Maurice accepted the notion of development as the growth of living minds, but said: 'There appears to be a strange fluctuation in [Newman's] mind between this idea and another—the most diametrically opposed to it: one, namely, which would identify development with accumulation . . . [Mr Ward] has no dream of a development except in this last sense . . . The bigger the heap the greater his admiration' (quoted in Ward, W. [1889] p 322). It would, perhaps, be more accurate to suggest that the 'fluctuation' which Maurice detected in Newman's thinking on development prior to the writing of the *Essay*, and which persists in the *Essay* itself, represents the tension between two ways of conceiving of the history of 'ideas'. The first, concentrating on the theoretical component in christian history (the history of statements and propositions), tends to envisage the process of development as linear and cumulative. In the second, more episodically considered perspective, the focus of concern is the concrete 'reality' of the history of the 'idea'. The element of continuity is seen to reside, not in the linearity of the process, but rather in the fact that, at every stage in the process, the same eternal 'idea' is expressed, 'realised', in the life and teaching of the church.

The 'linear' conception of development is at work, for example, in so far as individual statements in scripture are put forward as supplying the biblical warrant for the claim that individual contemporary doctrines or practices are 'developments' of primitive christianity (cf *Dev* 2.1.14). 'Logical deduction' is offered as an analogy for the process of development: 'all parties appeal to Scripture, that is, argue from Scripture; but argument implies deduction, that is, development' (*Dev* 2.1.3; cf *Diff* I pp 394–5). This view of doctrinal history is that which predominates in Newman's treatment of the 'fourth note' (*Dev* 5.4; 7.3.1; 9). Newman's sensitivity to the complexity of history prevents him from pressing the analogy of 'deduction' too far: he is aware that the history of the idea admits, as Congar puts it, 'des cheminements . . . zigzagants' ([1970d] p 611), and he would have agreed with de Lubac that 'Là où l'on ne semble apercevoir qu'un développement linéaire, par voie de conséquences, la réalité nous montre une réaction perpétuelle aux données ambiantes, par voie de défense, d'élimination, de triage, de transformation, d'assimilation' ([1948] p 139).

It is when he is arguing from within a broadly linear, cumulative, framework, that Newman's view approximates most closely to those accounts of doctrinal development which existed before him in catholic theology, and which continued to flourish until fairly recently.[16] Such a view is easier to maintain in the measure that the starting-point of the process, the *revelatum*, is conceived of as an aggregate of divinely authenticated statements. We shall see that there is, in the *Essay*, a tendency (encouraged by New-man's Alexandrian, neo-platonic approach to revelation) so to regard the text of scripture (cf *Ess* I p 286; *US* p 334; *5.2*; *5.21*).

On the other hand, this same neo-platonism also provided him with the perspective for another, very different conception of doctrinal development. It is now the 'harmony' (see *4.3*), at each successive stage of its development, of christianity considered as a concrete whole, that is the focus of his apologetic concern. His typological approach to the study of history; his preoccupation with the comparability of the terms of the process of development (see *4.11*); his conviction that, at every period, the church's creed and rite are the complete, if inadequate and symbolic expression of the eternal 'idea' of christianity; such factors combined to enable him to view the process of development as that of the 'realization' (one might almost say 'incarnation') of the ineffable word of God in the life, institutions, worship and belief of a people :[17] the history of a 'living' and 'real' idea.[18] 'Ainsi la vérité divine, en s'incarnant dans la pensée humaine de son Eglise, y mènera une vie semblable en toutes choses à celle des idées humaines excepté l'erreur' (Walgrave [1964a] p 85).

This view is more appreciative of the essential, yet subordinate function of religious 'forms' (liturgical and institutional, as well as credal) than the previous one, and also more alive to the inevitable inadequacy,[19] almost arbitrariness of these forms as they are forged out of the dialectical tensions of the historical process.[20] It is here that Newman's sensitivity to the historicity (*Geschichtlichkeit*[21]) of christianity, and to the role played in doctrinal development by the 'logic of facts' (*VM* I p lxxxvi; cf *L&D* xx p 392; xxi p 457), is most evident.

It is hardly surprising that the presence of this second conception of doctrinal history has, for the most part, been neglected by Newman's commentators. Not only was he himself preoccupied with the problem of continuity (which is more easily handled in a 'linear' perspective) but, especially at the time of the modernist crisis, his defenders were concerned, above all, to show that his account of development did not succumb to that 'transformism' which they so feared.[22]

Nevertheless, when Newman came to revise the *Essay*, one of the first notes he pencilled suggests that he was envisaging the problem 'episodically', rather than within a 'linear' framework :

'I may have a new truth . . . conveyed to my intelligence by one set of words, then by another, then by a third . . . And then, when called upon, I may enunciate the doctrine, the very same doctrine, but again and afresh in my own words, and not in those which were used to teach it to me . . . Here there is an idea communicated, not indeed except thro' words, but not in dependence of any formula. Such is the nature of that communication to us afresh of the truth of what we call revelation'. (*BOA* D.7.6, quoted in Chadwick [1957] p 246, who has 'communicate (?)' for 'enunciate' : cf Stern [1967] p 216).

Underlying both the tendencies which, for the sake of clarity, have been rather sharply distinguished in this section, is that 'Platonic' cast of mind which, negatively, allowed Newman to underestimate the 'literary' nature of scriptural statements,[23] and provided support for a christological perspective which hardly does justice to the humanity of Christ.[24] Yet, on the other hand, it provided his strong doctrine of the providential guidance of the church with a convenient conceptual framework.

It is not my intention to suggest that these two broad conceptions of doctrinal history are to be found, fully elaborated, and clearly distinguished one from the other, in the *Essay*. Rather, by drawing attention to the rudimentary presence of two such different conceptions, my aim has been to illustrate, once again, the extreme caution which is necessary in the face of systematically unified accounts of Newman's 'theory of development'. Throughout his life, Newman's respect for the complexity of historical process ensured a certain fluidity in his conceptualisation of the structures of that process. Thus, in 1874, he said that those truths 'which are sometimes called developments of Christian doctrine' are 'evidently the new form, explanation, transformation, or carrying out of what in substance was held from the first' (*Diff* II p 313–4).

4.2 *The analogy between society and the individual mind*

The presupposition that the process of thought in the mind of an individual provides an illuminating analogy for understanding the development of an 'idea' in society lies so near the heart of Newman's philosophy that it is seldom explicitly stated or critically examined (cf *Dev* 2.1.1–2; 5.4.1; 5.5.2; 9.0.1; *4.1*). One of the grounds of the analogy is the theological conviction that 'the heart of every Christian ought to represent in miniature the Catholic Church, since one Spirit makes both the whole Church and every member of it to be His Temple' (*SD* p 132). Similarly, in 1847 : 'Nam spiritus ille, in quo verbum est totum quid, vivit in universis ejus partibus, per singulas autem communicatur' (*Perrone* p 408). A presumed analogy between two processes, however, does not necessarily justify the assumption that they are more or less identical. Walgrave seems to make this assumption when, early in his chapter on 'The Social Psychology of Development,' he says that : 'An idea develops and matures within a society *in the same way* as a thought in the mind of a philosopher' ([1957] p 171, referring to *Perrone* pp 414–5; my stress). The analogy is more closely pressed in the last of the *University Sermons* than in the *Essay*, a fact which may have influenced those commentators who, in their search for Newman's 'theory' of development, devote the greater part of their analysis to the sermon rather than to the *Essay* (cf Davis [1967a]; Potts [1964]; Stern [1967] pp 210–18).

The aim and method of the *Essay*, however, are significantly different from those of this sermon (cf Lash [1970] p 51; Guitton [1933] pp 66–7). The descriptive context in which the development of an idea is discussed is far broader in the *Essay* than in the sermon. Of the five 'kinds of development' described in the *Essay*, and declared to be relevant to the development of christian doctrine (*Dev* 1.2.10), only one is directly comparable to the process of development in the mind of an individual. This is that which Newman calls 'metaphysical', and it is significant that the account of this type of development is the only place in the *Essay* in which the sermon is quoted (*Dev* 1.2.9; see *4.32*).

In 1847, in the *Perrone Paper*, Newman made extensive use of the analogy : 'when his *Essay* was attacked by eminent theologians in Rome, it was this . . . analogy to which he sought to lead them by way of explaining what he intended' (Chadwick [1957] p 151). Our concern, however, is with the *Essay* itself, in which the analogy 'does not appear, or appears only in passing' (*ibid*). If Newman 'had a theory of development' only in the sense described in the previous sections (*4.11, 4.12*), then it is not surprising that different controversial needs, and different aims, should give rise to different specifications of that 'theory' in the sermon, the *Essay*, and the *Perrone Paper*.

In other words, whether or not the analogy, when pressed to the extent that it is in other writings, will withstand serious criticism, is not our immediate concern. In the *Essay*, the range of 'types' of development under consideration is sufficiently wide to enable Newman to avoid the consequences of too rigid an application of the analogy. Nevertheless, the presupposition, in the *Essay*, of the general validity of such an analogy raises two important questions. The first, which we have touched on elsewhere in regard to the *University Sermons* (cf Lash [1970]), concerns the use of the notions of 'implicit' and 'explicit' reason in Newman's argument. This will be discussed in the following chapter (5.4). The second concerns Newman's insistence on the ethical component in an individual's growth in the knowledge of God.

It has sometimes been assumed that to regard the history of christian belief and practice as a process of 'development' is necessarily to adopt a 'progressive' view of the church's history, with the implication that the later stages in that history are somehow to be seen as an improvement on the earlier.[25] While there are several passages in the *Essay* which would lend support to the view that Newman saw the history of doctrine in this light, the contrary evidence is so strong that Chadwick is entitled summarily to assert : 'Newman never believed in progress'.[26]

In so far as the history of the individual is concerned, 'The development of the religious man is a dialectic of fidelity to conscience. The philosophy of the rationalist is wrought by reason to the exclusion of conscience' (Walgrave [1957] p 148). Again and again, especially in his sermons, Newman expresses the conviction that growth in holiness is a necessary condition of growth in the knowledge of God.[27] In the light of the analogy between the intellectual history of an individual and that of a society, it would seem possible to claim that the contemporary church had a deeper grasp of God's revelation than had the primitive church only if, at the same time, it could be claimed that the church had grown in holiness.[28] For all his confidence in the providential guidance of the church, few ideas would have been more foreign to Newman than this one.[29] Indeed, he never completely abandoned the view that the primitive church possessed a degree of sanctity never again attained in its subsequent history (cf *PS* ii p 29; iii pp 161–2, 233–4; vii pp 81–3, 250; *SN* pp 202–3; *VM* i pp 7, 132–3, 201–2).

It could be suggested that even the most thorough systematisation and reflexive ('explicit') appropriation of the truth 'held' in the apostolic consciousness, although it may, from some points of view (for instance, by analogy with the emergence of a secular science) be plausibly described as progress *quoad nos*, does not necessarily imply a more profound grasp of the mystery of the living God.[30] But even this suggestion would not rule out the possibility that the development of an 'idea' in history, the irreversible reflexive appropriation by the church of God's revelation, since it is not accompanied by a proportionate growth in holiness, represents a decline into just that 'rationalism' which Newman most feared. It seems that, from the apologetic standpoint of the *Essay*, this is a serious problem which Newman never adequately considered.[31]

The claim that the institutionalisation of christianity (which 'came into the world as an idea rather than an institution'[32]), and the crystallisation of christian belief in credal and liturgical forms, were inevitable, is grounded on the general methodological principle that 'Christianity has been long enough in the world to justify us in dealing with it as a fact in the world's history' (*Dev* Int 1; see *3.1*). If such a process had not taken place, christianity would have perished; but it does not follow that the occurrence of this process necessarily constitutes a progressive increase in or deepening of man's knowledge of God.

Newman's lifelong dedication to the 'dogmatic principle' is the expression of his conviction that the truth of God is prior to and objective in respect of the human mind, and not a creature of that mind's construction. It is significant that the description of this principle in the *Essay* includes the phrase : 'the mind is below truth, not above it, and is bound, not to descant upon it, but to venerate it' (*Dev* 8.1.1). Later in the same chapter, he says that 'What Conscience is in the history of an individual mind, such was the dogmatic principle in the history of Christianity' (*Dev* 8.1.5). In other words, even the most vivid 'realisation' of the 'idea' in history, while it may be necessary to ensure the survival of 'living faith' (man's reception of the 'idea' of the living God), does not necessarily imply any notion of progress.

Nevertheless, must we not say that, inasmuch as Newman sees the process of doctrinal development as including the necessary solution of urgent problems which the primitive church had not tackled (cf *Dev* 2.1.5–6), there is an element of 'progress' in that process, in which case the objection we are considering still stands? For, in so far as one of the elements in the history of doctrine consists in the formal, explicit appropriation of 'aspects' of the mystery which have hitherto simply been 'held', prereflexively, in the general consciousness of the believing community (as suggested by the arguments of the *Perrone Paper*; see *6.21*), and in so far as such achievements are claimed to be of enduring, normative significance, must we not claim that there is an element of 'progress' in doctrinal history? And yet, if the church has not grown in holiness, what justification can we have, on Newman's own principles, for claiming that the church has 'progressed' in its grasp of the *revelatum*, of the mystery of God disclosed to man?

Since Newman never adequately considers this objection in the *Essay*, it is unprofitable to speculate on how he would have dealt with it. But it does seem to follow that we are left with a serious and unanswered problem which, at the least, imposes severe limitations on the extent to which the analogy between the history of an individual and the history of the church may, on Newman's own principles, legitimately be employed. The difficulty would be lessened if, instead of considering the history of christianity primarily as a continuous process, the key achievements of which are irreversible, greater emphasis were laid upon those features of that history which enable us also to consider it more episodically (see *4.12*). In this connection, it is interesting to notice that, closing his description of the 'kinds of development', Newman says that, 'in many cases, *development* simply stands for *exhibition*' (*Dev* 1.2.10; cf 2.1.7; 5.2, discussed in *5.42*)

4.3 'Homogeneous evolution'

In twentieth-century Roman catholic theology, the concept of 'homogeneous evolution' has been the most influential formulation of the attempt to reconcile the facts of historical change with the apparent claim of christian belief to substantial doctrinal immutability.[33] The dominance of this concept was especially due to the influence of Marin-Sola's study of the problem.[34] Marin-Sola, in common with many subsequent writers, saw Newman's *Essay* as a major source of inspiration for theories of 'homogeneous evolution'. In order to understand the significance of the repeated ascription to Newman of a theory of 'homogeneous evolution', the desire to clear his name of the charge of modernism must be borne in mind.[35] In view of the restricted problematic within which scholars such as Marin-Sola operated, this concern for Newman's orthodoxy inevitably hindered an adequate understanding of the complexity of the *Essay*.

Amongst scholars who have attributed to Newman a theory of 'homogeneous evolution' or 'homogeneous development', cf Baum [1968] pp 148–9; Bent [1969] p 14; Dupuy [1964] p 162; Dupuy [1968a] p 67; Nédoncelle [1962] p 140; Jossua [1968] p 194; Moeller [1952] pp 351–2; Nicholls [1965] p 378. Because of the consistent oversimplification of the argument of the *Essay* involved in this attribution, the recognition of the inadequacy of theories of 'homogeneous evolution' sometimes goes hand in hand with too swift an assumption that the *Essay* has thus ceased to be of interest. According to Baum, for instance, we have to ask 'whether it is possible to formulate the Christian Gospel in a new way, not simply as a homogeneous development of the doctrines once defined—this was Newman's position—but as a reinterpretation ... in a new cultural context' (Baum [1967a] p xii; cf Echlin [1970] p 10; Lindbeck [1970] p 101. See 7).

Although the *term* 'homogeneous' is rarely used by Newman,[36] and never in the *Essay*,[37] it can nevertheless be said that the view that the process of development is homogeneous, expanding and irreversible has a significant place in his argument. In the present section we shall briefly examine each of these aspects in turn. The following sections will be devoted to two more specific questions : namely, the role which organic analogies play in the *Essay* (*4.31*), and the problem of how, on Newman's principles, the process of doctrinal development reaches a term (*4.32*).

If Roman catholicism is 'corrupt'; if its present teaching and practice represent a significant departure from the christianity of the early church; then it should be possible to indicate at what point in the historical process such 'corruption' began to enter in. Thus Newman introduces the concept of doctrinal homogeneity with the claim that it is only reasonable 'to take it for granted, before proof to the contrary, that the Christianity of the second, fourth, seventh, twelfth, sixteenth, and intermediate centuries is in its substance the very religion which Christ and His Apostles taught in the first'. (*Dev* Int 3). The argument is pre-emptive : he does not deny the 'abstract possibility of extreme changes . . .

[but] The *onus probandi* is with those who assert what it is un-natural to expect' (*ibid*).

This apologetic use of the argument from homogeneity is stronger in *1878* than in *1845*. This is especially true of the key passages, summarising the preceding or subsequent discussion in which the argument occurs. (For example, the argument is strengthened in *Dev* 3.1.1—cf *1845* p 146; 4.2.1 and 5.7.4 are additions in *1878*; 5.0.1 is rewritten, and its new situation, in-troducing a key chapter, heightens its significance (cf *1845*, p 203). Cf also *Dev* 7.0.1.) Several of the 'Instances in Illustration' are designed to substantiate the general presumption expressed in the Introduction (eg *Dev* 4.2, 4.3). If 'these existing doctrines are universally considered . . . in each age to be the echo of the doc-trines of the times immediately preceding them' (*Dev* 3.1.1; cf *DA* pp 135–7), 'Where then was the opportunity of corruption'?[38] Although some phrases stressing the particular importance of the 'first note' were dropped in *1878* (cf Dev 5.1.1, *1845* p 58), the new paragraph added to summarise chapter 5 insists that 'the point to be ascertained is the unity and identity of the idea with itself through all stages of its development from first to last' (*Dev* 5.7.4).

The emphasis on the homogeneous development of doctrine suggests that the history of christianity resembles, as it were, a stick of rock : wherever you cut it, the image or pattern is sub-stantially the same. Thus the force of Newman's argument, in the passages we are considering, rests upon one form of what Moeller has described as the 'psychologie du cylindre'.[39] However, central to the 'difficulty' with which Newman was concerned in the *Essay* was the presence of 'additions' in the Roman catholic church to the doctrines and practices of primitive christianity. In order to reconcile these 'additions' with the claim that the 'pattern' or 'image' of christian doctrine is substantially identical at every stage of the historical process, he had recourse, on the one hand, to his characteristic stress on the unity of the catholic system (see 5.3) and, on the other, to the concepts of 'expansion'[40] or, especi-ally in *1878*, of 'enlargement'.[41] It is rather as if we were being invited to view the history of christianity as a cone, and not merely a stick, of rock.[42] Newman's own favourite image is that of the growth of the human body : 'Let the soul's religion . . . imitate the law of the body . . . Small are a baby's limbs, a youth's are larger, yet they are the same'.[43] The subsequent discussion is confused, but there is little doubt that Newman sees, in such changes as may reasonably be interpreted as an 'enlargement' of the original 'image', a 'note' of the preservation of the original 'idea'. Thus, in *1878*, he quotes with approval a passage from the *Apologia*: 'The idea of the Blessed Virgin was, as it were, *magnified* in the Church of Rome, as time went on, but so were *all* the Christian ideas, as that of the Blessed Eucharist'.[44] To an adversary who protested that because Roman catholicism teaches 'more' about the Virgin than is found on the surface of scripture, therefore it is obviously corrupt, Newman would surely have answered that, on the contrary, the mere fact of 'enlargement' is evidence of vitality.

In order to show, however, that doctrinal 'enlargement' constitutes true development, and not 'corruption', the crucial consideration is surely the extent to which the overall 'harmony' of the various constituent elements of the doctrinal 'image' has been maintained: 'mere enlargement is not organic development. Warts, and wens, and obesity, form no normal part of the human system' ('The theory of doctrinal development', anon, *The Biblical Quarterly and Congregational Magazine*, i, 1846 p 185). According to Gore 'one of the most effective points in Mozley's reply to Newman is that he calls our attention to the slight consideration paid by Newman to one of the most characteristic features in developments all the world over . . . viz onesided exaggeration of some tendency or feature which was always present in the system, but which had been balanced originally by other tendencies or features which in course of time were suppressed or ceased to act'.[45] Gore is right. To rebut the charge of 'distortion', or 'corruption', it is insufficient to show that the history of this or that individual doctrine may plausibly be described as an 'enlargement'. It is also necessary to assess the extent to which this 'enlargement' was achieved at the cost of neglecting or suppressing other aspects of christian doctrine.[46] It is one thing to say that the 'distinct aspects' of the 'idea' may, 'for the sake of convenience' be considered 'as if separate ideas' (*Dev* 1.1.3. See *4.11*). It is another simply to assert that 'The harmony of the whole, however, is of course what it was'.[47]

In other words, while the general notion of homogeneity in development might be said to offer a prima facie case for the 'substantial identity' of the church at various stages in its history, it does not seem that even this much can necessarily be claimed for the contention that the 'additions' to primitive doctrine and practice are merely 'enlargements' of the primitive 'realisation' of the 'idea'.

Many different forms of historical process (or 'types of development') are described in the *Essay*, and some of the finest prose is reserved for accounts of history's turbulent complexity (eg *Dev* 1.1.4–7; 2.2.1–2; 5.1.3–7; 5.5.1; 12). Nor is Newman unaware of the possibility of discontinuity and revolutionary change, but he undoubtedly regards gradual, homogeneous growth, in which nothing of the past is lost or forgotten, as the ideal. (Cf the description of 'corruption' in *Dev* 5.0.3; 5.6.1–2; 5.7.1–3; 12.2, and *VM* II p 31. Even the relationship between the old and new covenants is described as 'development' and not 'revolution': cf *DA* p 30; *SD* pp 180–217.)

The history of the catholic church has obviously not, on even the most generous interpretation, consisted simply in a smooth 'déroulement linéaire' (de Lubac [1969a] p 245). In order to uphold the claim of homogeneity and maintained substantial identity, Newman has recourse to two arguments which are found alongside each other, for example, in chapter 12. Firstly, there is the claim that 'these disorders were no interruption to the sustained and steady march of the sacred science' (*Dev* 12.4; see *4.31*). Secondly, a dialectical, rather than a linear or organic analogy, is sometimes invoked: 'The series of ecclesiastical decisions . . . alternate between the one and the other side of the theological dogma in question, as if fashioning it into shape by opposite strokes' (*Dev* 12.4; cf *Apo* p 252, and critique in Egner [1969] pp 169–197; Cross [1933a] pp 169–70). Related to this is the important theory that heresies are 'indices and anticipations of the mind of the Church' (*Dev* 8.1.6; see *5.41*; Artz [1968] p 192).

As with so many of the arguments in the *Essay*, the interpretation of such passages is difficult, both because description and prescription (as to what would count as a 'true' development) are inextricably intertwined, and because, in so far as they embody a descriptive claim, they are cast in such general terms that it is not clear what historical evidence would count against them. There is, moreover, a prima facie conflict between the dialectical model and that of continuous, 'harmonious' growth or 'expansion'.

It is, however, clear that Newman regards any reversal of the process of development as impermissible: 'a developed doctrine which reverses the course of development which has preceded it, is no true development but a corruption' (*Dev* 5.6.4; cf 5.6.1–3). Hence the admission, in an addition in *1878*, that 'the hypothesis which I am advocating is at once shattered' if 'the Church herself, acting through Pope or Council as the oracle of heaven, has ever contradicted her own enunciations'.[48] Even here, the question remains: what would count as contradiction? (see *3.21*).

The attempt, throughout the *Essay*, to view the process of development as gradual, homogeneous and irreversible, is partly motivated by apologetic concern, and partly by the conviction that the church has never lost any portion of what was once entrusted to its keeping.[49] It is also partly due to autobiographical considerations. Newman was convinced that, in becoming a Roman catholic, he was but being faithful to his own lifelong principles; hence the claim that 'a gradual conversion from a false to a true religion, plainly, has much of the character of a continuous process, or a development . . . [it] consists in addition and increase chiefly, not in destruction'.[50]

The argument of the 'first note' is a special case of the general argument which we are considering. It is therefore possible to generalise Chadwick's observation that arguments 'from resemblance of impression . . . [are] a curious and surprising form of the Vincentian Canon that Christianity is always the same'.[51] While it is true that the very broad terms in which Newman conducts the discussion enable him to take in his stride the most dramatic shifts in doctrine and practice in the course of the church's history,[52] it is also the case that he is less concerned to discover the extent to which christianity could change without betraying the gospel than he is to sustain his conviction that, fundamentally, it has not changed at all.[53]

According to Walgrave, for Newman's 'type of mind, the main thing is that doctrinal development should be shown to be homogeneous as a whole. If, after that, there still remain problems of detail and individual difficulties, that does not trouble him at all' ([1957] p 261). It can reasonably be argued that the cumulative effect of the arguments in the *Essay* of the type with which we are concerned in this chapter, is to establish a prima facie case (at least as strong as the contrary claims which he was concerned to rebut) for the claim that Roman catholicism is not only not obviously 'corrupt', but is, from several points of view, the nearest approximation in type, ethos and principles, to the church of the first five centuries (cf *L&D* xii p 332; *LG* p 365). But this achievement, however important it may have been to Newman personally, and however useful it might be in interdenominational polemic, may nonetheless be seriously misleading in so far as it creates the impression that the history of christian doctrine and practice has been shown to have been a fundamentally smooth and consistent process.

So far as the 'upper blade' of the scissors is concerned (*3.21*), the claim that, on doctrinal grounds, the history of christian belief and practice must be presumed to be homogeneous until the contrary is proved, must be questioned. This is not to say that christian faith has no grounds on which to trust that the essence of the gospel message will be found proclaimed and embodied, now more, now less adequately, in the belief and practice of successive generations of christians. But, from the standpoint of contemporary historiography, the working hypothesis of homogeneous development seems little more than an 'historicist transposition of [that] fixity' (Jossua [1970] p 259) which had, in an earlier age, been considered the hallmark of orthodoxy. In other words, the 'upper blade' of the argument is a pioneering attempt to reconcile an awakening sense of historicity (*Geschichtlichkeit*) with the apparent claims of christian belief; an attempt which, for apologetic reasons, was pushed further in the direction of immutability in the *Essay* than in those of Newman's writings which had a purpose other than the demands of interdenominational controversy and the justification of a crucial personal decision.

So far as the 'lower blade' is concerned, it is not a question simply of 'detail and individual difficulties'. If it would be the 'work of a life' adequately to 'apply the Theory of Developments' (*Dev* Int 21), it would equally be the work of a life adequately to examine, adjust and correct the historical illustrations which abound in the *Essay*. However, to mention just two examples, any standard account of the history of the sacrament of penance (eg Poschmann [1963]), or of ecclesiology (eg Congar [1970c]), discloses far more variety, regression, and rediscovery, both in doctrine and practice, than is compatible with even a broadly conceived view of 'homogeneous development'.

4.31 Organic analogies

'Catholic theology, as well as liberal and modernist, was somewhat puzzled, even bewildered, by Newman's psychological theories. They asked if he was speaking of logical or biological development, and failed to obtain a precise answer' (Walgrave [1957] p 283). That they so failed is hardly surprising, and Walgrave adds, correctly, that 'No doctrinal development can be fully achieved in terms of formal logic; but, for all that, it is not a biological process either' p 295). However, Walgrave's own categorisation of Newman's 'theory' as 'psychological' is inadequate.[54] Organic analogies play an important part in the Essay, but they are analogies for a historical process.

'It was undoubtedly on the analogy of biology that Newman hit upon his seven notes or tests of genuine development'.[55] He was assisted in doing so by the fact that this analogy was implied in the charge which he was concerned apologetically to rebut, and that the image of 'growth' seemed to provide a clue to the problem of reconciling maintained identity with change.[56] There is, moreover, a strictly theological dimension to the argument of the Essay, the presence of which helps to account for the principle that 'life' in a society is itself a criterion of 'reality'. In this section, we shall briefly examine each of these factors.

The charge against the Roman catholic church was that it had 'corrupted' christian doctrine. The organic metaphor employed in the criticism invited the employment of a similar metaphor in the rebuttal (cf Dev 5.0.3). Yet in the last of the University Sermons organic analogies hardly appear. Palmer regretted this and 'wished, that the eminent writer . . . had taken some notice of a view, which is undoubtedly prevalent in some quarters' (Palmer [1843] p 61, quoted Stern [1967] p 190; cf Chadwick [1957] pp 118, 230). In the Essay, Newman did so in no uncertain fashion, attempting to answer Palmer's objection that 'A germ infers growth, indeed, and change, but it also infers corruption and death' by setting up criteria for distinguishing 'true' from 'false' development (Palmer [1843] p 62, quoted Stern [1967] p 204—on the use of the concept of 'germ' by Hawkins and Sumner, see Stern [1967] p 179). He never lost sight of the fact that the use of organic imagery and terminology in the Essay is only metaphorical or analogical.[57] This is explicitly asserted in Dev 1.2.1 (see 4.1) and Dev 5.0.4, and alone accounts for his curious description of the conservative tendency which prevents that excessive development, or over-ripening, which would be corruption. (*Dev* 5.6.1). At this point, the metaphorical usage breaks down : it appears that a 'true' development is one which has halted or slowed down the process of development (cf *Apo* p 265)! The source of the muddle is Newman's desire to answer his own earlier charge that 'Romanism' is 'fruit over-ripe' (*VM* I p 43; cf p 41). In 1877, he hesitated : 'who would not prefer that "Romanism" which has an excess of life to that Protestantism which is deficient in it?' (*VM* I p 42; cf *Diff* II p 79).

The sixth note illustrates the important and paradoxical fact that Newman, in using the language of 'growth' to describe the process of development, far from attempting to cut christian belief and practice free from its normative realisation in the apostolic church, was expressing his fundamental conservatism and mistrust of innovation. Confronted with that 'apparent variation and growth of doctrine, which embarrasses us' (*Dev* Int 20), the use of organic imagery, together with the stress on the unity of the 'idea', seemed to provide a perspective within which the unchanging identity of the church and its isomorphism with its primitive form could plausibly be maintained.[58]

It is this conservatism in the programme (whether or not that programme is successfully executed) which marks the *Essay* off sharply from the modernist approach. Three centuries previously Jewel had protested : 'This is open blasphemy, to compare the Church of Rome that now is to a perfect man . . . and the primitive Church of the apostles and martyrs unto an infant' (quoted Tavard [1959] p 238). For a modernist such as Williams, who would, one suspects, have encountered the full blast of Jewel's wrath, the mind of the primitive church might be said to contain the 'germ' of an idea which has subsequently developed (eg Williams, W. J. [1906] pp 99–100, 102–9). For Newman, the religious beliefs, practices and institutions of primitive christianity may be said to be the germinal realisation, or 'image', of an 'idea' which is nevertheless in some sense prior to and transcendent in respect of the process of development (cf *VM* I p 293, quoted *Dev* 2.1.11 : for an earlier version, see Stern [1964] p 134, [1967] p 182). We shall have occasion, in the next chapter, to examine the extent to which this paradoxical claim is supported by the appeal to the notion of 'implicit' reason. For the moment, it is sufficient to insist, once again, that the *Essay* does not contain any single, elaborated 'theory' of development and that, however frequently they occur, organic images represent only one of the various classes of analogy to which Newman had recourse.

By the end of 1841, Newman's waning confidence in the catholicity of the anglican church led him to insist, in four important sermons,[59] on those marks of holiness and 'inward' vitality in the church which are 'truer and more precious tokens' to the believer than the 'external notes' which are 'practically superseded' by them (*SD* p 328). Although, in the *Essay*, the pendulum has swung the other way and (as befits an historical investigation) he concentrates on the aspect of 'visible growth', the preoccupation of those sermons, written during the darkest period of his personal struggle, enabled him to make the 'life' or vitality of the church a central feature of his apologetic. The fact that the history of the church may be seen to be the history of a *living* idea is powerful evidence of its 'reality' or truth (see *4.1*). 'I believe *I* was the *first* writer who made *life the* mark of a true church' (*L&D* XI p 101, in discussing the four Advent sermons of 1841; cf pp 175, 191).

Far from a biologistic interpretation of historical process leading Newman to interpret that process in organic terms, it was rather his conviction that the church, indwelt by the Spirit of the risen Christ, uniquely 'lives', that led him to employ organic imagery to describe its history. The arguments and claims of the *Essay* are unintelligible unless sufficient weight is given to the presence of christological motifs which have been too often neglected. We shall mention three: certain overtones to the concept of 'principle'; the influence of the 'growth' parables; and the use of other images which imply a close identification of the 'idea' of christianity with the risen Christ.

The concept of 'principle', which occurs some 220 times in *1878* (cf *5.42*), or 'first principle', in the *Essay* is 'highly analogical' (Walgrave [1957] p 121). It is sometimes methodological (eg *Dev* Int 21; 1.2.4; 3.1.9; 3.2.4; 5.2.1; 6.1.21; 9.6.1), and sometimes refers, more generally and dynamically, to the deep psychological springs motivating understanding and activity (eg *Dev* 1.1.1; 1.2.3; 1.2.7; 5.2.2–5; 5.6.2; 7.6.3; 8.1.5; 10.1.1). To restrict its reference, however, to psychological description, as Walgrave tends to do, would be to miss the significance of those passages in which, usually in the context of organic language and imagery, the notions of 'active principle' or 'principle of life' also seem to carry ontological overtones (cf Lash [1969] pp 345–6). Thus, for example, a 'living idea' is said to be one which becomes an 'active principle' within society, leading men 'to an ever-new contemplation of itself' (*Dev* 1.1.4; cf 1.1.6; 5.2.3; 5.2.6; 5.3.5; 5.7.2; 8.1.3). Nowhere in the *Essay* is there any explicit indication that such passages are more than a symbolic or metaphorical device, heightening the dramatic impact of the description of the 'process of development'. The 'idea' in question, however, is that of revelation, of God's self-disclosure in his living word in history (see *4.1*). Adequately to grasp the notion of 'principle' in the *Essay*, account must be taken of the numerous passages in Newman's writings in which the risen Christ, or his Spirit, is described as the 'principle of life' in the church: 'That divine and adorable Form, which the Apostles saw and handled, after ascending into heaven became a principle of life, a secret origin of existence to all who believe, through the gracious ministration of the Holy Ghost'.[60]

The sermon just quoted also describes the church as 'the fruitful Vine', whose members are 'internally connected, as branches from a tree, not as the parts of a heap' (*PS* iv p 170); the use of organic analogies in the *Essay* is partly attributable to the influence of such biblical images. The 'growth' parables are explicitly appealed to (*Dev* 2.1.16; *Jfc* p 273. Cf the text of Wiseman's 1839 sermon, quoted Ward, W. [1897] i p 314) and the 'harmony' characteristic of a 'true development' is likened to 'the tall growth, and graceful branching, and rich foliage, of some vegetable production' (*Dev* 5.4.1).

Although, in the *Essay*, the Johannine image of the vine is not explicitly employed, it is possible to detect its influence: 'As the Church *grew* into form, so did the power of the Pope develop; and wherever the Pope has been renounced, *decay* and division have been the consequence' (*Dev* 4.3.8—my stress). The argument that separation from the papacy results in corruption is spelt out more fully in a polemical passage in *The Second Spring*: 'That old Church in its day became a corpse . . . and then it did but corrupt the air which once it refreshed, and cumber the ground which once it beautified'. (*OS* p 170). This situation is said to have come about once 'The vivifying principle of truth, the shadow of St. Peter, the grace of the Redeemer, left it' (*ibid*). As early as 1824, in a passage which referred explicitly to Jn 15, Newman described the 'fruitless' soul as 'cumbering the ground, worthless, and fit only to be cast into the fire' (*BOA* A.17.1, quoted in Linnan [1968] p 168).

The tendency, in the *Essay*, to express the transcendence of the 'idea' by hypostatising, or personalising it, is grounded in the identification of the 'idea' with the presence of the risen Christ, God's living Word.[61] The image of Samson, 'the strong man bound', as a type of Christ who, in his resurrection, broke the bonds of death, is a classic christian symbol. One of the most explicit evocations of this image in Newman's writings occurs in the *Lectures on Justification* : 'Truth always avenges itself; and if kept in bondage, it breaks forth irregularly, burying itself with the strong man in the overthrow of its oppressors'.[62] If *Dev* 1.1.6–7 and *Dev* 12.9 are read with this and similar passages in mind, the resonances are unmistakeable.[63]

The use made of organic analogies in the *Essay* is an excellent illustration of the fugal nature of Newman's method of argument : they provide him with a convenient controversialist's gambit, a flexible model for use in the attempt to set up an overall 'view' of christian history, and a set of images evocative of the doctrinal claim that 'The Christian history is "an outward sign of an inward spiritual grace" ' (*Ess* II p 188; see *3.13*).

According to one exasperated critic, Newman 'habitually associated—some might say "confused"—logical, psychological, ethical and biological categories' (Stephenson [1966] p 466). It is true that the criteria and techniques severally appropriate to historiography, apologetic and theology, necessitate their separate exploration. It is also true, however, that even a christian with less thirst than Newman for personal synthesis may feel the pressure to connect the disparate features of his world. In many ways, the *Essay* represents an attempt to achieve the impossible (cf Culler [1955] p 191). But to attempt the impossible may, so far as the 'personal conquest of truth' is concerned, be sometimes more fruitful than the attainment of more modest goals.

4.32 Does the 'process' tend towards a term?

If the history of christian belief and practice is a process of development, is it the kind of process which, of its nature, tends towards a term? It would seem that four of the eight kinds of development described in *Dev* 1.2 could continue indefinitely (namely : 'mathematical'; 'material'; 'political'; and 'logical'). 'Physical' developments inevitably reach a term in death, but they do not 'come into consideration' (*Dev* 1.2.1); we have already seen that Newman's use of organic concepts and imagery is only analogical or metaphorical (see *4.31*). The brief account of 'historical' developments hints at the possibility of at least asymptotic approximation to a terminal state, and there are undoubtedly some historical questions which admit, in principle, of definitive solution, such as the dating of historical events (cf *Dev* 1.2.10). While there seems no reason why, in general, 'ethical' processes should not continue indefinitely, Newman includes under this heading Guizot's theory of the origins of religious institutions (because this will strengthen his argument, in *Dev* 2.2, that the development of an 'infallible developing authority' is 'antecedently probable'). But, even in this instance, the institutional forms which appear are in turn capable of indefinite further development and even reversal (see *3.23*).

Thus the only kind of development which Newman recognised as relevant to the subject-matter of the *Essay* and which of its nature tends towards a term, is that class of '*metaphysical* developments . . . [which] are a mere analysis of the idea contemplated, and terminate in its exact and complete delineation' (*Dev* 1.2.9). That article echoes the argument of the fifteenth *University Sermon* (the greater part of the article consists of the only quotation from that sermon in the *Essay*). In order, therefore, to answer the question with which we began, it is necessary to turn first to this sermon, and then to examine the extent to which the type of development discussed there plays a significant part in the argument of the *Essay*.

Early in the sermon there is an outline rhetorical description of the history of christianity, ending : 'at length a large fabric of divinity was reared, irregular in its structure, and diverse in its style . . . but still, on the whole, the development of an idea' (*US* p 316; see *3.22*). The impression that the appearance of this 'large fabric', even if this is patent of further 'expansion', in some sense marks the term of a process of development, is reinforced when Newman turns from the 'survey of the general system' 'to the history of the formation of any Catholic dogma' (*US* p 316;

in the terminology of the *Essay*, the history of an 'aspect' of the 'idea'). Eventually, 'the whole truth "self-balanced on its centre hung", part answering to part, one, absolute, integral, indissoluble, while the world lasts' (*US* p 317; cf *GA* p 126; *VM* I p 118). This is clearly the description of the term of the process of development 'from its first disorders to its exact and determinate issue' (*US* p 316).

The main concern of the passage which was later quoted in the *Essay*[64] (a passage strongly influenced by the analogy with the process of thought in the mind of the individual believer: see *4.2*) is to stress the symbolic function of creeds, enabling the believer to give real, and not merely notional assent to the object of faith: 'we form creeds as a chief mode of perpetuating the impression'[65] The believer's 'view does not depend on such propositions . . . they are but specimens and indications of it. And they may be multiplied without limit . . . their multiplication is not intended to enforce many things, but to express one' (*US* p 336; cf *Apo* pp 256–7; *Ari* p 147; *Jfc* p 316).

Although this process of 'multiplication' of dogmatic propositions may continue indefinitely, it is clear, as in the earlier section, that the *prior* stage in the development reaches a term, or 'results in a . . . body of dogmatic statements, till what was at first an impression on the Imagination has become a system or creed in the Reason' (*US* p 329; 'at first' added 1871. Cf Newman [1844] p 331; *Ari* p 144).

Turning to the *Essay*, the influence of the sermon on *Dev* 1.1.4 is clear, prescinding from the problem of interpretation mentioned in *4.1*: the emergence of a 'body of thought, laboriously gained . . . little more than the proper representation of one idea' is the term of a process which began in 'agitation' and 'confusion' (cf the 'first disorders' of *US* p 316). In this article, however, the description is completely general: whether it refers equally to the process as a whole, and to the development of individual 'aspects', is unspecified. Elsewhere, however, Newman insists that there are no signs of the general process 'coming to an end' (*Dev* Int 20), and that we are 'unable to fix an historical point at which the growth of doctrine ceased, and the rule of faith was once for all settled' (*Dev* 2.1.12).

In so far as the development of individual doctrines is concerned, Newman does seem, as in the sermon, to envisage a point at which their development reaches a term : the doctrine of original sin is said to be 'completed' or 'fully developed' at the time of Augustine (cf *Dev* 4.1.4), and the development of the doctrine of infant baptism is said to reach a 'conclusion' when 'the infallible Church confirmed, that observance of the rite was the rule, and the non-observance the exception' (*Dev* 4.1.7).

In the light of these texts, the following general observations are in order. In the first place, both the overall development of the christian 'idea', and the development of a particular doctrine, or 'aspect' of that idea, are two-stage processes. The first stage is the development from implicit awareness to explicit articulation in a body of doctrine. The second stage is the further elaboration and expansion of that body of doctrine.

In the second place, it seems that the model for the first stage is that of 'metaphysical' development, but that this model is differently applied to the general and particular processes. So far as the former is concerned, even if the emergence of the creed (which seems to correspond to the termination of this first stage) may be regarded as an 'exact and complete delineation' (*Dev* 1.2.9) of the 'idea', it does not follow that the creed is an exhaustive statement of christian doctrine, but only that it is a normative interpretation of scripture (see *5.4*. Newman does not lose sight of the inadequacy of human statements of divine truth; cf *GA* p 120; *4.12*). From another point of view, the general process never reaches a term; as Newman wrote in 1877 : 'whatever is great refuses to be reduced to human rule, and to be made consistent in its many aspects with itself' (*VM* I p xciv. *Dev* 1.1.4 should be read with this in mind. Cf *Dev* Int 20; *2.1.12*). The 'complete delineation' of the idea remains only an ideal. So far as the development of individual doctrines is concerned, Newman does, in regarding their crystallisation in dogmatic statements as the term of a process of 'metaphysical' development, betray an inadequate appreciation of their historically conditioned nature. Moreover, both the doctrines of original sin and of infant baptism have clearly 'developed' beyond the point which Newman regarded as their 'completion'.

In the third place, whether or not the concept of homogeneous development plausibly describes the second stage in the process (see *4.3*), it is quite unserviceable as an account of the turbulent, dialectical first stage.

In the fourth place, Newman's apologetic preoccupation in the *Essay* accounts (as we have so often insisted) for his failure to ask certain critical questions concerning the adequacy of this or that feature of the process of development.[66]

In the fifth place, in so far as the distinction between the two stages in the process is marked by the formation of the creed, or the definition of a dogma, it would seem that the perspectives of the *Via Media* survive more strongly in the *Essay* than is apparent when this distinction is overlooked.[67]

In the sixth place, it is not necessary to endorse the epistemology of the sermon (in particular, of passages quoted in *Dev* 1.2.9; Cameron [1962] p 205) to appreciate the importance of Newman's insight into the religious function of creeds.[68] The confusion consequent upon his attempt to apply this insight to a situation in which the propositions of the early creeds had 'multiplied' (*US* p 336) is due to the fact that he did not appreciate the extent to which creeds have served different functions at different periods in the church's history, or to which 'The unfortunate result of . . . mixing . . . the confessional with the doctrinal is that interpretations become items to be believed, and so the doctrinal interpretation and expansion becomes an object of faith' (*Concilium* [1970] p 317; cf Brekelmans [1970]; Dulles [1968]; Lash [1971b]; Schlink [1967]).

Finally, even though the model of 'metaphysical' development plays an important part in the interpretation of both the general and particular processes, it must not be forgotten that the development of christian belief and practice is, according to Newman, also marked by four other 'kinds of development'. This should, once again, serve as a warning against abstracting any particular feature from the total argument of the *Essay*, and identifying it alone with 'Newman's theory of development'.

5

Interpreting the 'earlier'
by the 'later'

If 'time is necessary for the full comprehension and perfection of great ideas' (*Dev* Int 21), then, according to Newman, later stages in the history of an idea may legitimately be used to interpret its comparatively obscure and ambiguous beginnings. This principle, which is the hermeneutical counterpart to the themes with which the previous chapter was concerned, has received comparatively little attention from the commentators. Walgrave only once refers to it explicitly (and then with surprise) ([1957] p 246). Chadwick discusses it, but only in the context of Newman's use of historical evidence ([1957] pp 145–7). Atkins, who recognises that 'One of Newman's cardinal principles was that primitive adumbrations of a doctrine are to be interpreted in the light of later more detailed statements of it', refers to Whitehead, in this context, as Newman's 'legitimate heir' (Atkins [1966] p 539). The particular problems with which the sections of this chapter are concerned have, it is true, often been discussed but, in order to locate them within the overall argument of the *Essay*, it seems desirable to situate them within the broad context of that principle of which they are the specific expression and implementation.

An introductory description of the use of the principle (*5.1*) will be followed by an examination of Newman's use of scripture in the *Essay* (*5.2*); then we shall discuss the relationship between this principle and two of Newman's favourite themes : his stress on the unity of the 'idea' (*5.3*), and his insistence that the whole 'idea' of christianity has been present from the beginning (*5.4*). While, so far as possible, repetition of problems already discussed will be avoided, the method of the *Essay* makes it progressively less easy to avoid overlapping as we proceed.

5.1 A general principle of interpretation

The previous chapter has sufficiently indicated that, although Newman himself described the central insight, or hypothesis, with which the *Essay* is concerned, as a 'theory of development', his heuristic achievement was not exploited further than the generation of a number of rudimentary 'theories', the further elaboration of which would have shown them to be, at least in some instances, mutually incompatible. It is not surprising that what is true of the 'theory' of development is also true of the interpretative principle with which we are now concerned.

In the present section, some general introductory remarks concerning the status of the principle, and its relationship to the themes discussed in *4*, will be followed by a discussion of Newman's use, in this connection, of the analogy of literary criticism (*5.11*). Finally, it will be necessary briefly to ask to what extent the *Essay*'s standpoint of interdenominational apologetic affects the possibility of profitably using the principle (*5.12*).

Chadwick has shown that Newman 'wished to apply later evidence to an earlier epoch, not as an old-fashioned argument *de praescriptione* . . . but as a genuine use according to the strict canons of historical scholarship' ([1957] p 147). It is significant that one of the earlier passages in which the principle is invoked is the description of 'historical' developments : '. . . the Poet makes Truth the daughter of Time . . . History cannot be written except in an after-age' (*Dev* 1.2.5). Keogh drew attention to the centrality in Newman's thinking of the conviction that truth is the 'daughter of Time'. He said of the *Essay* that it pioneered 'the introduction of historical intelligibility, with its own norms and methods, into the method of theology' (Keogh [1950] p 17).

We have already seen that Newman defends his historiographical method, his method of argument in 'concrete matters', and his conception of the history of an 'idea' in a society, on the grounds that, independently of doctrinal considerations, they are legitimate or inevitable methods and conceptions, and that therefore they are applicable to religious questions : 'We must be content to follow the law of our being in religious matters as well as in secular' (*Dev* 3.2.5). Similarly, he justifies the principle that the earlier evidence for a doctrine or practice is to be interpreted in the light of a later state of affairs on the grounds that it is simply the doctrinal or apologetic application of a principle the general validity of which owes nothing to religious considerations. Whether or not that application is successful is the question with which we are concerned in this chapter.

It would not be difficult to select isolated passages from the *Essay* which would make it seem that, in recommending that 'the early condition . . . of each doctrine . . . ought consistently to be interpreted by means of that development which was ultimately attained' (*Dev* 3.1.7), Newman was replacing the Vincentian canon by the *securus judicat orbis terrarum* in such a way as to encourage the view that 'The Pope may at any time "interpret" tradition in such a manner as to change it completely' (Inge [1919] p 124), and that Newman's 'theory marks . . . the complete and final apotheosis of the Pope and the hierarchy, who are thereby made independent even of the past history of the Church' (*ibid* p 144). This caricature points to a real difficulty which will be discussed in 6. For the moment it is sufficient to notice that, in intention, the principle with which we are concerned is a principle of interpretation of the church's past, and not a device to render the contemporary church independent of that past.[1] As Newman wrote to Mrs Froude in 1844 : 'Granting that the Roman (special) doctrines are not found drawn out in the early Church, yet I think there is sufficient trace of them in it, to recommend and prove them, *on the hypothesis* of the Church having a divine guidance, though not sufficient to prove them by itself. So that the question simply turns on the nature of the promise of the Spirit, made to the Church' (*Apo* p 197; cf Svaglic [1967] p 558; cf *VM* I p 217 for an earlier sketch, 1837).

In so far as the major themes of the previous chapter are concerned, the following general observations are in order. In the first place, the effect of this principle on Newman's preoccupation with the 'terms' rather than with the 'process' of development (see *4.11*) is to encourage him to isolate those features of the patristic church which correspond most closely to his image of contemporary Roman catholicism (cf *Dev* 6.1.30; 6.2.17; 6.3.1.10; 6.3.3.23). In the second place, the principle is more obviously of assistance when the first, rather than the second model of doctrinal history sketched in *4.12* is under consideration. In the third place, in so far as the analogy between the individual and society is legitimate (see *4.2*), later stages in the history of the church may be used to interpret earlier, ambiguous evidence in the same way that, in evaluating an individual's behaviour, 'we use the event as a presumptive interpretation . . . of those past indications of his character which, considered as evidence, were too few and doubtful to bear insisting on at the time' (*Dev* 3.2.5).

In the fourth place, the use of the principle introduces some circularity into the attempt to see every stage in the history of christian doctrine and practice as 'homogeneous' in respect of every other (see *4.3*): does the decision to read the earlier stages in the light of the later enable one to discern the substantial identity of 'type', of the 'ethos' of christianity throughout its history, or does the antecedent presumption that this has been the case control the selection and reading of the evidence?

Finally, the principle is more freely used to interpret the first, rather than the second of the two stages in the development of doctrine which we distinguished in *4.32*. The 'later' period that Newman has in mind is as often the fifth as the nineteenth century: 'the simple question is, whether the clear light of the fourth and fifth centuries may be fairly taken to interpret to us the dim, though definite, outlines traced in the preceding' (*Dev* 4.3.17; cf *DA* p 238).

5.11 The analogy of literary criticism

According to Stephenson, 'Literary criticism is a good (rough) model for theology and doctrinal development' ([1966] p 464). It is only in the light of this model that Newman's use of the principle with which we are concerned in this chapter can be understood. A passage in the section entitled 'Method of Proof' (*Dev* 3.1) appeals to literary criticism in general to justify the exegetical and theological use of the principle, but it contains some puzzling ambiguities. The conclusion seems straightforward enough: 'We elucidate the text by the comment, though, or rather because, the comment is fuller and more explicit than the text' (*Dev* 3.1.3). But what is the 'text' that Newman has in mind, and what the 'comment'?

It is significant that none of Newman's illustrations in this article is a straightforward instance of literary criticism. The justification of offering 'a more explicit statement' in Cicero's *Ad Familiares* as the 'true explanation' of a 'concise or obscure passage' in one of his letters would presumably be that both texts have the same author. But the remaining illustrations, of cases in which the author of the 'comment' is other than the author of the 'text', are obscure and elliptical. While there is some plausibility in the suggestion that 'St Anselm is interpreted by St Thomas,' the suggestion that Thucydides is 'illustrated' by Aristophanes 'in point of history' is even more startling than the claim that 'Aeschylus is illustrated by Sophocles in point of language' (*Dev* 3.1.3). Newman seems to be suggesting that we are helped to understand Thucydides' historical and political attitudes by reading the plays of his supporter, and that the ideas expressed by the supposed 'primitive', Aeschylus, are presented in a clearer, or more 'developed' manner in the language of Sophocles, with whom he stood in supposed continuity. In these two cases the focus of concern is not so much the 'literal sense', or meaning, of the texts of Thucydides and Aeschylus, but rather the 'reality' or 'ideas' which they attempted to express. The distinction is not unimportant : throughout this chapter we shall see that Newman's interest, in studying the texts of scripture or of the ante-nicene Fathers, is not so much in the texts themselves as in the 'reality' or 'ideas' which the earlier writers are attempting to express with a clarity only achieved at a later period (cf *Jfc* p 121). The presumption throughout is that this 'reality' or these 'ideas' have a platonically conceived existence prior to and more or less independent of the work of the authors in question (see *4.1*).

In brief, some of the puzzling features of *Dev* 3.1.3 begin to make sense when it is recognised that the model of literary criticism, as Newman uses it, has not simply two terms (the text and the comment), but three : the text, the comment, and the 'real idea' with which both are concerned (cf *DA* pp 147–8). In the remainder of this section, we shall presume that the various uses of the analogy of 'text' and 'comment' are to be read with this general epistemological structure in mind.

It is possible to distinguish, in the *Essay*, three distinct uses of the analogy. In some passages, the 'text' is scripture, and the 'comment' is subsequent doctrinal statement (eg *Dev* 2.1.5; 2.1.9; 4.2.8; *5.2*). In others, the 'text' is scripture, and the 'comment' is subsequent *events* (eg *Dev* 4.3.9; 7.4.1; *5.43*). In a third group, the 'text' is the doctrine and practice of one period in the history of the church, and the 'comment' is the doctrine and practice of a later period. (eg *Dev* 4.1.3; 4.1.11; 4.3.17. As far back as 1834 Newman had described the Spirit as the 'illuminating' agent, who has 'commented' on the 'text' of 'the birth, the life, the death and resurrection of Christ' *PS* II p 227; cf *Ess* I p 234; *GA* p 119.) The distinctions are not, of course, as sharp as this categorisation suggests (some passages are impossible to classify: eg *Dev* 2.2.2; 5.6.1); it does, however, indicate the more or less metaphorical use of the model of textual criticism. If the passages in the first group, for instance, are read as prescriptions for good theological method, and not simply as descriptive, they indicate a traditional view of theology as the interpretation of scripture. The passages in the third group, in contrast, are highly metaphorical. Since the justification of such metaphors, and their function in the argument of the *Essay*, constitute the problems with which this whole chapter is concerned, it is sufficient, for the moment, briefly to indicate the way in which their use raises questions concerning the credentials of the commentator, the criteria for distinguishing good comment from bad, and the authorship of text and comment respectively.

In so far as all developments are to be regarded as 'comments' on the text of scripture or the teaching of the ante-nicene church, the first four chapters of the *Essay* are concerned to establish the case for the 'need' for a trustworthy commentator and 'the fact of its supply' (*Dev* 2.2.13). As we would expect, the consequence of the apologetic standpoint of the *Essay* is that the question of the commentator's credentials is not approached in the abstract, or theoretically: even the arguments from antecedent probability are rather intended to persuade the reader that an existing claimant, the Roman catholic church, has, by the fact and style of its existence, established a strong claim to be regarded as the only authentic 'commentator' on the 'text' (see *5.12*).

The question of the criteria for distinguishing good comment from bad is closely linked with the problem of authorship. When the author of the comment is someone other than the author of the text, it seems clear that good literary criticism consists in determining, as exactly as possible, what the original author 'really' meant. As we shall see when discussing the use of scripture in the *Essay* (*5.2*), Newman's insistence on the identity of the author of both text and comment considerably influences his use of the analogy of literary criticism. Stephenson says that 'the expert literary critic finds more in the play, but he finds it in the play' ([1966] p 465). However, at the heart of the problem with which this chapter and 6 are concerned, is the difficulty of giving any critical value to the analogy when divine authorship is claimed for the play and divine ratification (*Dev* 3.1.1) for the comment (cf *Dev* 3.2.11 : 'developments cannot but be, and those surely divine, because it is divine').

In short, the specification of the general prescription to 'understand the earlier by the later' in the form of an analogy from literary criticism is complicated not only by the fact that the argument is often highly metaphorical (especially when applied to historical events), but also by the presence of an underlying theological appeal to God, as the author of the 'text', providentially safeguarding the authenticity of such 'comment' as the 'text' receives in the events, doctrines and practices of christian history.

5.12 The apologetic use of the principle

If Newman's primary concern had been to understand the process of doctrinal development, then the recommendation to understand the earlier in the light of the later might have been taken to mean, for example, that the forms and expressions of christian belief and practice in different historical and cultural contexts could be expected to throw light, from a number of different standpoints, on what the apostolic church, confronted with unprecedented experiences and unforeseen hopes, had been attempting to express and embody. Theologically, the more weight that is placed upon the providential guidance of the church in history, the more justifiable it would be to regard the fruit of subsequent reflection and experience as clarificatory and interpretative of primitive, undifferentiated doctrine and practice.[2]

In practice, however, Newman's adoption of the standpoint of interdenominational apologetic, and his theological conservatism, triply distort his use of his chosen principle of interpretation.

In the first place, even if it were permissible to take the doctrine and practice of nineteenth-century Roman catholicism as a standard by which to interpret primitive christianity, it would hardly be possible to understand the former except through an examination of the whole of that history which gave it birth and, especially, of medieval and tridentine catholicism. It is not enough simply to ask whether traces of later catholic ecclesiological and sacramental doctrine and practice can be discerned in the early church. The later forms may be put as 'questions' to illuminate the earlier situation, but only on condition that these later forms themselves are 'questioned' and illuminated by the process from which they derived. In other words, if Newman's adoption of the principle with which we are concerned indicates his sensitivity to hermeneutical problems, the effect of the apologetic standpoint of the *Essay* is to preclude the implementation of one of the two interdependent procedures which constitute the 'hermeneutical circle'. In 1841, in a plea for the study of ecclesiastical history that shows considerable sensitivity to both procedures, Newman wrote : 'the present is a text, and the past its interpretation' (*Ess* II p 250; cf pp 250–2).

In the second place, it may be reasonable 'To give a deeper meaning' to the comparatively undifferentiated doctrinal statements of the ante-nicene Fathers by interpreting them 'by the times which came after' (*Dev* Int 11), but the decision, on ecclesiological grounds, to allow interpretative status only to particular features of those later times, inevitably calls in question the adequacy of the interpretation.[3] It would be anachronistic to expect Newman adequately to have considered questions which have only become sharply focused in our own day under the combined pressure of ecumenical convergence and a heightening consciousness of the theological significance of cultural and linguistic pluralism. It is nevertheless possible to ask : in so far as later developments represent a specification, or 'realisation' of the undifferentiated and 'obscure' expressions of primitive christianity (see *4.12*), on what grounds, other than those of prior ecclesiogical conviction, is the possibility ruled out of different, and apparently mutually exclusive, later developments being proposed, with equal plausibility, as interpretations of the early evidence? In so far as Newman asked this question, part of his answer is to be found in the stress he placed upon the enduring unity of the idea (see *5.3*). But this theological conservatism, together with the epistemological structure to which we referred in the previous section (*5.11*), inhibited the clear emergence of the question. A brief comment on this point may conclude the present section.

The practice of administering communion under only one kind is a good prima facie case of Roman 'corruption'. Discussing the relevant decree of the Council of Constance, Newman says that 'the question is, whether the doctrine here laid down . . . was entertained by the early Church, and may be considered a just development of its principles and practices' (*Dev* 4.1.8). At first sight, it would appear to be obvious that these are two distinct questions, and not one. By 'theological conservatism', in the present context, I mean precisely this tendency to collapse these two questions together, so that only those views or doctrines are admitted as 'true developments' which may be said to have been 'entertained' or 'held' (cf *Dev* Int 10) by the primitive Church (see *4.3*. A good instance of this weakness in Newman's sense of history is his defence, in 1888, of the anachronisms in *Callista: Call* p ix.) Such a position will be easier to sustain in the measure that the 'idea' of christianity is envisaged as in some way external to, or independent of, those who 'entertain', 'hold' or 'profess' it. We are here at the heart of the tension, crucial for an understanding of the *Essay*, between Newman's historical sensitivity and his belief in the immutability of christian doctrine. The problem will be more fully discussed in *5.4*.

5.2 *The use of scripture in the Essay*

While still an undergraduate, Newman had learnt from Hawkins[4] that 'the method of the Christian writings affords indeed the very strongest *proofs* of doctrines interwoven by allusion, implication, and every indirect mode, with the texture of the sacred books; but it is often the least adapted to the purpose of *teaching* those doctrines, which was the end we should have expected them to have in view'.[5] In view of Newman's purpose in the *Essay*, it is not surprising that this perspective occupies a dominant role (cf *Dev* 2.1.3), and references to the 'disappointing' (*Dev* 2.2.12; cf *US* p 268 and Cameron [1962] p 205), 'unsystematic' (*Dev* 2.1.14; cf *Ari* p 147) or 'inchoate' (*Dev* 2.1.6) nature of scripture need to be read in its light.[6] It is no accident that the majority of the apparently disparaging references to scripture occur in chapter 2, in which Newman is arguing for the inevitability of development, and for the antecedent probability that the church will have been provided by God with the authority necessary to enable it, in later situations, confidently to interpret the scriptures and to apply their message.[7]

The absence of 'arguments from scripture' in the *Essay* is largely a tactical device. In the *Lectures on the Prophetical Office* he had elected to fight 'the controversialist of Rome' on 'the ground of Antiquity' (*VM* I p 37). He now selects the same ground from which to refute his earlier position (cf *L&D* XIV pp 369–70).

Moreover, 'If, as an Anglican, he accepted the maxim that all truths necessary to salvation were to be found in scripture, as a Catholic he could affirm that the whole of revelation was, in a certain sense, contained in scripture'.[8] It is possible, however, to maintain the 'material sufficiency' of scripture, while yet describing the relationship of scripture, tradition and church teaching in such a way as to deny to the scriptures any effectively normative role. There are two principal reasons why the *Essay* suffers from this crucial methodological weakness.

In the first place, Newman's tendency to stress the authority of 'living tradition' at the apparent expense of the authority of scripture is partly the fruit of his pastoral concern. There is a close parallel here with his defence of 'implicit' reason. 'If children, if the poor, if the busy, can have true Faith, yet cannot weigh evidence, evidence is not the simple foundation on which Faith is built' (*US* p 231). Similarly, 'I would not deny as an abstract proposition that a Christian may gain the whole truth from the Scriptures, but would maintain that the chances are very seriously against a given individual' (*VM* I p 158; cf pp 164, 244).

In the second place, while the perspective he had acquired from Hawkins had been powerfully corroborated by his study of the Fathers, he did not sufficiently distinguish between the methods appropriate to theological inquiry and dispute, on the one hand, and the teaching of christian doctrine, on the other. Nor did he sufficiently appreciate the extent to which shifts in theological method, and the criteriological disputes of the sixteenth century, made it difficult, if not impossible, to relate patristic patterns of argument to the problems of the nineteenth century.[9]

Thus, for example, it may be true that 'all parties appeal to Scripture', but it is less certain that 'Here there is no difference between early times and late' (*Dev* 2.1.3). Not only did he too uncritically endorse patristic methods of exegesis, but his trust in the 'living tradition' made him insufficiently sensitive to the exegetical unsoundness of the contemporary habit of supporting theological conclusions by invoking, more or less arbitrarily, individual passages of scripture (cf Hutton [1891] p 175).

It may be true that 'all the definitions or received judgements of the early and medieval Church rest upon definite, even though sometimes obscure sentences of Scripture' (*Dev* 2.1.15; cf *US* p 219); it does not necessarily follow that they soundly 'rest' upon them.[10]

The incompleteness and imbalance of Newman's treatment, in the *Essay*, of problems concerning the relationship between scripture and subsequent doctrinal statement, which is partly due to particular applications of the principle with which this chapter is concerned, does not mean that he had any intention, in principle, of understating the unique role of scripture in the life of the church : 'The divines of the Church are in every age engaged in regulating themselves by Scripture . . . Scripture may be said to be the medium in which the mind of the Church has energised and developed' (*Dev* 7.4.2). In other words, prescinding from criteriological questions, Newman takes it for granted that the process of doctrinal elaboration in the church as a whole is the fruit of its meditation on scripture 'by the unconscious growth of ideas suggested by the letter and habitual to the mind' (*Dev* 2.1.3). As so often in the *Essay*, it is implied, rather than explicitly stated, that the guarantee of the faithfulness of this process is the guiding presence of the Spirit, 'promised to all Christians . . . to impress the *contents* of Scripture on their hearts, and to teach them the faith through *whatever* sources' (*VM* I p 164).

If the whole of revelation is, in some sense, contained 'in' the scriptures, how are we to understand that 'in'? Does it follow from the principle that 'the earlier is to be understood in the light of the later' that, in the search for the 'real' meaning of a biblical passage, the results of scientific exegesis count for less than those events of christian history and their theological interpretation which are claimed to be the authentic 'comment' on the original and 'obscure' text? (cf *Dev* 4.3.9). In the following section we shall attempt to provide part of the answer to these questions by examining Newman's defence of the 'mystical interpretation' of scripture.

5.21 *The 'mystical sense'*
According to Newman, the ante-nicene creeds 'make no mention in their letter of the Catholic doctrine' (*Dev* Int 11) of the Trinity. 'Of course we believe that they imply it, or rather intend it . . . But nothing in the mere letter of those documents leads to that belief. To give a deeper meaning to their letter, we must interpret

them by the times which came after' (*ibid*). The drift of this passage is to the effect that the patristic texts in question have two meanings : a 'literal' meaning, found 'on the surface' of the text, and a 'deeper' meaning 'implied' by the original writers and explicitly embodied in the subsequent form of the doctrine (in the context, it is clear that 'the catholic doctrine' in question is that formulated in the Athanasian creed). This is the framework within which, in the *Essay*, Newman tackles the problem of the 'senses' of scripture. The way in which he does so sharply illustrates the problems involved in the application of the principle with which we are concerned.

Even if Newman's concern had been merely historical, his enthusiasm for the Alexandrians (and especially for Athanasius) would have made it difficult for him adequately to appreciate the Syrian achievement. De Lubac can both acknowledge that Newman was one of the few nineteenth-century theologians to achieve any real understanding of patristic 'mystical' exegesis ([1969b] p 62; significantly, three of the four authors mentioned by him were pioneers in problems of doctrinal development: Drey, Möhler and Newman) and at the same time say of the Antiochenes that 'Their attitude of mind and their form of work entitle them to be considered as the real founders of biblical exegesis' (p 47). In contrast, Newman's concept of the 'literal sense' of scripture was, as we shall see, restrictively conditioned by the fundamentalist tendencies against which he was reacting and, for him, Antioch was 'the very metropolis of heresy' (*Dev* 7.4.5; cf *TT* p 145). In this section, we shall briefly examine those contemporary preoccupations which influenced his handling of the problem, the imbalance they produced in his treatment, and the concepts of the 'literal' and 'mystical' senses with which he worked.

In the first place, his tendency to accept a deductivist model of theological method[11] invites a particular exegetical perspective. If the 'multitude of propositions' which constitute the eventual 'form of a doctrine' (*Dev* 2.1.4) are deductively derived from scripture; if it is assumed that the process of deduction is guided, and its results authenticated, by the Spirit of Truth; then those results may be said to embody the 'deeper' or 'mystical' meaning of the original texts.

A second, and more important factor underpinning Newman's

claim that 'the mystical interpretation of Holy Scripture' is 'one of the characteristic conditions or principles on which the teaching of the Church has ever proceeded'[12] is the analogy he constructs between the Jewish rejection of Christ and the protestant refusal to 'follow the course of doctrine as it moves on' (*Dev* 5.1.8; cf 7.4.5; see *5.43*). Theodore of Mopsuestia, 'Maintaining that the real sense of Scripture was, not the scope of a Divine Intelligence, but the intention of the mere human organ of inspiration' (*Dev* 6.3.2.5; cf 5.4.5; 6.3.2.3–4; 7.4.1), becomes the symbol of the 'rationalist' who was Newman's perennial foe. In Newman's mind, the exclusion of the 'mystical interpretation' is closely bound up with the denial of 'the verbal inspiration of scripture' (*Dev* 6.3.2.3). It is this connection which he intuitively perceived between conservative fundamentalism, the 'abuse of private judgement' (cf *VM* i pp 145–88), and the 'rationalism' against which he inveighed in the *University Sermons* and *Tract 73*, which accounts for his 'superficial and misleading account of German religious development since the Reformation' (Chadwick [1957] p 225, on *Dev* 5.4.4).

In view of the fact, therefore, that a static literalism was, for Newman, not simply a defective exegetical perspective, but a symptom of weakening faith and a threat to the vitality of christian belief and christian holiness, it is hardly surprising that he does not tackle the problem with scholarly impartiality. As usual, he plays the advocate rather than the analyst. Because it was not currently called in question, there was no need to emphasise the importance of the 'literal sense'.[13] His polemic is directed against those who '*confine* themselves to the mere literal interpretation of Scripture' (*Dev* 7.4.5, my stress). In practice, however, the effect of his polemic is seriously to tilt the balance in the other direction,[14] thus dangerously weakening the tension between the historical and the transcendent, the 'human' and the 'divine'.[15]

Newman's tendency to identify the 'literal sense' with the 'mere letter' (*Dev* Int 11; cf 2.1.4), the most restrictive possible interpretation of a text, is partly due to an acceptance of his opponent's terms: 'The literal, plain, and uncontroversible meaning of Scripture . . . without any addition or supply by way of interpretation, is that alone which for ground of faith we are necessarily bound to accept' ('the latitudinarian Hale', quoted *Dev* 7.4.7), and partly to his own unsatisfactory analysis of the notion of 'objectivity' (see *4.12*). Given this view of the 'literal sense', and his acceptance of a deductivist account of theological method, it was inevitable that the claim that later church doctrine embodied a meaning which was, in some sense, 'contained in' scripture, could only be sustained by positing an additional, 'larger' (*Dev* 3.1.6) or 'deeper' (*Dev* Int 11; 3.1.6) meaning the relationship of which to the 'literal sense' is exceedingly fragile. Once abandon the principle that 'un énoncé . . . ne peut *pas* avoir *deux sens différents*' (Haag [1969] p 220), and that, as a result, 'Le "sens plenier" ne fait que prolonger et approfondir le sens littéral',[16] and the application of the principle that 'the earlier is to be interpreted by the later' releases the 'allegorical' or 'spiritual' interpretation of scripture from its necessary control by the text on which it purports to 'comment'.[17] Once separate the 'literal' (or 'human') and 'mystical' (or 'divine') meanings of a biblical passage, and the way is open, through the claim that 'the justification of the larger and higher interpretation lies in some antecedent probability, such as Catholic consent' (*Dev* 3.1.6), to the dangerous admission that 'We make it no objection . . . that the sacred writer did not contemplate' the interpretation in question (*Dev* 3.1.4). The pattern of argument here is similar to that by which, in a letter of 1841, he justified the method of *Tract 90* (cf *Moz* ɪɪ pp 335–6 and, with insignificant variations, *Apo* p 137).

The tension between the fruits of biblical exegesis and the claims of christian belief is structurally similar to that which we found to be central to the problem of Newman's christian historiography (see *3.13*). We shall return to it in the context of the wider problem of christian history viewed as the fulfilment of biblical prophecy (see *5.43*).

The problem with which Newman was concerned is undoubtedly a real one, and he was able to do greater justice to the concerns of patristic exegesis than many of his contemporaries. If, nevertheless, his treatment is distinctly unsatisfactory, this is only partly due to the unfortunate way in which that problem is posed. More basically, it is due to his characteristic technique of attempting to outflank the opposition. His opponents, anglican and protestant, maintained that all true doctrine is contained in scripture. He accepts the premise but, rather than enter immediately into discussion of particular 'developments', he concentrates on the 'upper blade', on making a case for the interpretative principle that 'Of no doctrine whatever, which does not actually contradict what has been delivered, can it be peremptorily asserted that it is not in Scripture' (*Dev* 2.1.14).

5.3 *The unity of the 'idea'*

In a lecture written in Dublin in 1855, but never delivered because it was judged to be 'inexpedient in view of the prevailing temper on matters theological' (Ward, W. [1912] I p 409), Newman said : 'I . . . would open my heart, if not my intellect (for that is beyond me), to the whole circle of truth' (*Idea* p 456). Throughout the *Essay*, the complexity, polyvalence and interdependence of its arguments bear witness to his restless search for 'the total reality . . . He find it quite impossible to think otherwise than in continual reference to the whole' (Walgrave [1957] p 6; cf *PN* p 8).

We have already had occasion to observe, in a number of contexts, that emphasis on the *unity* of the 'idea' of christianity which permeates the *Essay*. In this section we shall examine the relationship between Newman's characteristically 'circular' thinking and his concern to stress the unity of the 'idea', and draw attention to the historiographical, apologetic and theological components in this concern.

According to Schlink, certain 'basic forms of human perception . . . are pre-eminently represented by certain men who persistently apply their particular type of thought-progression to all kinds of objects of perception'.[18] One such form of 'thought progression' he describes as 'Circular thinking [which] corresponds to a contemplative movement round the object of perception—whether this is concrete or abstract—and the mutual connexion of features constitutes the truth about the object perceived' ([1967] p 56; cf Burgum [1930] p 322). If we read 'real idea' for 'object of perception', and 'aspect' for 'feature', that description is strikingly similar to the process described in *Dev* 1.1.1–2 (see *4.1*).

Schlink also observes that 'Such figures as a triangle or a circle may be of enormous systematic significance if they dominate the progression of thought and the organisation of facts' (p 54; cf Lash [1971d] pp 56–9). In the *Essay*, the image of a 'circle' of 'doctrine' (or 'revealed truth') is employed on three occasions (*Dev* Int 10; 20; 7.4.2; *DA* p 145). In the *Idea of a University*, the dominant image for expressing Newman's metaphysical concern is that of a 'circle' (cf Culler [1955] p 184, who locates the source of the image in translations of 'encyclopaedia' by Bacon and Elyot; pp 173–88). Here it is sometimes used, as in *Dev* 1.1, to describe the cognitive process (*Idea* p 151); sometimes to highlight the interdependence of different disciplines; (*Idea* pp 20, quoting Mosheim, 26, 51, 59, 67, 73, 451; *PN* p 173; *VM* i p 123); and sometimes to indicate the boundaries of a particular field of inquiry. (*Idea* pp 36, 62, 217, 508). Since many of the lectures are concerned with the relationship between secular and religious knowledge, it is not surprising that reference is frequently made to either or both of these '*two* great circles of knowledge' (*Idea* p 430—my stress; cf pp 26, 36, 62, 211, 451, 508). But there is an implicit appeal to the unity of all truth, as of the world it interprets.[19] A circle not only unites the segments of its circumference, and encloses a certain space, it is also defined in terms of its centre : 'formation of mind' is said to consist in 'the actual acceptance and use of certain principles as centres of thought around which our knowledge grows and is located' (*Idea* p 502—the background for understanding passages such as *Dev* 7.1.3. Cf *US* pp 287, 341).

In the *Essay*, the appeal to the unity of christian doctrine at one and the same time indicates a particular conception of revelation (*Dev* 2.1.9; see *5.4*); serves as an historiographical device for interpreting scanty evidence (*Dev* 3.1.8–10); and grounds the apologetic argument that 'You must accept the whole or reject the whole' (*Dev* 2.3.2; cf *Apo* p 297; *DA* p 398; *Idea* p 182; *SD* p 391; *VV* pp 144–5). However important this last argument may have been for Newman personally, justifying his acceptance of those details of the Roman catholic 'system' which still left him uneasy, it is nevertheless misleading. In order not to overestimate the force of the injunction, we need to keep in mind the patterns of persuasion that run through all the arguments of the *Essay*. In a passage such as *Dev* 2.3.2, Newman is not saying that there is no difference between the 'acceptance' to be accorded to the veneration of relics and to the doctrine of the eucharistic presence. The fundamental issue is, as always, the choice between 'faith' and 'reason' considered as 'habits of mind' (see *3.22*) : the claim to the unity of the catholic system is being employed to structure the appeal to 'receive it unsuspiciously . . . whatever may be our eventual judgement about' the details (*Dev* 3.1.10. Cf his advice in 1826 to take 'our old divines *as a whole*'—*Moz* i pp 142–3).

The claim that 'A living idea becomes many, yet remains one' (*Dev* 5.3.2; cf 2.1.1) is not only an affirmation of the interdependence of the aspects at each stage in the history of the 'idea'; it is also a claim that the 'idea' is substantially identical in its earlier and later stages : 'The point to be ascertained is the unity and identity of the idea with itself through all stages of its development from first to last'. (*Dev* 5.7.4). This article, added in *1878*, as a summary of a key chapter, is important for its stress that all the seven 'notes' are concerned with establishing the 'unity' of the 'idea' (cf *Dev* 3.1.1). Newman's occasional use of the term 'oneness', rather than 'unity', is significant (cf *Dev* 2.3.5; 5.0.1).

The close link which exists between Newman's insistence on the 'unity' of the 'idea' of christianity and his attempts to persuade us to see the history of christian doctrine as a process of 'homogeneous evolution' (see *4.3*) is made explicit in the *Apologia* : 'Infallibility cannot act outside of a definite circle of thought . . . The new truth which is promulgated, if it is to be called new, must at least be homogeneous, cognate, implicit, viewed relatively to the old truth' (*Apo* p 253).

As with so many arguments in the *Essay*, the complex nature of the appeal to the unity of the 'idea' (both materially : in that argument's range of content, and formally : in the interweaving of historical, theological and apologetic components) makes summary evaluation impossible. As we have suggested in *4.3*, it is unconvincing as an historical description. The failure to differentiate sufficiently clearly between descriptive and prescriptive claims is common to much discussion of the problem of doctrinal development. This lack of differentiation is partly obscured by, and partly the result of the characteristic structure of argument in the *Essay*. The arguments from antecedent probability are not simply intended to ease our acceptance of a particular description of christian history (which could then be tested, simply as descriptive, according to purely historiographical criteria). Grounded in the theological assumption that all christian doctrine and practice is to be interpreted in the light of the one mystery of Christ (an assumption which is one of the 'central elements in the Tractarian vision of the world and of God'—Allchin [1967] p 53, see *6.3*), they also embody prescriptive recommendations, generated by Newman's appreciation of contemporary needs (cf

Egner [1969] pp 132–3, 136). The use of the political analogy of 'monarchy' (see *3.23*) is interesting in this regard. Newman observed that the apparently monolithic Roman catholicism of the mid-nineteenth century readily expressed its self-understanding in terms of this analogy. His own political tastes predisposed him to welcome the analogy. He does not simply argue, however, that we have reason to expect, on historical grounds, that christianity would take this form (and we find that it has done so in Roman catholicism). He also argues, prescriptively, that only by taking this form can it escape, in practice, from the dilemma in which other christian bodies find themselves: 'Else . . . you will have to choose between a comprehension of opinions and a resolution into parties, between latitudinarian and sectarian error' (*Dev* 2.2.13).

In other words, the appeal to the unity of the 'fact' of christianity (and therefore of its 'idea') is, at one and the same time, an historical, descriptive claim, a heuristic recommendation (creating the expectation that things would turn out this way), and a complex prescriptive argument. The strength of the prescription, in its dependence on the unity of revelation (see *5.4*), is the strength of traditional arguments from the 'analogy of faith'. The excesses and distortions consequent upon the isolation of any particular aspect of the christian mystery (whether in practice—in structures and forms of piety, or in theoretical statements) can only be prevented and corrected in so far as the attempt is continually made to set that aspect in the context of the whole. (The criteriological questions which arise at this point, and the extent to which, in the *Essay*, Newman shows himself sensitive to them, will be discussed in *6.3* and *6.31*).

The weakness of the prescription consists in the fact that it becomes almost impossible to pin down any one of the strands in Newman's argument and test it to destruction: he can always, when attacked, shift his angle of vision. Both the strengths and the weaknesses are the fruits of that epistemological style, that 'circular thought progression' which seems to be, not so much a freely chosen technique, but rather the expression of particular psychological type.

From the point of view of the principle with which we are concerned in this chapter, the claim that 'the earlier is to be interpreted by the later' rests upon the assumption, to which we must now turn, that the whole 'circle of doctrine' has, in some sense, been present from the beginning of christianity.

5.4 Newman's concept of revelation

'The question then for those who think Newman's theology is Catholic, is this : these new doctrines, of which the Church had a feeling or inkling but of which she was not conscious—in what meaningful sense may it be asserted that these new doctrines are not "new revelation"?'.[20] Misner remarks that 'Although several authors have pointed out in defence of Newman his stress on the unity, wholeness and indivisibility of the idea-impression which underlies all true expressions of revealed doctrine, no one has found in Newman a corresponding refinement in his notion of revelation' ([1970] p 46; cf the reactions to Chadwick in Davis [1958], Léonard [1958], Nédoncelle [1958] and Stern [1967] pp 210–24).

In this section, therefore, we shall, firstly, comment on the notion of revelation in the *Essay* and, secondly, make some general observations concerning the claim that the whole 'idea' of christianity has been present from the beginning. We shall then examine three arguments which are used to support this claim : the argument that earlier doctrines 'tend towards' later ones (*5.41*); the use made of the distinction between 'principle' and 'doctrine' (*5.42*); and the analogy drawn between the development of christian doctrine and the fulfilment of prophecy (*5.43*).

Newman's complex and varied uses of the term 'revelation' in the *Essay* may be divided into three main groups : those which refer to the *content* of revelation, to the *process*, and to its *expression*. So far as the first group is concerned, 'revelation' is more or less identical with the 'idea' of christianity (see *4.1*). The inadequacy of Newman's treatment of revelation in the *Essay* is in no small measure due to the fact that, while his use of the notion of a 'living, real idea' demands a concept of revelation far wider and richer than that current in nineteenth-century theology, he does not seem clearly to have recognised that demand, with the result that he insufficiently appreciated the extent to which 'his pioneering effort to do justice to dogma and history, actually required a more adequate notion of revelation than was then available' (Misner [1970] pp 46–7).

We remarked earlier that Newman's use of the model of literary criticism involves three terms: the text, the comment, and the 'real idea' with which both are concerned (see *5.11*). Since scripture (the 'text') is the privileged expression of that revelation which has been given 'once for all' (*Dev* Int 21), he sometimes loosely refers to it as 'the revelation' (*Dev* 2.1.2; 2.1.5; 2.1.6; 2.2.2; 7.6.1). The concept of the 'development of revelation' is invoked to describe our present relationship to the past, definitive expression of that new personal relationship of God to man (the 'reality') which still endures (*Dev* 2.1.5; 2.1.6; 2.1.9; 2.2.3; 2.2.5; 2.2.8; 2.3.1; 7.6.1). It is significant that he speaks of the need to seek in history not for revelation, but for 'the matter of that revelation which has been vouchsafed to mankind' (*Dev* Int 4; cf 3.2.2). Emphasis on the enduring presence of that 'Object' which is revealed (*Dev* 1.2.9; 2.1.1; 2.1.16) results in those expressions which most strongly suggest that revelation is an ongoing process (*Dev* 2.1.2; 2.2.8; 2.2.12; see *5.43*).

As a process, revelation is 'a message and a lesson speaking to this man and that' (*Dev* 2.2.12). It is not simply the disclosure of information but, as we would expect (cf *4.32*, note 68) it is primarily in the order of command or invitation, evoking an 'ethical' or 'practical' response (*Dev* 1.1.3; 1.2.6–7; 2.1.16; 8.1.1). Far from being merely 'verbal' (even metaphorically: as *locutio Dei*), it is the 'manifestation of the Invisible Divine Power' (*Dev* 2.2.11; cf 1.2.9; 8.2.1). Its originality and uniqueness lies in its constitutive 'facts' rather than in its 'principles', in which it simply reinforces what is discoverable in 'all the works of God'.[21] Whereas, prior to this revelation, the will of God is discernible only through the activity of conscience, Newman's characteristic defence of the 'dogmatic principle' leads him to emphasise the 'objectivity' (ie 'giveness' and public availability) of this revelation (*Dev* 2.1.1; 2.2.5; 2.2.8; 2.3.1–2).

In spite of the stress, throughout the *Essay*, on the unity of the 'idea' (see *4.1, 5.3*) the problem of locating the origin of individual doctrines which were eventually definitively appropriated by the church sometimes leads him to speak, in a manner which echoes the distinction between the 'episcopal' and 'prophetic' tradition, of the 'idea of Christianity' as containing 'much which will be only partially recognised by us as included in it and only held by us unconsciously' (*Dev* 2.3.2; cf 2.2.5. The same difficulty was

already present in the argument of the last *University Sermon*—
cf Lash [1970]).

Because Newman believed that 'new' revelation, subsequent
to the events to which the scriptures bear witness, was impossible,
he had need of a hypothesis on the basis of which the structures,
devotional life, theological and dogmatic achievements of the
church could be said, with varying degrees of confidence, to be
'contained in' the original revelation. He argued that the relationship of the 'later' to the 'earlier' was one of comment, interpretation, explicitation, application, fulfilment, 'that is, . . . development' (*Dev* 2.1.5). The range of terms indicates not mental confusion, but sensitivity to the richness and variety of the 'fact', and
therefore of the 'idea', whose historicity he struggled to comprehend.

Because Newman believed that 'new' revelation was impossible,
and because he believed in the ongoing substantial identity of the
christian 'fact', he held that, in some sense, the whole 'idea' must
have been present from the beginning. This was partly a historical,
and partly a doctrinal claim. Because of the inadequacy of the
categories within which he attempted to formulate the doctrinal
claim, he was led into making assertions which are historically
untenable.

It is not difficult to point out the weaknesses and inconsistencies in his argument, and to show that, as a result of his failure
rigorously to maintain his own insistence on the unity of revelation, much of the argument in the *Essay* is difficult to reconcile
with any coherent defence (other than a thorough-going fideism
such as he never contemplated) of the claim that 'revelation
closed with the death of the last apostle'.[22]

Unfortunately, this claim, thus formulated, seems to imply
that revelation consists in the divine provision of items of information. Certainly Newman's treatment of revelation in the *Essay*
would have gained in coherence if he had more clearly perceived
that the categories within which the christian claim to the finality
of the Christ-event was, at the time, expressed, were inadequate
to their intention.[23] It is difficult correctly to answer the wrong
question : whether or not 'Newman's theology is Catholic' is not
something that can today profitably be discussed on the basis of
a formulation of the problem that has been superseded.

There is, indeed, a 'certain unsurmounted "extrinsicism" in

Newman's thought in regard to revelation' (Misner [1970] p 47). This is evident from the way in which he formulated his affirmation of the 'objectivity' of God's word in respect to man.[24] But, although there are passages in which, as we have noticed, he tends to speak of the scriptural propositions in which the apostolic witness to revelation was expressed as themselves 'the revelation', there is no doubt that his central concern was to insist on the 'continuing action of God who reveals and communicates *himself* to the successive generations of those who receive his word in faith'.[25] But the privileged *locus* of that word, for those who still hear today, remains the scripture. Therefore Newman tried to show that the 'whole idea' has been present from the beginning.

Several of the passages in the *Essay* which point in this direction remind us, in the dynamism they attribute to the 'idea', of the christological component in the claim that Newman is making (see *4.3*): 'forcing its way into its normal shape' (*Dev* 4.1.4); 'from the first a certain element at work' (*Dev* 4.3.1); the dogmatic principle was 'active, nay sovereign . . . in every part of Christendom' (*Dev* 8.1.4). Other passages, with their similar use of dynamic terminology, seem to be suggesting both the latent presence of the 'reality', the 'whole idea', behind its particular human expressions, and also an awareness that what men are 'trying to say' may be more significant than the 'obvious' meanings of the formulations they actually achieve (*Dev* 4.2.1; 4.2.6; 4.2.11; 9.4.3; 10.0.1; see *5.41*).

In 1837, Newman spoke of 'Prophetical Tradition' as: 'partly written, partly unwritten, partly the interpretation, partly the supplement of Scripture, partly preserved in intellectual expressions, partly latent in the spirit and temper of Christians' (*VM* I p 250). Many years later, to express this awareness of the variety of forms by which the one 'idea' is mediated to us, he spoke of the 'diffraction' of 'The pure and indivisible Light' (*GA* p 132). In such passages, the appeal to the unity of the idea in the mind of the community that receives and embodies it (see *4.1*) is understated, and he can plausibly be described as conceiving of revelation as 'donnée sous forme fragmentaire' (Stern [1967] p 37, on *Ess* I pp 41–2). In the *Essay*, however, the emphasis on the underlying unity of the 'idea' is evident throughout, and Chadwick, in saying that the 'original revelation . . . was given partly in explicit doctrines, partly in feelings which were left to be subse-

quently drawn out into doctrines' ([1957] p 157), is perhaps describing the conception that Newman had in 1839 of the 'Romanist' position (cf *Ess* I p 12), rather than that which he sought to
express in 1845. Chadwick's use of 'partly . . . partly', in the
passage just quoted, distorts Newman's thought in that it does
not sufficiently respect the complexity, in Newman's view, of the
relationship between the 'fundamentals' and others aspects of
christian belief and doctrine (see *6.21*). Moreover, Chadwick's
isolation of the term 'feelings' understates the cognitive component in Newman's view of the manner in which doctrine may
be 'held', even before it is reflexively appropriated. (Cf my comments in *2.11* on the use of 'feeling' by Newsome and Geoffrey
Faber.)

If the 'whole idea' was present from the beginning *per modum
unius* (*L&D* XIII p 82; *Consulting* p 63) does it necessarily follow
that every subsequently elaborated 'aspect' of that 'idea' was
'known' by the church from the beginning? To that question
(which, on the basis of a different theology of revelation, might
have been differently posed), there was no easy answer. Newman,
the theologian, convinced that later doctrines were not in any
absolute sense 'new', was unable to answer, simply : 'No'. Newman, the historian, was unable to answer, simply : 'Yes'. The
least persuasive of his attempts to escape the dilemma in which he
found himself is the claim : 'the holy Apostles would without
words know all the truths concerning the high doctrines of theology, which controversialists after them have piously and charit-
ably reduced to formulae, and developed through argument'.[26]

It is, perhaps, a pity that Newman did not incorporate into the
revised version of the *Essay* the formula he hit upon, in a letter
to Richard Hutton, in October 1871 : 'A Catholic believes that
the Church is, so to call it, a standing Apostolic committee—to
answer questions, which the Apostles are not here to answer, concerning what they received and preached. As the Church does
not know more than the Apostles knew, there are many questions
which the Church cannot answer' (*L&D* XXV p 418).

5.41 The earlier 'tends towards' the later

In his study of Newman's views on the primacy, Misner notes
that 'two different interpretations of the origins of the papacy are
present in Newman's discussion of the question in *Development*

. . . The one constitutes an admission that there was a considerable period of time in the early history of the Church when popes and their supremacy over the whole church neither existed nor were thought of (but when this divinely willed institution was only present in the elements out of which it was to take shape in the course of centuries)' ([1968] p 213). According to the other interpretation, 'the papacy being of divine institution for the church of all ages, it must have existed in some real sense as such from the beginning, though of course impeded in its exercise'.[27] Moreover, in *1878*, 'this second strand . . . assumed a much more important place, with a corresponding weakening of the first strand'.[28]

The two 'strands' in the argument, to which Misner refers, can be detected not only in Newman's discussion of the primacy, but also in most of the other sections of chapter 4 of *1878*, and the shift in emphasis between the two editions is nowhere more striking than in the important article, added in 1878, which introduces this chapter. This shift in emphasis, which would seem partly to be the result of Newman's attempts to make his views acceptable to the cautious theologians of the Roman school,[29] cannot adequately be construed as a removal of the appeal to history (see *3.11*). Not only were both arguments present, as Misner notes, in *1845*, but the first strand is quite compatible with the claim that the 'whole idea' was present from the beginning as 'a vast body of thought within it, which one day would take shape and position' (*Dev* 10.0.1. Some of the most significant changes were introduced as early as 1846: see Appendix). 'My argument then is . . . that, from the first age of Christianity, its teaching looked towards those ecclesiastical dogmas, afterwards recognised and defined, with (as time went on) more or less determinate advance in the direction of them' (*Dev* 4.0.1).

What does it mean to say that doctrine at one period 'looked towards' or 'tended towards' the teaching of a later period? In order to answer that question, it is necessary to distinguish between accounts of the direction which events were taking during a particular period (A), and Newman's assessment of the 'state of the evidence' for a given doctrine at a given moment in time (B). These two operations are sometimes performed separately and sometimes in conjunction.

Thus, for example, he argues (A) that 'the tendency of the

controversy with the Arians was to raise our view of our Lord's Mediatorial acts, to impress them on us in their divine rather than their human aspect' (*Dev* 4.2.3; cf 4.2.4; 5.5.1; *Ess* I p 268). This type of description presents few difficulties from the point of view of method.

The passages in which he combines the two procedures, in an attempt to discern, from the state of the evidence at a given period, the seeds of that future development which in fact took place, are more problematic (and here, as so often, Newman's illustrations are his own worst enemies: cf *Dev* 5.5.2–3). Although the early evidence for a doctrine may be both fragmentary and ambiguous, its later form may enable us to detect what the earlier writers were trying to say: 'when we have reason to think, that a writer or an age *would* have witnessed so and so, but for this or that, and that this or that were mere accidents of his position, then he or it may be said to tend towards such testimony. In this way the first centuries tend towards the fifth' (AB).[30] The unsatisfactory form of many such arguments, such as the treatment of original sin in *Dev* 4.1.4 (added *1878*) or communion in one kind, *Dev* 4.1.8, the purpose of which is to make a case, in the teeth of the evidence, for the substantial immutability of doctrine, should not lead us to dismiss them out of hand. They contain an insight of considerable interest: the 'deep' writer 'has something before him which he aims at, and, while he cannot help including much in his meaning which he does not aim at, he does aim at one thing, not at another' (*DA* p 174; cf *Dev* 5.5.1–4, esp 5.5.2). Newman here comes close to a distinction, indispensable for the attempt to understand doctrinal pronouncements in their historical context, between what is 'stated' and what is 'formally affirmed'. Moreover, while the recommendation to use the 'clear light of the fourth and fifth centuries' to 'interpret to us the dim, though definite, outlines traced in the preceding' (*Dev* 4.3.17) is not without its dangers and ambiguities, it does seem to be the case, for example, that christians who receive the decrees of Chalcedon interpret the christology of the new testament in their light—not, indeed, as a principle of scientific exegesis, but as a matter of religious fact.

We have already considered, in *4.11* and *4.3*, Newman's fondness for comparing the form or shape of christian doctrine and practice at different periods in the history of the church. Some of the passages in which he does so (eg *Dev* 6.1.30; 6.2.17; 6.3.3.23) approximate to the type of procedure referred to above as 'B'. This tendency to conceive of history episodically cannot simply be attributed to the influence of the Fathers on his historical method (cf Smyth [1955] p 166). More basically, it is the expression of a particular conception of memory and of historical apprehension. This is less clear in his published works than in his *Philosophical Notebooks*, in which he returns to the problem more than once (*PN* pp 35–9, 45, 123). He objected to phrases such as 'I can trust my various acts of memory' (Ward, W. G. [1860] p 14) on the grounds that the faculties of memory, or sensation, are not distinct from the conscious subject, but are the 'mind in its several modes, viz the mind feeling, the mind remembering, the mind reasoning' (*PN* p 45), and that 'As I have not faith in my existence, much less can I be said that I have faith in my consciousness' (*PN* p 33). Thus, at the period when he wrote these notes (1861 and 1859), Newman had come to conceive of the memory as a mode of apprehension. He tended to regard the 'objects' of memory as 'present' in much the same way as other objects of consciousness: 'What is *time* that it should make a *real* difference between memory and consciousness'.[31] He here makes explicit a tendency to conceive of history, or at least the personal history of the individual, synchronically rather than diachronically.

Sillem has indicated that one of the probable sources of Newman's philosophy was the Associationist school with its emphasis that 'the *coalescence* of our past experiences into a pattern . . . enables the knower to apprehend an object as the whole it is'.[32] He draws attention to 'Newman's often repeated observations about the direction in which letters of the alphabet seem to be looking' ([1969] p 215: cf *GA* p 374; *PN* pp 11, 75, 169). Newman used this device in his last letter to William Froude, in 1879: 'which way does B look? to the right or to the left?' (quoted Ward, W [1912] II p 590, discussing the 'principle' of the *Essay*). Later in the letter he wrote: 'There were circumstances in the mode of conducting the Vatican Council which I could not like, but its definition of the Pope's Infallibility was nothing short of the upshot of numberless historical facts *looking that way*'.[33]

By now, the purpose of this apparent digression should be clear.

The key article added in 1878, in which Newman claims 'that, from the first age of Christianity, its teaching *looked towards* those ecclesiastical dogmas, afterwards recognised and defined' (*Dev* 4.0.1, my stress), can only be understood against the background of certain characteristic features of Newman's conception of historical apprehension. I would wish to argue that, by implication, many of the passages in which he speaks of earlier doctrine 'tending towards' the later, should be similarly understood.[34] We are thus reminded, once again, that Newman is less concerned with 'demonstration' or 'proof' than with coaxing the reader to 'see' the (ambiguous) evidence in the way in which he himself has come to see it.[35]

Newman's claim that the seeds of later development can, with hindsight, be detected in the early history of a developing 'idea' is, as usual, not an exclusively doctrinal argument, but the theological application of a general historiographical principle (see *3.1*). It is, for example, possible that Newman's use of terms such as 'tends' or 'tending' carries overtones of the organic analogy, in the sense in which Coleridge spoke of the 'tendencies of the life of Nature to vegetation or animalisation' (Coleridge [1848] p 48). Thus he argues that 'Changes in society are . . . commonly preceded and facilitated by the setting in of a certain current in men's thoughts and feelings in that direction towards which a change is to be made' (*Dev* 6.1.3; cf Sorel [1912] p 7). His application of the argument to the history of doctrine leads him to an assessment of heresy that is at once historically more sensitive and theologically more constructive than was common in the catholic theology of the period : 'heresies in every age may be taken as the measure of the existing state of thought in the Church, and of the movement of her theology : they determine in what way the current is setting, and the rate at which it flows'.[36]

5.42 'Principles' and 'doctrines'

Amongst the arguments which Newman employs to support his claim that the whole 'idea' of christianity has been present from the beginning, one of the most interesting is that contained in the second 'note' of a true development : 'Continuity of Principles' (*Dev* 5.2; 7). This second note is, in many ways, the complement of the first : it is because 'developments . . . have been conducted all along on definite and continuous principles that the type of the Religion has remained from first to last unalterable' (*Dev* 7.1.1; less categorical than *1845* p 319).

In this section, we shall summarise the notion of 'principle' employed in the *Essay*, and say something of the implications of *Dev* 5.2 for the general problem of doctrinal development. Before doing so, it is necessary to draw attention to the added significance which the second 'note' acquired in *1878*.

Extensive as is the re-ordering of the material in *1878*, and although hardly a page of the *Essay* escaped at least trivial retouching, very little new material was added for the revised edition. The chapter devoted to the detailed illustration of the 'second note' contains more new material than any other chapter.[31] It may therefore be presumed that Newman attached greater importance to this 'note' in 1878 than he had done in 1845.

The notion of 'principle' and in particular of 'first principles' occupies a very important place in Newman's thinking, and has therefore attracted the attention of several of his commentators. As with any key term in Newman's writings, summary definition is impossible : one can only observe the use which he makes of it in different contexts. In general, it can be said that, in the *Essay*, the range of meaning covered is similar to that covered, in ordinary English usage, by the term 'law' (cf *Dev* 5.2.1; 5.2.4–6; *4.31*). One basic notion is that of an 'active' or 'living' principle : a 'living idea' is said to be one that 'becomes an active [*1845* : living] principle within [the public throng of men], leading them to an ever-new contemplation of itself, to an application of it in various directions, and a propagation of it on every side' (*Dev* 1.1.4; cf 1.1.6; 5.3.5; 5.7.2; 8.1.2; *Diff* I pp 43–4, 54). It thus refers to the motive forces at work within an individual or a society, to deeply implanted attitudes and convictions. Unlike doctrines, which 'grow and are enlarged, principles are permanent' (*Dev* 5.2.1) and do not develop, except in the sense that they are gradually reflexively appropriated by the society that is animated by them.[38] To the extent that principles, which lie 'deeper in the mind [than doctrines], and are assumptions rather than objective professions' (*Dev* 5.2.2; cf 1.2.3; 1.2.7; *Prepos* pp 271–314), are consciously adverted to, they may be formulated in ethical maxims or statements of principle (cf *Dev* 1.2.4; 5.2.5; 9.6.1; *Jfc* p 333).

The basic distinction that Newman draws, in the *Essay*, between 'principles' and 'doctrines', is that the former refer to the animating forces in a society, indicating the presence of a 'living idea', whether or not the members of the society are reflexively aware of them, while the latter are the propositions in which a society formulates its beliefs : 'The life of doctrines may be said to consist in the law or principle which they embody'.[39] By insisting on the permanence of the principles of christianity, Newman is able to admit the possibility of considerable variety, and even contrariety in doctrine (cf *Dev* 2.1.3; 5.1.3; 5.2.2–3; 5.6.2; 7.1.5; 7.6.1), without calling in question his fundamental claim that the 'idea' of christianity is immutable 'in itself' (cf *DA* pp 12–13; *Diff* I pp 129–30; *SD* p 216). The underlying appeal is, as usual, theological. Although this is not explicitly asserted in the *Essay*, it may legitimately be inferred from other passages in his writings, in which he refers to the presence of Christ and his Spirit as the 'principle' of christianity (cf *DA* p 379; *GA* pp 465–6; *Jfc* pp 53, 198; *PS* II p 288; IV pp 170, 315; V pp 41, 93; VII pp 208–9; *US* p 29), and from the central place which the doctrine of the divine indwelling occupies in his thought (cf Dessain [1967]).

The insistence that principles are more fundamental than doctrines allows Newman to stress the subordinate role of doctrinal statements in a manner more characteristic of *Arians* than of the *Essay* as a whole (cf *Ari* pp 36–7, 133–50). It does not follow, however, that continuity of principle is a sufficient condition for the authenticity, the ongoing obedience of the church.[40] The relationship between principle and doctrine is one of complementarity : 'Doctrine without its correspondent principles remains barren, if not lifeless . . . On the other hand, principle without its corresponding doctrine may be considered as the state of religious minds in the heathen world' (*Dev* 5.2.3). In other words : 'The Church has never laid it down that we are justified by Orthodoxy only' (*Jfc* p 314). Throughout his life, Newman remained faithful to Bishop Butler's maxim : 'The form of religion may indeed be where there is little of the thing itself; but the thing itself cannot be preserved amongst mankind without the form' ([1896] II p 405). ' "I did not say a creed was everything," answered Reding, "or that a religion could not be false which had a creed; but a religion can't be true which has none" ' (*LG* p 119).

The selection, in *1878*, 'For the convenience of arrangement', of the incarnation as 'the central truth of the gospel' (*Dev* 7.1.3), although difficult to reconcile with the principle laid down in *Dev* 1.1.3 (cf *1845* pp 34–5; see *4.1*, *4.11*, *6.31*), is hardly surprising in view of Newman's conviction that it is only through the medium of those 'forms' which enable the 'divine and adorable Form' (*PS* IV p 170) of the word to be present to man, that man may 'realise' his relationship to God. A version of christianity whose experience of God was not publicly symbolised (or 'realised') in a form available to all its members (ie in creed and rite) was as repugnant to him as one whose public articulation of belief in doctrinal formulae was not the expression of the life, the holiness, the ethical concern which activated it (cf *Apo* pp 48–9; *Campaign* p 253; *DA* p 233; *PS* II p 74). The attempt, in the second 'note', to ground the continuity of the church in the consistency of its motivating 'principles', more fundamentally than in the identity of its doctrinal statements, is in harmony with Newman's insistence, especially in his sermons, that faith is a 'principle of action' (see *3.22*, *6.32*). 'Principle is a better test of heresy than doctrine' :[41] nowhere in the *Essay* are we further than we are in this 'note' from 'logical' theories of doctrinal development (cf *4.12*, the second conception of development).

Nevertheless, however valuable the analysis of the relationship between the notions of 'principle' and 'doctrine' may be, the apologetic use to which Newman puts this analysis runs into difficulties. It may be granted that 'the political principles of Christianity . . . are laid down for us in the Sermon on the Mount' (*Dev* 5.2.5). But, in order to show that the church has been faithful to its 'principles' not merely in theory, but also (which is essential to his argument) in fact, it would be necessary to show that the 'lines of thought or conduct' (*Dev* 5.2.6) laid down in the sermon on the mount have determined the characteristic ethical 'spirit' of some branch of historical christianity. Which might be difficult.

5.43 The fulfilment of prophecy

According to Newman, the relationship between prophecy and its fulfilment is a special case of the relationship between a 'text' and its elucidatory 'comment' : 'Thus too we deal with Scripture when we have to interpret the prophetical text and the types of the Old Testament. The event which is the development is also the interpretation of the prediction; it provides a fulfilment by imposing a meaning' (*Dev* 3.1.4; see *5.11*). Insisting that 'the whole Bible, not its prophetical portions only, is written on the principle of development',[42] Newman sets up a general analogy between the fulfilment of prophecy and the development of doctrine. In this section, we shall consider Newman's use of this analogy, his appeal to Butler in this context, and the difficulties which the use of the analogy raises for the problem of the 'closure' of revelation.

The interpretation of the old testament in the light of the new is so familiar a feature of christian theological method that it would have been extraordinary if Newman had not seen it as an instance of the principle with which this chapter is concerned. It has a twofold importance for him.

In the first place, he rejects the idea that prophetic revelation consisted of the 'accumulation' of 'separate predictions' : 'It is not that first one truth is told, then another; but the whole truth or large portions of it are told at once, yet only in their rudiments, or in miniature, and they are expanded and finished in their parts, as the course of revelation proceeds' (*Dev* 2.1.9). The implicit argument running through this article is to the effect that, however fragmentary and even disconnected individual prophetic 'predictions' may appear to be, 'Every word requires a comment' (*ibid*), and that 'comment', fulfilment, or development is ultimately found in the person of Christ and his church, in respect of which the earlier prophecies can be seen to be 'pregnant texts . . . types'. (*ibid*). One difficulty raised by this form of the argument that the 'whole idea' has been present from the beginning was voiced by Newman in a letter of 1856 : 'I conceive that new Truths *were* given in Christianity; though it is very difficult to assert *what*' (*L&D* xvii p 421).

In the second place, it is important for Newman that the 'comment' elucidating the prophetic 'text' is usually an historical event or series of events (cf *Dev* 3.1.6), and not simply a further statement : 'the very course of events, as time went on, interpreted the prophecies about the Church more truly'.[43]

Although, in his use of the analogy from prophetic fulfilment, Newman often appeals to Butler (*Dev* 2.1.8–9; 2.1.14; 3.1.5–6), he is aware of the fact that he is bending the latter's argument (which has more in common with the tenor of *Tract 85* than with arguments from 'antecedent probability' in the *Essay*) to a new use.[44] He argues that he is entitled to do so because, not only was Butler 'far from denying the principle of progressive development' (*Dev* 2.1.8), but his objections against a use of analogy apparently similar to that indulged in by Newman were directed against *a priori* theorising, whereas Newman's arguments from 'antecedent probability' are an element in his attempt to interpret a process which has, in fact, already taken place. (Cf *Dev* 2.1.8; 2.2.9–10 : the structure of both passages is very similar). Moreover, Butler had admitted that 'it might be intended, that events, as they come to pass, should open and ascertain the meaning of several parts of scripture' ([1896] I p 235).

Chadwick's suspicion that the argument of the *Essay* is incompatible with the decree *Lamentabili* ([1957] p 160; *5.4*) is nowhere more amply justified than in the use which Newman makes of the analogy from prophetic fulfilment. According to Newman, the later stages in the history of prophecy and its fulfilment (within the biblical era) were 'contained within' earlier prophetic utterances, and yet were later stages in the *revelation*. The '*effata* of Our Lord and His Apostles are of a typical structure, parallel to the prophetic announcements' (*Dev* 2.1.10; cf 2.1.12). On what principle can one deny to the 'developments', in word or event, of these *effata* the status of further revelation? (Cf *Ari* p 58). He could not be unaware of the problem since, in 1837, he had accused 'the Romanist' of believing 'in a standing organ of Revelation, like the series of Jewish prophets' (*Ess* I p 159), but he seems never to have satisfactorily resolved it.

As we suggested in *5.4*, the possession by Newman of a more adequate theology of revelation than was available to him might have enabled him to reconcile the apparently unavoidable implications of his use of this analogy with his conviction that the 'whole idea' is revealed in Christ 'once for all' (*Dev* Int 21), and embodied in the new testament that bears witness to him.[45]

Today, it is not uncommon for theologians to speak of revelation as a continuing process while, at the same time, affirming that the word in its fullness was spoken in Christ and that, therefore, the new testament witness continues to enjoy unique and normative status. However, attempts to draw analogies between the biblical period and the history of the post-apostolic church without admitting that there is 'new' revelation (in some unacceptable sense) in the latter period are not always completely convincing (eg Darlap [1969] p 138).

There are at least two distinct problems here. In the first place, the parallel between 'doctrinal development' in the old testament period and in the history of the christian church could only be exact if, as in some 'liberal' theology, little emphasis were placed on the eschatological finality of the work of Christ. Nevertheless, it may still be asked whether a closer application of the parallel would not have been consistent with Newman's insights into historical process, although the results of such an application would have been disturbing to him. In the second place, should not Newman's recognition of the complexity of 'development' in pre-christian judaism (eg *SD* pp 308–80) have led him to question the validity of his assumption that the field of data relevant to his inquiry into christian development could, on historical and exegetical grounds, legitimately be restricted to the life of one denomination? (see *2.2, 3.23, 3.32*).

The claim that the 'whole idea' of christianity (of which later doctrines and institutions are 'realised aspects') has been present from the beginning would seem to be strengthened in proportion to the plausibility of the claim that these later doctrines and institutions may be regarded as the fulfilment of 'prophetic' words and gestures in the new testament. Discussing the early history of the papal primacy, Newman observes that 'The *regalia Petri* might sleep . . . as an unfulfilled prophecy' (*Dev* 4.3.3; cf 4.3.9; Misner [1968] p 182). Throughout *Dev* 4.3.1–3, Newman is attempting to draw a distinction between the 'existence' of the papacy and its 'operation' (*Dev* 4.3.1, both *1845* and *1878*, despite alterations). But if the only sense in which the papacy can be said to have 'existed' in the world in the early centuries was as an 'unfulfilled prophecy', would it not be simpler to say of the papacy what Davison said of christianity as a whole: 'There was a time when Christianity was not in the world, but only foretold: a time when it had no being, but in prophecy'? ([1861] p 278).

The difference between the two descriptions, in terms of their underlying ontology, is partly accounted for by Newman's 'platonic' or 'sacramental' view of the 'idea' of christianity. As we remarked earlier, his various uses of the model of literary criticism embody three terms: the 'text', the 'comment', and the 'real idea' which both attempt to express (see *5.11*).

However unsatisfactory we may feel the arguments to be, if only on the ground of their complexity, it must be admitted that Newman is more sensitive to the 'political' factors which account for the emergence of the papacy than many apologists have been.[46] Moreover, it should be noticed that as throughout the *Essay*, his purpose is more restricted than, at first sight, it might appear to be : 'Supposing there be otherwise good reason for saying that the Papal Supremacy is part of Christianity, there is nothing in the early history of the Church to contradict it'.[47] As he himself admits, 'All depends on the strength' of the 'presumption' that the existence of 'a monarchical principle in the Divine Scheme' is 'antecedently probable' (*Dev* 4.3.7).

6

The problem of the normative standpoint

If Newman's purpose in writing the *Essay* had been non-comittally to describe the process by which an 'idea' may be said to 'develop' in history, and the methods by which such a process of development may be discerned, this chapter would have been unnecessary. But 'mere development is no criterion by which to distinguish the true from the false' ('The theory of doctrinal development', anon, *The Biblical Review and Congregational Magazine* i, 1846, p 188). 'It is never enough . . . to show that later doctrine is a development of earlier. Our search is for criteria which will enable us to say why one development is true and another false, or even why one development is in some respects truer than another' (Wiles [1967] p 168). In this chapter, therefore, we shall discuss some aspects of the problem of the normative or criteriological standpoint of the *Essay*. (Normative considerations were inevitably operative in early chapters. In particular, the themes discussed in *4* and *5* have normative significance in view of the fact that all the arguments in the *Essay* are subordinate to the over-riding claim that the Roman catholic church is, amongst existing christian denominations, that which is least dissimilar to the primitive church.) In the first place, we shall examine the meaning of 'true development' in the *Essay*, and the extent to which Newman succumbed to a form of the 'naturalistic fallacy' (*6.1*). By correlating Newman's use of 'development' with the notion of 'tradition' in contemporary theology, we shall be led to discuss his view of the role of ecclesiastical authority in authenticating 'developments' (*6.2*). Finally, we shall discuss the stance which Newman takes, in the *Essay*, on the problem of the 'essence' of christianity (*6.3*). By way of introduction, some further comments on the concept of a 'theory of development' may be useful (see *2.3, 4.11, 4.12*).

The function of the theoretical component in the *Essay* is justificatory. Newman is not primarily concerned to elaborate an argument that might count, in the abstract, as a 'theory of development', but rather to interpret the process of teaching, worship, and institutionalisation which has occurred between the initial preaching of the gospel and time of writing. The purpose of this interpretation is to render plausible the claim that such changes as have taken place do not constitute a 'corruption' of the gospel message.

But a justificatory theory or argument may take different forms. On the one hand, the elaboration of a theory may initially be the fruit of a search for intelligibility or coherence in the pattern of events under consideration (a). In order to be justificatory, such a theory will then have to embody the further claim : as coherent, these developments are faithful to, or true to, the origins or goals of the movement in question (A). (At this point I am, for the sake of simplicity, prescinding from those problems with which we shall be principally concerned in *6.1*).

On the other hand, the attempt could be made theoretically to justify the later developments without appeal being made to the intelligibility or coherence of the historical process which gave rise to them (B).

For example, those theories of doctrinal development which are usually referred to as 'logical' clearly belong to type (A). In contrast, those 'theological' theories in which, in practice, a 'true' development in doctrine is defined as one that has been adequately endorsed by ecclesiastical authority, belong to type (B). In the latter case, the function of theological or historical inquiry is derivatively justificatory in the sense that it seeks to provide some conceptual plausibility for developments that have already been accepted as 'true', have been held to be formally justified, through the application of theory (B). We may refer to these subordinate, or consequent, fruits of the search for intelligibility as (b).

Formally, arguments of types (a) and (b) will often be very similar. But their function, criteriologically, is significantly different. In the first case, (a) is a necessary condition without which the value-judgement embodied in (A) cannot be arrived at. In the second case, the value-judgement embodied in (B) is reached quite independently of, and logically prior to, the elaboration of (b).

In view of the apologetic purpose of the *Essay*, the emphasis placed on the authenticating role of acts of ecclesiastical authority is not surprising. As we shall see, the *Essay* has often been accused of undermining the possibility of any effective criteriological control being exercised by scripture or tradition. The crucial question, however, is not: does Newman place considerable emphasis on the authenticating function of ecclesiastical authority? but rather: what is the relation between this authenticating function and the intelligibility and coherence of those developments which are thus authenticated?

Although the distinction between (aA) and (Bb) has, for the sake of clarity, been presented here in a schematic manner which is alien to Newman's method of argument and analysis, it is of considerable importance.

Finally, it should be noticed that a good theory of type (a) may be expected to have some predictive power, on the basis of which decisions of ecclesiastical authority could be critically evaluated.[1] We shall see that the fact that the tentatively adumbrated theories of development in the *Essay* lack, for the most part, any such predictive power does not reduce them from type (a) to type (b), but is merely due to the fact that it was not Newman's aim, in *this* sense, to elaborate a 'theory of development' at all.[2]

6.1 The concept of 'true development'

According to Guitton, the term 'development' undergoes a change of meaning between the two parts of *1878*. In part ii 'Il ne s'agit plus maintenant d'une explication, mais d'une interprétation de l'histoire. Disons que la notion de développement est prise désormais au sens normatif' ([1933] p 89; cf Laframboise [1946] p 149* and for criticism, Walgrave [1957] p 52). Any interpretation of *1878* which thus ascribes to its two parts a fundamental difference of aim and method either rests on the unwarranted supposition that, in reordering the material in 1878, Newman intended to change the nature and scope of the constituent arguments, or else implies that the pattern of argument in *1845* is very confused.[3] There is no need for either hypothesis. We have sufficiently indicated, in earlier chapters, the apologetic (and thus justificatory, and not merely analytic) intention of the themes and arguments in the first part of the *Essay*.

The introductory articles to part ii (*Dev* 5.0.1–4) distinguish different senses in which a later 'religious system' may be said to be the 'successor, the representative, the heir', of an earlier one. As throughout the *Essay*, Newman takes it for granted that the contemporary catholic church is the '*historical* continuation of the religious system, which bore the name of Catholic . . . in every preceding century . . . The only question that can be raised is whether the said Catholic faith, as now held, is *logically*, as well as historically, the representative of the ancient faith'.[4] In the earlier chapters, Newman regarded the incontrovertible 'historical' or material continuity as grounding the antecedent probability that this continuity was also formal or 'logical' : that '*external* continuity . . . argues a real continuity of *doctrine*' (*Dev* Int 3, my stress).

Whereas a claim to 'historical' or 'external' continuity would be simply descriptive, the argument that the continuity is also 'logical' already implies the adoption of a normative standpoint : ie if a process of development can be shown to have been 'logical', it can therefore be claimed that the outcome of such a process is a 'legitimate . . . natural and necessary development' from its initial stages.[5] Thus, as summarised in *Dev* 5.0.1, the argument of part 1 is claimed to be of the general type (aA). The fact that, as in *Dev* 1, the argument in *Dev* 5.0.1–2 is presented as an analysis of any 'intellectual development' (*Dev* 5.0.2), and not merely of religious developments, also suggests that the perspective within which Newman presents his normative arguments is of type (aA) rather than type (Bb).

In *Dev* 5.0.2, Newman admits that the demonstration of 'logical' coherence, even if a necessary condition of 'true' development, is not a sufficient condition. A 'development may be in one sense natural, and yet untrue to its original' (*Dev* 5.0.2). The function of the 'tests' is to suggest criteria by which 'true' developments may be distinguished from developments which, although consistent and 'logical', are nevertheless 'corruptions' of the original.

In this section we shall first ask whether, in spite of the distinction made in *Dev* 5.0.2, Newman tended to succumb to a form of the 'naturalistic fallacy' by regarding such developments as have taken place to be 'necessary' and, because necessary, 'true'. Secondly, we shall look more closely at the concept, in the *Essay*, of a 'true' development. Before doing so, the respective roles which Newman ascribes to theological and historical inquiry, on the one hand, and to the decisions of ecclesiastical authority, on the other, may provisionally be indicated by a glance at the last paragraph of *Dev* 2.2.3.

In theories of doctrinal development of the type (Bb) the decisions of ecclesiastical authority are regarded, in principle, as a sufficient authenticating factor, independently of whatever historical or theological arguments may be produced to support them.[6] For Newman, however, such arguments have a positive role : 'they may aid our inquiries . . . and are instruments . . . of right decisions' (*Dev* 2.2.3). Nevertheless, in practice, 'they are insufficient for the guidance of individuals' (*ibid*, cf 2.2.1). The one sentence in which Newman apparently ascribes to his 'tests' a type (b) status ('they . . . serve as answers to objections brought against the actual decisions of authority'—*ibid*, added *1878*, cf *1845* p 117) is, in fact, a characteristic denial that the outcome of such 'tests' can be 'demonstration' or 'proof' (see *2.3*).

In the search for evolutionary 'laws' during the nineteenth century, many observers adopted a stance that was at once determinist (in assuming that what had happened must continue to happen) and optimistic (in assuming that such inevitable evolution as had occurred constituted, by the very fact of its inevitability, 'progress' or improvement). This stance, a characteristic expression of which was Spencer's claim that 'Progress is not an accident, not a thing within human control, but a beneficent necessity' (Spencer [1966] p 195), was strongly criticised by Huxley, of whose Romanes lecture Inge wrote : 'The alliance between determinism and optimism was thus dissolved' ([1922] p 167). We have seen that Newman was no optimist (*4.2*); nor, in view of his sensitivity to the complexity of history and the incomprehensibility of divine providence, was he likely to be a determinist. Nevertheless, there is a strand of argument in the *Essay* which laid him open to the charge of assuming that the 'mere historical eventuation of dogmas . . . is a sufficient evidence of dogmatic *truth*'.[7]

According to Guitton, for a protestant, 'il n'y a pourtant pas après Jésus dans la durée d'axe privilégié' ([1957] p 85). However exaggerated that observation, it does draw attention to the fact that, in principle, less criteriological significance is usually attributed, in protestant theology, to any such 'privileged axis', than has been the case in catholic theologies of tradition. From this point of view, the *Essay* undoubtedly embodies a characteristically 'catholic' perspective or tendency. The effect of this tendency, in an extreme form, would be to attribute exclusive normative significance, in practice, to the currently obtaining state of affairs.[8] Were this the case, then Newman could reasonably be accused of jettisoning tradition.[9]

Especially in chapter 2 of *1878*, Newman is at pains to persuade us that such developments as have, in fact, occurred, should be regarded as 'natural' (*Dev* 2.2.1, 2.2.5, 2.3.1, 5.0.1), 'legitimate' (*Dev* 2.1.17, 2.2.5, 2.3.2, 5.0.1), 'inevitable' (*Dev* 3.1.1), 'necessary' (*Dev* 2.3.1, 2.3.2, 5.0.1), and 'true (cf *Dev* 2.2.1, 2.2.5, 2.3.2), . . . that is . . . contemplated by [their] Divine Author' (*Dev* 2.1.17; cf 2.1.8, 2.2.1). It is of crucial importance, however, to notice that Newman is not, in these passages, establishing the principles of a systematic criteriology. As throughout the *Essay*, his aim is only to persuade the reader that there are good grounds for meeting the 'developments' in question 'not with suspicion and criticism, but with a frank confidence' (*Dev* 3.1.2; see *4.31* on his use of organic analogies). To derive, from Newman's arguments, inflexible criteriological principles, is to do violence to the form and method of the *Essay*.

For the most part, the critics of *1845* had little influence on Newman when he came to rewrite the *Essay*. The exception seems to be Mozley, by whose criticisms Newman had said that he 'felt . . . much aggrieved'.[10] Mozley pointed out that 'There is the corruption of exaggeration and excess, as well as that of decay' ([1847] p 121), and accused Newman of so defining 'corruption' that 'this definition simply omits the whole notion of corruption by excess . . . So long as an idea is simply pushed out, extended, added to . . . its career is *ipso* right' (p 139).

Newman added an article in response to this 'important objection',[11] but the point at which he inserted it suggests that he believed that his seven 'tests' did, in fact, sufficiently take into consideration both forms of corruption to which Mozley referred. As he wrote, in 1861, referring to the *Essay*: 'I lay down, that no one can religiously speak of development, without giving the *rules* which keep it from extravagating endlessly' (*L&D* xx p 54). Mozley's criticism was taken up by Gore ([1926b] p 835; cf Lash [1967] p 24), and Wiles claims that 'the real difference between the approach' to problems of doctrinal development 'called for today and that of men like Newman' is that we are unready 'to accept in advance that doctrinal development . . . can be assumed with confidence to have been wholly true in direction and in conclusion' ([1967] p 11). Is it the case that Newman's distinction between 'true' and 'false' developments amounts to an assertion that a development, if not a corruption, is 'wholly true in direction and in conclusion'? The best way to answer this question is to examine the concept, in the *Essay*, of 'true development'.

A development is said to be 'true or not true' in so far as it is 'faithful or unfaithful to the idea from which it started' (*Dev* 1.2.1). The complexity and comprehensiveness of Newman's concept of the 'idea' of christianity (see *4.1*) ensures that any system of doctrine and practice which represented a significant impoverishment of the original 'idea', or which had 'suppressed' significant 'tendencies or features' of it (Gore [1926b] p 835), would fail to satisfy this definition.[12] Moreover, Newman's evaluation of the 'faithfulness' of the Roman catholic church is comparative : that church is claimed to be the 'nearest approximation in fact to the Church of the Fathers, possible though some may think it, to be nearer still to that Church on paper' (*Dev* 2.3.5). There are, indeed, some minimum conditions to be fulfilled without which a development cannot be said to be 'faithful'. In particular, 'the changes which have taken place in Christianity' must not have been such as to 'destroy' the original 'type' (*Dev* 7.0.1; see *4.3*), or to have involved the substitution of 'another Gospel for the primitive Creed' (*Dev* 5.6.4; cf Int 3). Newman's assertion that the Roman catholic church is a 'true' development of the original christian 'idea', far from resting on the assumption that it is 'wholly true in direction and in conclusion' (Wiles [1967] p 11), amounts only to the claim that, on the one hand, it is not radically unfaithful and, on the other hand, that it is the least unfaithful of the existing varieties of christianity (see *2.3*, *3.23*).

In other words, criteriological questions are, as we should by now expect, subordinated throughout the *Essay* to apologetic considerations. As a result, the arguments which we discussed in *4* and *5* are dangerously inadequate and onesided if divorced from their original context and erected into a systematic criteriology. (In the former case, by tending towards the assumption that what has taken place is what ought to have taken place; in the latter, by giving later stages in the history of the process excessive normative significance).

Within the *Essay*'s framework of inquiry, to decide that any given system of church teaching and practice is not a 'true' development is to judge it a 'corruption'. But the shift from Newman's carefully qualified concept of 'faithfulness' to a more absolute and less critical evaluation of the adequacy of an existing church system is too easily made. In the concrete, the fear underlying the criticisms of Mozley and Gore has too often been amply justified. If, especially in the light of his experience of the Vatican Council, Newman had seen fit, when rewriting the *Essay*, to confront criteriological problems more directly, the history of subsequent 'theories of doctrinal development' might have been rather different. As we shall see in *6.21*, Newman's mature thought in this matter found expression, not in the *Essay*, but in other writings that were not destined to have a comparable influence.

6.2 Scripture, tradition and church authority

The fundamental issues at stake in debates on scripture and tradition have always been criteriological.[13] *Scriptura sola* affirms that christian life and teaching must be subject to critical evaluation by the biblical witness to the gospel. To affirm the principle of *scriptura sola* is not necessarily to deny the authoritative function of the believing community in determining the message of the scriptures. However, in the polemical climate in which the principle was generated, it was more or less inevitable that the question should unfortunately have been posed in terms of alternatives: either the authority of the church or the authority of scripture.

Similarly, to affirm that both scripture and tradition are to be received *pari pietatis affectu* (Trent IV Dz 783) is not necessarily to deny either the primacy of scripture, or that 'Holy Scripture containeth all things necessary to salvation' (*39 Articles*, 6), but to insist upon 'the relevance of history to the understanding of the Word of God' (Tavard [1959] p 109). However, inadequate theologies of revelation, the Spirit, and the church, and the degeneration of an already impoverished concept of tradition produced a situation, in post-tridentine Roman catholic theology, which 'can be characterised as a moving away from a conception of tradition as content and deposit received from the apostles, to one of tradition considered from the point of view of the transmitting organism, seen as residing above all in the magisterium of the Church' (Congar [1966] p 182).

One of the factors that has contributed most powerfully to the striking convergence, in recent years, of catholic and protestant positions on this problem, has been the recovery of a far richer, more flexible, and more traditional concept of tradition. In this recovery, the distinction between, on the one hand, tradition considered as the concrete history of the church, the entire process of christian life, teaching and worship and, on the other hand, 'traditions' considered as the precipitate of this process in 'the forms of expression that the transmission of the Gospel takes according to places, times, and cultures' (Schutz [1968] p 31), has been of considerable importance.

In order to appreciate the extent of Newman's achievement in the *Essay*, it is necessary to set it in this context of centuries of debate concerning the problem of revelation, scripture and tradition. Newman points out that he is using the term development 'on the one hand for the process of development, on the other for the result' (*Dev* 1.2.1). If we read the *Essay* with this in mind, then the distinction between 'development', in the sense of the historical process of the christian 'idea', and 'developments', the particular expressions of this process in the doctrine and life of the church, is seen to be strikingly similar to the now widely accepted distinction between 'tradition' and 'traditions'.[14]

Even if it is permissible to recognise, in the *Essay*, the elements of a theology of tradition which has today proved acceptable, in broad outline, to most major christian denominations, it does not follow that there are not outstanding problems of considerable importance. In particular, the question of the normative status to be attributed to official church teaching (or 'magisterium') in the 'hearing' of that word to which the scriptures bear uniquely privileged witness, is one area which still bristles with unresolved difficulties.[15] In the following two sections, therefore, we shall examine, first, the notion of an 'external developing authority' in the *Essay* (*6.21*) and then, secondly, the role occupied in Newman's thinking by the idea of the 'reception' of official teaching on the part of the believing community as a whole (*6.22*).

6.21 An 'external developing authority'

According to Congar, 'Newman . . . made a decisive contribution to the problem of the relationship between magisterium and history in tradition' ([1966] p 211). The context of that remark is the observation that, with Newman's *Essay*, 'the idea of development becomes an inner dimension of that of tradition'. And yet, at first sight, the relationship between the process of development, and the authenticating function of church authority, constitutes one of the most puzzling features of the *Essay*. Thus in admitting the inadequacy of the 'tests' for the 'guidance of individuals' in 'ascertaining the correctness of developments', Newman claims that, while 'it is probable that some means will be granted for ascertaining the legitimate and true developments of Revelation, it appears . . . that these means must of necessity be external to the developments themselves' (*Dev* 2.2.3). It would certainly be intolerable if every individual christian had personally to undertake massive exegetical and historical research before he could, with integrity, trust that the existing church system was, on the whole, a faithful 'development'. But to point to the practical necessity of an authenticating function (or 'magisterium') in the church, is one thing;[16] to claim that such an authenticating office must be 'external to the developments themselves', is quite another. How can such office be immune from that historical process of development to which all 'aspects' of the 'idea' are necessarily subject? After all, many passages in the *Essay* are devoted to arguing that the historical development of forms of authority in the church, and of the papacy in particular, have been 'true' developments.

In order to deal with this problem, it is necessary first to examine, at some length, the history of Newman's thought on the problem of tradition from the publication of *Arians*, in 1833, to 1845 and, second, briefly to notice such further developments as took place between 1845 and 1878.[17]

In *Arians*, 'Apostolical Tradition' is that summary of the essentian christian message which 'granting that the Apostles conversed, and their friends had memories' (*Ari* p 54), must have existed from the first. Newman is in no doubt but that 'creeds and teachers have ever been divinely provided' (p 51). This 'Apostolical Tradition', which was corroborative, illustrative, and subordinate to 'the inspired records' (p 55), he also describes as a 'traditional system of theology, consistent with, but independent of, Scripture' (p 220). He gives three reasons why considerable time elapsed before this tradition crystallised into 'authoritative forms' (p 35). In the first place, the catechetical emphasis, especially in

Alexandria, was on moral education, rather than on satisfying intellectual curiosity; hence the creed and the eucharist were only made available to those who had been 'distinguished . . . by a strictly conscientious deportment'[18] In the second place, the 'imposition' of a fixed form of words for the creed only became necessary as questions were raised which demanded an answer, and to protect the church from heresy. In the third place, the more 'the cogency of Apostolic Tradition was weakened by lapse of time' (p 133), the more fragile became the link of 'Apostolical Tradition'; hence the necessity of having 'recourse to the novel, though necessary measure, of imposing an authoritative creed' (p 36).

The life of the church in general was fed by the scriptures, which were 'addressed principally to the affections' (p 146), rather than to the intellect. It is in this sense that 'the Sacred Volume was never intended . . . to teach us our creed' (p 50). The function of the latter is to concentrate the 'general spirit' of the message of the scriptures, 'so as to give security to the Church, as far as may be' (p 147. A 'symbol' acts as a 'guide to the memory and judgement of the eager disputant,' p 32, 'fixing and stimulating the Christian spirit', p 146).

By 'the time of the Nicene Council, the voices of the Apostles were but faintly heard throughout Christendom' (p 35) and 'In the creeds of the early Councils', the message, hitherto orally transmitted, 'may be considered as having come to light' (p 55).

While Stern is correct in observing that 'Newman éprouve de la nostalgie pour l'âge qui précéda la systématisation' ([1967] p 91, cf pp 77–96), Biemer goes rather beyond the argument of *Arians* in saying that 'tradition was given a fixed and *unaltered* expression in the Creeds of the Church' ([1967] p 38, my stress).

It is important to notice that, as well as the frequent references to 'Apostolical Tradition', Newman already recognises, in 1833, that factor in the process of development to which he will later refer as 'Prophetical Tradition'. Two streams contribute to the elaboration of the 'ecclesiastical' (as distinct from the 'Scripture') doctrine of the Trinity : 'There will . . . be difference of opinion, in deciding how much the ecclesiastical doctrine . . . was derived from direct Apostolical Tradition, and how much was the result of intuitive spiritual perception in scripturally informed and

deeply religious minds' (*Ari* p 179, cf p 149). The 'minds' in
question are principally those of the early Fathers.

Thus, in *Arians*, 'Apostolical Tradition' is both the process of
oral transmission, and the content of that process, the creed (p
135), in so far as the latter term is understood to refer, formally,
to 'the great doctrines of the faith' (p 134). 'Apostolical Tradition',
however, is distinguished from the creed in so far as this term is
taken to refer to that explicit crystallisation in authoritative conciliar formulae of the message previously transmitted by word of
mouth.

In the same year Newman wrote the paper which was eventually entitled 'How to accomplish it'.[19] Here he admits, as he had
in *Arians*, that, considered as 'historical . . . testimony', the authority of apostolic tradition 'has long ceased, or, at least, is indefinitely weakened' (*DA* p 11). He recognised that this admission, if
handled 'without care . . . would practically tend to the discarding
the precedent of Antiquity altogether' (*DA* p 12).

During 1834 and 1835, the debate with Jager gave Newman
the opportunity significantly to develop his position (cf Stern
[1967] pp 111–36; [1964]; Tristram [1945c]). In the first letter
to Jager he invoked the doctrine of 'fundamentals', inherited
from the Caroline divines (Stern [1967] pp 114–15): 'Newman
admet comme fondamentales uniquement les doctrines contenues
dans le Symbole des Apôtres et celui de Nicée' (p 125). He also
distinguished between a tradition which interprets scripture, a
tradition independent of scripture (but which can be justified by
it, such as infant baptism), and a tradition concerned with
customs and discipline.[20] There is a fourth category, which Newman believes is admitted in Roman catholic doctrine and which
he rejects: 'You consider Tradition *per se* the sufficient authority for the Church's considering a doctrine fundamental' (*BOA*
D.6.1, quoted Biemer [1967] pp 43–4).

In a letter to Froude of 20 July 1835 (and in the second letter
to Jager) Newman explicitly formulates, for the first time, the
distinction which will be fundamental to the *Lectures on the
Prophetical Office*, between 'The popular sense of Tradition . . .
the voice of the body of the Church . . . which I may call *prophetical Tradition*', and 'that strict Tradition from one hand to
another . . . which I may call *Apostolical* or *Episcopal*' (quoted
Stern [1967] p 133; cf Biemer [1967] pp 46–7; Stern [1967]

pp 128–36; Tristram [1945c] p 215). He still insisted that tradition was, in matters of faith, only interpretative of scripture (letter
to Froude, 23 Aug 1835, Moz II p 126). He also recognised that
'prophetical Tradition' had no independent normative value.[21]
Froude disliked the concept of 'fundamentals', and objected to
Newman's rather vague references, in his letters to Jager, to 'development' and 'expansions'. He recognised, perhaps more clearly
than Newman did at this period, that the independent normative
value of 'Apostolical' or 'Episcopal' tradition would seem to rest
upon the immutability of the creed : 'Will not the Romanists say
that their whole system is an expansion of the Holy Catholic
Church and the Communion of Saints?' (Moz II p 127; cf Stern
[1964] p 140).

In 1836, in the article usually known as 'The Brothers' Controversy',[22] Newman's principal concern is to refute Hampden's
claim that 'tradition is nothing more than expositions of the text
of Scripture, reasoned out by the Church and embodied in a code
of doctrine'.[23] Concentrating on the ante-nicene period, he argues
that 'The doctrinal statements of the creeds are not to be viewed
as mere deductions from Scripture . . . but as the appropriate expressions and embodying of apostolical teaching . . . handed down
in the Church as such from age to age'.[24] This, as we have seen,
was his position in 1833. The relationship between scripture and
'Apostolical Tradition', however, now finds more systematic expression : 'Scripture is the sole verification of the creeds, as of all
professed Apostolical traditions . . . creeds are the legitimate expositions of Scripture doctrine' (Newman [1836b] p 170; cf
p 190). Therefore, as in the debate with Jager, he continues to
deny 'the independent and substantive power of Tradition in
matters of faith, where Scripture is silent' (p 184).

The distinction between 'Prophetical' and 'Apostolical' or 'Episcopal Tradition' is not explicitly mentioned, and barely hinted at
in passing.[25]

In Newman's attempt to justify an affirmative answer to the
question 'are the dogmatic statements of the Creeds . . . of Apostolic origin?' ([1836b] p 187), one can detect the recognition of the
problem with which this section is principally concerned. He is
aware, not only that the 'articles varied somewhat in the different
branches of the Church', but also that 'the very articles of the
Creed are not Apostolic', that is, 'literally spoken by the Apostles'.

Nevertheless, he claims that, taken together, they 'go to convey that view which is Apostolic', and that verbal differences 'argued no difference in the Tradition of which they were the formal record', since they were but 'heads and memoranda of the Church's teaching' (*ibid* pp 187–8; cf *Ath* II, p 65).

Finally, it is important to notice that the process by which 'Bishop compares notes with bishop', enabling them to recognise in each other's local credal formulae the profession of a common faith, 'implied time and accurate thought, freedom of discussion, questioning, reviewing' (*ibid* p 189. We shall see that a similar concern is central to his disquiet at the conduct of affairs in 1870).

In the *Lectures on the Prophetical Office*, Newman's basic view of the relationship between scripture and tradition is unchanged: 'Scripture is interpreted by Tradition, Tradition is verified by Scripture . . . Tradition teaches, Scripture proves'. (*VM* I p 274). Scripture is 'the document of ultimate appeal in controversy, and the touchstone of all doctrine' (*VM* I p 309; cf pp 28, 244; *Ath* II p 51). He continues to reject what he believes to be the Roman claim that 'points of faith may rest on Tradition without Scripture' (*VM* I p 273). In pushing this criticism a stage further, and accusing the Roman catholic church of claiming the power of 'discerning the Scripture sense without perceptible human *Media*' (p 268), he is, in effect, ascribing to Roman catholics a criteriological perspective of the type (Bb) (cf *VM* I pp 48–9, 214–38, 282–3).

He argues for the indefectibility of the church in retaining 'what is called in Scripture "the Faith", the substance or great outlines of the Gospel' (p 196; cf p 214). It is this 'substance' which is enshrined in the creed. The creed derives its authority both from the fact that the evidence for its apostolicity is 'of a plain and public nature' (p 269; cf pp 51, 190), and from the fact that the church 'teaches it' (p 190). The former claim, which is given far more emphasis than the latter, rests on the historically perceptible immutability of the creed: 'The creed of Rome is ever subject to increase; ours is fixed once for all' (p 212). The problems that arise here are not treated as seriously as they were in *Arians* or 'The Brothers' Controversy': Newman unconvincingly distinguishes between 'adding a word and adding a doctrine' (p 225), and is content to affirm that 'we must consider the Nicene and the Apostles' Creed as identical' (p 227).

K

Episcopal tradition is distinguished from prophetical both from the point of view of the *mode* of transmission and of the content transmitted : the former is 'received from Bishop to Bishop' (p 249), and consists of the 'essentials' (p 258), of doctrine 'necessary for salvation', of 'certain definite subjects' (p 128) delineated in the creed (p 254). The latter, the scope of which is the whole rich complexity of the life, teaching and worship of the church, is seen as *'existing* primarily in the bosom of the Church itself, and *recorded* in such measure as Providence has determined in the writings of eminent men' (p 250, my stress), and in the 'Decrees of Councils' (p 254).

The fact that the line of demarcation between the 'Fundamentals', transmitted by 'Episcopal Tradition', and the 'non-essentials' (p 258), transmitted by 'Prophetical Tradition', is impossible to draw precisely, does not disturb him (p 254). Indeed the recognition of this fact is described by Stern as 'Le fruit le plus précieux de la controverse avec Jager' ([1967] p 126). Similarly, because the content of prophetical tradition consists of non-essentials, it does not worry him that 'no such especial means were taken for its preservation as those which have secured to us the Creed' (*VM* I p 251). As we would expect, his main concern, throughout the *Lectures*, is pastoral rather than theoretical : hence the formulation of the prudential principle 'That when Antiquity runs counter to the present Church in important matters, we must follow Antiquity; when in unimportant matters, we must follow the present Church' (p 135).

When Newman describes the Roman catholic 'doctrine of the Church's infallibility'[26] as resting upon 'the notion, that any degree of doubt about religious truth is incompatible with faith, and that an external infallible assurance is necessary to exclude doubt' (pp 85–6), he clearly means 'external' to the mind of the individual believer.[27] The same is true of a passage in which 'The means which are given to us to form our judgement' are classified as 'partly internal, partly external' (p 131; cf *HS* III p 79). When, however, he says that 'we do not profess to judge of Scripture in greater matters by itself, but by means of an external guide' (p 153), he has in mind the episcopal tradition, guardian (p 224) of the creed, which is 'external' to the text of scripture.

With the publication of the *Lectures on the Prophetical Office*, Newman's anglican theology of tradition achieved its mature expression. Before turning to the *Essay*, however, it is necessary briefly to comment on *Tract 85* (*DA* pp 109–253) and the fifteenth *University Sermon*. In the former, published in 1838, Newman returns to the problem, which he had discussed in 'The Brothers' Controversy', of the state of the evidence for the creed before the fourth or fifth century. He claims that 'the abundance of the fourth [century] as to the Creed interprets, develops and combines all that is recondite or partial, in previous centuries, as to doctrine' (*DA* p 238; cf p 237, quoted *Dev* 4.1.3), but the drift of the argument seems to be that the doctrine of which the creed is a summary existed in the ante-nicene church, the incompleteness and ambiguity of the evidence being partly due to 'loss of documents once extant' and partly to 'misconceptions, which want of intercourse between the Churches occasioned' (p 237). The shift in position from that sustained five years earlier in *Arians* hardly amounts to more than a slightly greater attention to problems of historical evidence.

So far as the 'Fundamentals' are concerned, if protestants claim that what 'they sometimes call the essentials . . . the leading idea, the great truths of the Gospel . . . *are* plainly in Scripture' (p 128; see *6.3*), it follows that the doctrine of the Trinity, which is not 'brought out in form upon the surface of Scripture . . . either . . . is not included in the leading idea, or . . . the leading idea is not on the surface' (p 128; see *5.2, 5.21*). Finally, it should be noticed that 'the doctrines of the Church . . . were not in early times mere ideas in the mind . . . they were external facts, quite as much as the books of Scripture . . . Because they were embodied in rites and ceremonies' (p 241). Here 'external' is being used in the sense in which Newman habitually uses the term 'objective'.

Both Biemer and Stern lay considerable emphasis on the significance, for understanding the history of Newman's views on tradition, of the fifteenth *University Sermon*. It is true that this sermon marks a breakthrough in Newman's understanding of the *process* of tradition, or development. Nevertheless, the texts to which I have already appealed suggest that it simply is not true to say that 'Up to this time, Newman had really envisaged only the mechanical concept of tradition which was generally in vogue. He had cherished the idea that formulas verbally identical had been handed on, and that this repetition had assured the essential identity of the doctrine' (Biemer [1967] pp 51–2). Moreover, I propose to argue that the distinction between 'Episcopal' and 'Prophetical Tradition' and, with it, the doctrine of 'Fundamentals', are still substantially present in the *Essay* (and beyond, in Newman's catholic writings). If this is correct, then the doctrine of fundamentals is not 'overthrown' by the argument of this sermon.[28]

In the studies that we have so far considered, the existence of an 'Episcopal Tradition' is held to have become necessary as the distance in time from the originating 'Apostolical Tradition' increased, and as a result of the loss of that vitality and spontaneity attributed to the primitive church. The same perspective is adopted in the account, in the *Essay*, of the emerging authority of the papacy.[29] In the anglican writings, the content of this 'Episcopal Tradition' was held to be the creed and the liturgy. From one point of view, the creed only contains the 'fundamentals'; from another point of view, however, it contains, embodies, and safeguards the entire revealed 'deposit', since its articles are 'heads and memoranda of the Church's teaching' (Newman [1836b] p 187). The creed is authoritative both because it is 'of a plain and public nature' (*VM* i p 269), and because the church 'teaches it' (*VM* i p 190). In the *Essay*, there is a significant shift of emphasis from the former to the latter ground of doctrinal authority. But, as we shall see, it is only a shift of emphasis; the argument from public availability is not abandoned.

This shift is most clearly discernible in *Dev* 2.2. It is still 'assumed' that christianity is 'based on . . . a creed' (*Dev* 2.2.13) but, as a result of the apologetic purpose of the *Essay*, far greater stress is laid on the presence in the church of a 'power of deciding whether this, that, and a third, and any number of theological or ethical statements are true', than was previously the case. (*Dev* 2.2.4). By thus describing the meaning of 'infallibility', Newman correctly locates it in the area of decision, of judgement rather than, for instance, of 'revelation', 'inspiration' or 'new information' but, from the standpoint of the subsequent teaching of Vatican i, it must be said that he, in common with most writers, catholic and anglican, of the period, tends to use the term too widely and indiscriminately.

As a result of the perspective within which this claim is elaborated, attention is not focused on the distinction between 'essentials' and 'non-essentials', although it is taken for granted that 'No

one will maintain that all points of belief are of equal importance'.[30] Particular attention is paid to the ability of church authority to reach definitive judgements concerning those traditions
which are independent of scripture, but can be justified by it
(such as infant baptism), and those which embody the church's
historical response to questions 'so real, so practical, that they
must be answered' (such as the forgiveness of post-baptismal sin—
Dev 2.1.5). In effect, using the terminology of the *Via Media*,
the claim is that certain 'aspects' of the christian 'idea', which
have long been held in the 'Prophetical Tradition' alone, can, by
a definitive judgement of ecclesiastical authority, become also explicitly part of the 'Episcopal Tradition'.

We have seen that, in the anglican writings, the content of the
'Episcopal Tradition' is sometimes said to be 'external' to the text
of scripture (which does not mean, of course, that the content of
the tradition is not also in scripture) but more usually, it is described as 'external' to individual believers in the sense that, being
expressed and embodied in creed and rite, it is 'objective', publicly
available. When, in the *Essay*, reference is made to the 'external'
nature of ecclesiastical authority, it is the latter concept of ex-
ternality which is being employed.[31]

In other words, the key to the puzzling claim that the 'means
. . . for ascertaining the legitimate and true developments of
Revelation . . . must of necessity be external to the developments
themselves' (*Dev* 2.2.3) lies in the fact that, in such passages, the
process of 'development' is presumed to take place in the 'Prophetical Tradition',[32] while the outcome of the process ('development' as *term*) consists in its incorporation, by solemn ecclesiastical decision, into the 'Episcopal' (see *4.32*).

I should wish to argue, therefore, that the appeal to an authority
'external' to the process of development is not a massive incon-
sistency in Newman's argument, but rather bears witness to the
survival, in the *Essay*, of the broad outlines of that distinction
between 'Prophetical' and 'Episcopal Tradition' which characterised his earlier analysis of the problem. Nevertheless, even if the
structure of argument in the *Essay* shows far greater continuity
with his anglican thinking on the problem of tradition than has
usually been supposed, it is undoubtedly true that Newman fails
to confront the problem of the grounds on the basis of which the
content of the 'Episcopal Tradition' itself may be critically eva-

luated. He remained overconfident that 'The Creed . . . remains now what it was in the beginning, a popular form of faith, suited to every age, class, and condition' (*GA* p 144). Criteriologically, there is indeed a shift in emphasis from the normative function of antiquity to that of the 'living voice', today. Yet, in spite of the stress on the power of ecclesiastical authority 'infallibly' to adjudicate in 'theological and ethical' matters, the argument of the *Essay* still moves within the broad perspective represented by the claim that 'we must consider the Nicene and the Apostles' Creed as identical' (*VM* I p 227).

The claims made in the previous paragraph are borne out by the distinction, drawn by Newman in 1847, between the *Verbum Dei objectivum* and the *Verbum Dei subjectivum*, which broadly corresponds to that previously made between 'Episcopal' and 'Prophetical Tradition'.[33] The 'Verbum Dei objectivum' is said to be 'Simplex . . . et absolutum et immutabile' (*Perrone* p 405), and the process of catechesis, or personal appropriation of the word received in accepting the creed, is said to take place 'remoto non magisterio sed perpetuo ductu *auctoritatis externae*' (p 409, my stress). The third chapter of the *Perrone Paper*, 'De Verbo Dei in Ecclesia Catholica subjectivo' (pp 413–17), is principally concerned with the process whereby an aspect of revealed truth, which has hitherto existed only 'subjectively' in the church, now also acquires 'objective' status. From another point of view, this is regarded as the process whereby an aspect of the 'verbum objectivum' which was held in the deposit 'implicitly', acquires 'explicit' status.

The most significant advance in respect of the analysis in the *Via Media* consists in the fact that, whereas previously the distinction between 'Episcopal' and 'Prophetical Tradition' was material as well as formal (the 'essential' doctrines being ascribed to the former, and the 'non-essential' to the latter), now the distinction is simply formal, and the whole of revealed truth is presumed to be held in each form of the tradition (*Perrone* p 406). This development casts some light on the analysis, in the opening chapters of the *Essay*, of the *whole* process of christian tradition in terms of the history of a 'living' and 'real idea'.

Neither the *Apologia* nor the letter to Flanagan cast significant new light on the problem of the relationship between the process of tradition, or development, and the authenticating office of the

'magisterium'.[34] 'Great acts take time' (*Apo* p 169); the importance which Newman attached to the function of theological reflection, inquiry and debate in the church's appropriation of some
aspect of revealed truth is quite incompatible with a criteriological
viewpoint which would see, in an eventual judgement of ecclesiastical authority, the sole sufficient guarantee for the 'truth' of
a development: '. . . authority is called upon to pronounce a
decision, which has already been arrived at by reason' (*Apo*
p 267; cf pp 252–69). The chief ground of his opposition to the
conduct of the Vatican Council was that '. . . you are going too
fast at Rome . . . We need to try the doctrine by facts, to see
what it may mean, what it cannot mean, what it must mean'
(*L&D* xxv pp 93–4; cf pp 99, 101, Holmes [1969a]).

In the *Lectures on the Prophetical Office*, he had brought 'Two
broad charges . . . against the Catholic Religion' (*VM* ɪ p xxxvii).
The first of these, 'the contrast which modern Catholicism is said
to present with the religion of the Primitive Church', he had
dealt with in the *Essay*. The second, 'the difference . . . between
[the Roman Catholic Church's] formal teaching and its popular
and political manifestations', he replied to in the Preface to the
1877 edition of the *Via Media*. (On the importance of this Preface
see Bergeron [1971] and Coulson [1967] pp 123–4, 135–41; Coulson [1970] pp 165–83). It is this which must surely be regarded as
his 'final view on tradition' and, although it had little influence on
the revised text of the *Essay* published in the following year, an
answer to the questions with which this chapter is concerned needs
to take both texts equally into consideration. We shall return to
the Preface in the following section (*6.22*). For the present, it
suffices to stress, once again, that the ecclesiology of Newman's
mature years excludes, by its complexity and dialectical structure,
the possibility of ascribing exclusive normative significance to the
decisions of ecclesiastical authority.[35]

If this historical sketch of Newman's views on the problem of
tradition has shown that his references, in the *Essay*, to an 'external
authority' are not as inconsistent or incoherent as might at first
sight appear, it must still be admitted that he never sufficiently
confronted the problem posed by the fact that the content of the
'Episcopal Tradition' is itself subject to considerable historical
change. Newman would have agreed that the 'gulf between the
intellectual milieu of the New Testament texts and that of our own

present age' is so deep that 'no theology can understand itself any longer as "biblical" in the naive sense' (Pannenberg [1970a] pp 8–9). One alternative, from the normative viewpoint, to a crude *scriptura sola*, is an equally crude *traditio sola* or *auctoritas sola*. In the *Via Media*, it was with this latter error that Newman had charged Roman catholicism. In this section I have tried to show that the transition from the theology of the *Via Media* to that of the *Essay* did not entail a collapse into this alternative escape from the problems of faith and history. In the last resort, Newman's wisdom is shown by the fact that he understood, more deeply than many theologians have done, that man cannot stand outside his own history : 'it can hardly be maintained that in matter of fact a true development carries with it always its own certainty even to the learned, or that history, past or present, is secure from the possibility of a variety of interpretations' (*Dev* 2.2.1; cf *VM* I p xciv). Certainly Newman believed in the necessity of a 'living voice', whose definitive judgements could be trusted to be so guided by the Spirit of truth as not to betray the gospel. So far as the practical scope and implications of such an affirmation of trust are concerned, he admitted in 1868 : 'I wished to be vague' (*Flanagan* p 592, commenting on the discussion of infallibility in the *Apologia*). 'No one can see the form of a building but those who are external to it. We are within the Divine Dispensation; we cannot . . . pursue its lines, foretell their directions and coincidences, or ascertain their limits. We see enough for practice.'[36]

6.22 'Reception' by the community as a criterion of true development

'The maxim that the voice of the people is the voice of God is as old as Alcuin; it was . . . employed in our day by Newman to prop his theory of development' (Acton [1932] p 17). However great the stress which Newman lays in the *Essay*, for apologetic purposes, on the necessity of a 'peremptory', living authority in the church, it is fundamental to his argument that the gospel is communicated to, and lives in, the church as a *whole*. His ideas on the role of the laity in the process of doctrinal tradition clarified under pressure, and found controversial expression in the *Rambler* article of 1859 (Coulson [1961]). In this section, however, my concern is not specifically with the role of the laity in the preparation of doctrinal decisions, but rather with the wider question of the 'reception' of doctrine, by the community as a whole, as a factor in the evaluation of tradition or development as 'true'.[37] In order to connect this discussion with that of the previous section, some brief remarks will also be necessary on Newman's mature views on the 'regulating principle' in the life of the church.

In general, the description of the history of any 'real' and 'living idea' in *Dev* 1.1.4–7 is an account of the 'reception' of that 'idea' in the mind of that community which is its 'recipient' (*Dev* 1.1.4). The resolution of unsolved problems is the fruit of a 'slow process of thought . . . the influence of mind upon mind, the issues of controversy, and the growth of opinion' (*Dev* 2.1.5; cf 1.2.5). More particularly, Newman denies that the mere *text* of scripture can comprise 'a delineation of all possible forms which a divine message will assume when submitted to a multitude of minds' (*Dev* 2.1.2).

But does not the definitive explicit appropriation of some 'aspect' of revealed truth, in dogmatic or credal definition, bring this process to an end? Were this the case, then the only function of the christian community after this stage had been reached, would be passively to accept it. And yet, it is the active 'reception' of credal and dogmatic statements that generates and makes possible further stages in the process of development : only after 'the truths of the Creed had sunk into the Christian mind' (*Dev* 4.1.7, added *1878*), for example, did the adoption of a definitive stance on the question of infant baptism become possible (cf *Dev* 9.4.3, where he refers to its growth 'into general reception').

Criteriologically, the important question is whether the 'reception' of credal and dogmatic statements can be held to modify their meaning. In the section on 'Theology', added in *1878*, he speaks of the 'duty' of 'that loving inquisitiveness which is the life of the *Schola*'.[38] Even more important is the claim that 'the peculiarities of the recipient are the *regulating power*, the law, the organisation, or, as it may be called, the *form* of the development' (*Dev* 5.2.1, my stress).

In Newman's anglican writings, the distinction between the 'Prophetical' and 'Episcopal' traditions may be regarded as a distinction between the 'life' and 'form' of the church. Commenting on the Preface to the 1877 edition of the *Via Media*, Coulson argues that 'it is the prophetical office, not the unaided power of conscience, which has to be opposed to the institutional excesses of the Church' ([1967] p 135). In this Preface, 'By the introduction of theology as the regulating principle, Newman abandons his former distinction between life and form, returning to Scripture for a three-fold description of the Church as a community for teaching, worship and ministry'(Coulson [1967] p 136; cf [1970] pp 172–3). While it is true that, in his later years, Newman more than once refers to theology as 'the regulating principle' (*VM* I p xlvii; Ward, W. [1912] II, p 374), the tripolar dialectic which structures the ecclesiology of this Preface implies that the life and worship of the local community also plays a regulative, corrective, or interpretative function (*VM* I pp xl–xli). In other words, it seems to me that Newman was being quite consistent in leaving unaltered, in *1878*, the ascription of regulative power to 'the peculiarities of the recipient', that is, of the christian community, in general. This observation does not significantly qualify Coulson's argument, which is of considerable importance for an understanding of Newman's mature ecclesiology.

In the months leading up to the Vatican Council Newman insisted that he 'put the validity of the Council upon its reception by the orbis terrarum' (*L&D* XXIV p 355; cf *L&D* XXIII p 254). This emphasis on the normative function to be attributed to the reception of authoritatively proposed teaching by the community as a whole accounts for his hesitancy, after the Council, in accepting the definition of papal infallibility as a dogmatic statement. In 1871 'he startled Loyson by saying : Crescit in dogma. The old idea had revived. He was waiting for the echo' (Acton *CUL Add* MSS 4989.3. The reference is to a letter of 6 Jan 1871 from Loyson to Acton; cf CUL *Add* MSS 4989.2 and *L&D* XXV p 235, letter to Loyson of 24 Nov 1870). While he excluded the possibility of the Vatican definition being reversed, he was confident that it would be '*explained* and *completed* . . . Future Popes will explain and in one sense limit their own power'.[39]

If these words seem excessively cautious, we must remember that they were written in 1871. The principle to which they appeal is that 'Some power then is needed to determine the general sense of authoritative words . . . This power is virtually the *passive infallibility* of the whole body of the Catholic people' (cited Ward, W. [1912] II, p 564, Newman's stress). As Newman recognised, the use which—in these years—he made of the doctrine of 'reception' was simply the application of principles which structured the *Essay*; in particular, of the 'Securus judicat orbis terrarum'.[40]

Newman's ascription of a degree of normative significance to the manner in which the community 'receives', adapts and interprets the judgements of the 'Episcopal Tradition' thus constitutes an important modification of the sense in which, according to the *Essay*, the development of any particular aspect of christian doctrine may be said to reach a term in the course of that doctrine's history.[41]

6.3 *The Essay and the 'essence of christianity'*

A frequent complaint made by the early critics of the *Essay* was that 'Newman, having said that Christianity came into the world as an idea, does not offer any concrete suggestion as to what this idea is' (Brown, C. G. [1971] p 16). In the attempt to find a standpoint from which the life and teaching of the church may be critically assessed and evaluated, few programmes have proved more seductive during the last century and a half than the search for the 'essence' or 'leading idea' of christianity. When such a programme is announced in terms of organic analogies, the search is on for christianity's originating 'seed' or 'germ'. Thus, Fairbairn announced that 'we must do two things, a) find the germ . . . in its primitive or least developed state, and b) study the successive conditions under which it lived, their action on it, its action on them' ([1899] p 163). Fairbairn's confidence that his programme could be successfully executed accounts in large measure for the irritation with which he regarded the *Essay*.[42] Similarly, Mozley took Newman to task for not providing a detailed description of the original 'idea' : 'it is a theory of growth without a seed; development without an exordium'. ([1847], p 263). Milman's complaint was similar : 'From first to last there is no definition of the *Idea* of Christianity' ([1846] p 419).

Much of the argument of the *Essay*, however, is directed against the view that the 'idea' of christianity (or, indeed, any 'living' or 'real idea') can be reduced to any one of its constitutive features or 'aspects' : 'The idea which represents an object or supposed object is commensurate with the sum total of its possible aspects' (*Dev* 1.1.2); 'There is no one aspect deep enough to exhaust the contents of a real idea, no one term or proposition which will serve to define it' (*Dev* 1.1.3; see *4.1*). In the rare passages in which Newman speaks of the 'essence' or 'essential idea' of christianity, therefore, it is not some 'germ' or 'kernel' that he has in mind (in relation to which subsequent developments are merely the 'husk'—cf Abbot [1886]), but the whole mystery of God's activity in respect of and revelation to man in Christ which, while it may be embodied in the life of a community and symbolically expressed in creed and liturgy, can never be exhaustively or adequately expressed by any human institution or set of propositions. Among the early critics, the anonymous 'English Churchman' was almost alone in appreciating the significance of Newman's 'sacramental' epistemology for the problem of the 'leading idea' ([1846] pp 7–10).

In both editions of the *Essay*, Newman explicitly denied that it is possible 'to determine the "leading idea", as it has been called, of Christianity' (*Dev* 1.1.3). Nevertheless, especially in *1845*, his language is not completely free from ambiguity. A critic could hardly be blamed, for example, for detecting the presence of the model of 'germ' and 'husk' in a statement such as : 'Its vital element needs disengaging from what is foreign and temporary' (*1845* p 38; *Dev* 1.1.7).

The principal source of confusion has been the first 'note', the summary of which, in *1845*, ended : 'The first test, then, of a faithful or legitimate development is its *preservation of the essential idea* of the doctrine or polity which it represents' (*1845*, p 66, Newman's stress; omitted, with previous two paragraphs, *1878*). Yet, in the previous paragraph, Newman had admitted that this test 'is too obvious and too close upon demonstration to be of easy application in particular cases. It implies an insight into the essential idea in which a system of thought is set up, which often cannot be possessed, and, if attempted, will lead to mere theorising' (*1845*, pp 65–6). Maurice was surely justified in complaining that 'Mr Newman confesses that the knowledge of the essential idea, the type of Christianity, is necessary, or at all events would be most convenient, for the purpose of studying the actual history of Christianity. He confesses also that he cannot arrive at this type or leading idea, except by looking at those very developments, the soundness and faithfulness of which are to be ascertained by the help of it' ([*1846*] p xxi; cf pp xlix–lxxiv).

In *1878*, the argument is clearer. In emphasising, in *Dev*

5.1.1–9, the amount of 'external' change that is compatible with 'faithfulness' to the 'original type' (*Dev* 6.0.1, added *1878*), the appeal is, in one sense, to the 'essence' of christianity, but only in so far as that 'essence' is understood as comprising all the myriad ingredients that went to make up its 'original type' or 'ethos'. Nevertheless, it is still the case that Newman's account of the first 'note' does not provide a basis from which critical evaluation of the contemporary life and teaching of the church would be possible. Questions such as, how would we know if a society was changing its type, or whether it was doing so sufficiently to be regarded as corrupt, cannot, in practice, be answered by the 'application' of Newman's 'notes'. This is not surprising because, as we have already seen (*6.1*), Newman is more concerned cumulatively to elaborate a viewpoint from which it can be seen that Roman catholicism is 'not unlike' (*Dev* 6.1.30; 6.2.17; 6.3.3.23) the primitive church, than to provide us with a set of criteriological principles.

According to Alfred Fawkes, 'it is possible to detach the kernel from the husk, the idea from its setting, the unchanging substance of religion from its necessarily changing forms. This is the real issue between Professor Harnack and M. Loisy; and Harnack is right and Loisy wrong'.[43] On this analysis, Newman is clearly not on the side of Harnack. But, although 'He does not view the essence of Christanity as consisting of one or two simple principles given from the first and abiding unchanged beneath a bewildering mass of meaningless and mischievous encrustations' (Tyrrell [1909] p 148, describing a 'modernist'), neither does it follow that he is on the side of Loisy.[44]

Newman's effort to include, in principle, in the description of the 'idea', all the components of the complex concrete reality of the church (see *3.3*), is in striking contrast to 'the continually renewed attempt to reduce the totality of the many-sided and extensive dogmatic theology and institutions of a religion to a kernel, to what alone is truly important, however this single decisive element is named and discovered' (Rahner [1966g] p 21). But it does not thereby follow that he believed the 'circle of truth' to have no centre (see *5.3*, *6.31*), nor that he was not keenly aware that the 'essence' of christianity was only maintained with fragility (cf *VM* i pp 354–5), and its identity threatened by the changing languages, cultures, and polities in which it must become incarnate if it is to live. It is rather that his concern with the concrete 'objectivity' of the symbols of creed and liturgy indicates his awareness that although 'such a single essential element in religion does exist', it is not expressible 'by any reduction which remains within the framework of the categories, nor is it thereby experienced more directly or with more certainty' (Rahner [1966g] p 21).

6.31 The incarnation as the 'central aspect' of christianity

Although, in *1845*, Newman insisted that the task of ascertaining 'the "leading idea", as it has been called, of Christianity . . . is beyond us' (pp 34–5; *Dev* 1.1.3), in *1878* he admitted the propriety, 'For the convenience of arrangement', of considering 'the Incarnation the central truth of the gospel, and the source whence we are to draw out its principles'.[45] In this section, I propose briefly to consider the extent to which such passages constitute a significant shift in the argument and perspective of the *Essay*.

On the surface, the explicit selection of the incarnation as 'the central aspect of christianity', is a purely practical move, 'for convenience' (*Dev* 1.1.3). On reflection, however, it is clear not only that Newman had apologetic, theological and epistemological reasons for making it, but also that it simply makes explicit the stance or perspective from within which, throughout his life, he related to the mystery of christianity.

In the first place, the emphasis on the incarnation is partly due to apologetic considerations. This is especially clear from the list of 'Christian principles' which, in *1878*, he 'drew out' from the central doctrine of the incarnation : they represent those aspects of christianity which, in his polemic against 'liberalism' and 'latitudinarianism', he was accustomed most strongly to insist upon.[46]

In the second place, by stating that the incarnation is 'the central truth of the Gospel', Newman was only making explicit a theological conviction from which, throughout the greater part of his life, he never wavered.[47] It should be noticed that, in the passages which we are considering, he refers to the incarnation, not as the '*leading* idea', but as the '*central*' idea, aspect, (*Dev* 1.1.3) doctrine, (1.2.10) or truth, (7.1.3) 'in order to group others around it' (1.1.3). In other words, the underlying appeal is to the image of that 'whole circle of doctrines, of which our Lord is the subject' (*Dev* Int 10; see *5.3*). Thus Newman's ascription of 'centrality' to the incarnation, far from isolating any one aspect of revealed truth, performs a function similar to that performed by Luther's doctrine of the 'outer clarity' of scripture, as employed in our own day by Pannenberg: 'Jesus Christ is the one *res*, the proper content of Scripture, and this content comes to light through the outer clarity of Scripture, ie, through historical study of the Bible' ([1970c] p 197; cf pp 190–1). As early as 1830, Newman had insisted that the difference between 'Natural' and 'Revealed Religion' lay in the fact that only in the latter was there offered to man, in the incarnation, 'an object on which the affections could be placed, and the energies concentrated' (*US* p 23). Thus we are led to recognise, in the centrality which Newman accords to the incarnation, the influence of his distinctive epistemological concerns. 'Principles stimulate thought, and an idea concentrates it' (*Dev* 5.3.2; 'keeps it together' *1845* p 74). 'The doctrine of the Incarnation . . . establishes in the very idea of Christianity the *sacramental* principle as its characteristic'.[48]

On balance, it would seem that, in making explicit that centrality of the fact and doctrine of the incarnation which most deeply characterises his conception of christianity, Newman was not, in *1878*, reversing the judgement made, in *1845*, concerning the impossibility of ascertaining the 'leading idea' of christianity.[49] Undoubtedly, a theory or spirituality thus focused on the incarnation is only one of the possible perspectives within which the mystery of christianity may be structured and heuristically totalised by an individual or an epoch.[50] Nevertheless, Newman's employment of the adjective 'central', rather than 'leading' is, in the context, significant. In organising his christian experience and understanding round the mystery of the incarnation, he is not opting for a reductionist programme; and it is this, as we have seen, which is the recurring characteristic of that search for the 'essence' or 'leading idea' of christianity which, in *Dev* 1.1.3, he repudiated (see *6.3*). He continues to insist that the principles of Christianity must be 'many and positive . . . if they are to be effective' (*Dev* 7.1.2; cf 7.1.5), and that 'one aspect of Revelation must not be allowed to exclude or to obscure another'.[51]

6.32 'Right practice' as a necessary condition of true development

'Le Christ n'a écrit qu'une fois et c'était sur le sable. Quel dédain de tous les moyens humainement propres à conserver sa parole extérieure! Ce sont donc les actes des chrétiens qui prêchent cette vérité et qui en gardent l'empreinte ineffaçable' (Blondel, quoted in Nédoncelle [1964] p 105). That remark of Blondel's suggests a conception of religious truth, and of the means whereby that truth is safeguarded and promoted, according to which a certain style or quality of behaviour is acknowledged as a necessary condition for a 'true' development of doctrine. Such a perspective has affinities with Newman's insistence on the 'living' and 'real' nature of the christian 'idea'. In this section, I shall argue that, for Newman, an element of 'orthopraxis' is intrinsic to his criteriological perspective.[52]

We have already seen that, for Newman, the revelation of the christian 'idea' is not simply the provision of information, but is primarily in the order of 'command' or 'invitation', evoking an 'ethical' or 'practical' response.[53] His conception of revelation, and of the doctrinal statements in which the response of faith to that revelation is articulated and symbolically expressed, is such that the notion of truth which he employs cannot be restricted to 'notional', speculative, or theoretical truth, but also necessarily includes a personal, 'ethical', or existential dimension.[54] A 'true' development of doctrine or practice is, as we have seen (6.1), one that is 'faithful' to the 'idea' as originally communicated : to say that the church is 'faithful' to its origins is to say more than merely that its statements are consistent with, or logically derivable from, the primitive 'forms' of faith.

Once the ethical, personal or existential nature of christian truth is acknowledged, it is clear that in order to assess the truth, or 'faithfulness' of a particular 'development' of christian doctrine, it will be insufficient to ascertain that the 'development' is a theoretically justifiable interpretation or application of new testament teaching. It will also be necessary to ask whether the 'development' in question expresses or embodies a style of life, an ethical response, which is in conformity with the style of life commanded or recommended by the gospel. The truth of christian 'theory' is too closely bound up with the quality of christian 'practice' for it to be possible to press the necessary distinction between 'theory' and 'practice' to the point where they can be handled as fundamentally separate issues.

In 1837, Newman claimed that 'Action is the criterion of true faith'.[55] A necessary condition of a 'true' development is that it shall have been 'realised' in the concrete life and activity of the church (cf *Dev* 2.3.4; *VM* i p 16), for 'Realising is the very life of true developments' (*US* p 337; see *2.2, 4.12*). Moreover, on Newman's principles, there is surely a sense in which it should be said that 'The safeguard of Faith is a right state of heart' (*US* p 234), not merely for the individual christian, but also for the church as a whole (see *4.2*). While it is true that, in the Advent Sermons of 1841, Newman laid an uncharacteristically one-sided emphasis on life, or holiness, as a test of sound doctrine (*SD* pp 308–80), he never retreated from the broad criteriological standpoint from which he proudly proclaimed: 'I believe *I* was the *first* writer who made *life the* mark of a true Church' (*L&D* xi p 101; see *4.31*). Few features of the argument of the *Essay* more sharply distinguish it from those theories of doctrinal development which were debated in Roman catholic schools of theology during the first half of this century, than the stress which Newman consistently lays on 'life' or 'reality' as a criterion of true development in doctrine.

Newman's refusal sharply to separate the theoretical component of christian truth from its concrete embodiment in life and activity is by no means simply an apologetic device. It is grounded in his epistemology of belief (see *3.22* on belief as 'risk' or 'venture'). Thus, although he admits that 'development . . . comes . . . with the use of reflection and argument and original thought' (*Dev* 2.1.16), he insists at the same time that it comes 'with a dependence on the ethical growth of the mind itself'.[56] 'In essentials Newman's understanding of the symbolic function of the Church is closely akin to Coleridge's. She has to "act out what she says she is"; and for us to partake of the reality the Church renders intelligible, we must be prepared to act out the functions she prescribes in order to advance our understanding' (Coulson [1970] p 68). While he does not deny the rationality of true development, 'Arguments will come to be considered as suggestions and guides rather than logical proofs; and developments as the slow, spontaneous, ethical growth, not the scientific and compulsory results, of existing opinions' (*Dev* 7.2.10; cf 5.4.1; 7.2.4. See Chadwick [1957] p 248 for the shift of emphasis between *1845* and *1878*).

In discussing the significance of the distinction, in the *Essay*, between 'principle' and 'doctrine', we pointed out that Newman's

L

stress on the primacy of 'life' over 'form' never degenerates into an anti-intellectualism such as would call in question the indispensability of creeds and doctrinal propositions in ensuring the 'faithfulness' of the church to the gospel (see *5.42*). Thus, for example, W. J. Williams, although he believed himself to be faithfully capturing the spirit of the *Essay*, was in fact significantly distorting it when he said that 'vitality [is] . . . in the final resort, the only test, of religious truth' ([1906] p 62). Newman's emphasis on the normative significance of the 'truthfulness' of the church, its concrete obedience to the gospel it proclaims, never amounts to a denial of the necessity that its doctrines should be tested for their 'theoretical' truth, as descriptions, in some sense, of that state of affairs which is implied in, or promised by, the proclamation of the gospel.

According to J. A. Froude, the creed 'takes shape as a living germ develops into an organic body; and as you do not ask of a tree, is it *true*, but is it *alive*, so with an established Church or system of belief you look to the work which it is doing' ([1883] p 167). Newman's preoccupation with 'life', or 'holiness', as the 'mark of a true Church', always led him to 'look to the work which it is doing'. But he also maintained that this work was the fruit of man's communion with the living word of God, a communion mediated through that creed, liturgy and 'system of belief' which preserved, and symbolically contained, the memory of original events and statements which were fruitful because they were true, and not simply true in the measure that they proved fruitful.[57]

To read the *Essay* in the light of the debates that took place during the modernist crisis is to appreciate Newman's genius in attempting to hold together 'aspects' and dimensions of the christian 'idea' which, in the heat of polemic, would by others be isolated and erected into exclusive, theoretical systems of interpretation and assessment. Because Newman never lost sight of the complex, pluriform nature of a 'real idea', he never forgot the manifold nature of christian truth, and, therefore, of the 'various kinds of assents' correlative to it (cf *GA* p 243, commenting on the fact that 'a religion is not a proposition, but a system; it is a rite, a creed, a philosophy, a rule of duty, all at once'). Throughout this chapter, I have maintained that, as a result of the apologetic standpoint from which the *Essay* was written, it does not contain any systematically elaborated set of criteriological principles. By now, our familiarity with Newman's methods of argument and interpretation in 'concrete matters' renders it antecedently improbable that there could be, for him, any *one* criterion on the basis of which a 'development' in church teaching or practice is to be evaluated. If, as a result of the particular aims of the *Essay*, he lays considerable stress on the authenticating function of ecclesiastical authority, I have nevertheless tried to show that the mere fact of authoritative decision may not, according to Newman, be regarded as the sole sufficient criterion of the 'truth' of a development, independently of exegetical, historical and theological considerations, and of the role to be accorded to the 'reception' of doctrine by the church as a whole, in the concrete circumstances of its life and worship. In this final section, I have been concerned to show that, as a result of Newman's epistemology of belief, his preoccupation with the 'practical' nature of christianity, and his conception of religious truth, one of the conditions which must be fulfilled, before a 'development' of church teaching or practice may safely be judged to be 'true' to its origins, is the 'realisation' of that development in the hearts and minds and patterns of behaviour of the christian community.

7

The *Essay* in twentieth-century theology

It was remarked, in the Introduction, that the range of disagreement concerning the nature of Newman's aim and method of argument in the *Essay* is sufficiently wide to create a presumption that an analysis of the *Essay*, such as that which I have sought to provide, is a necessary prerequisite for tackling the further question : what light can the *Essay* cast on the significantly different situation in which christian theology today attempts to come to terms with the problem of change and continuity in christian doctrine? A detailed answer to that question lies outside the scope of this study. In conclusion, however, it may be useful to indicate the broad outlines of the more important reactions to the *Essay* since Newman's death, in order to suggest how some of the 'filters' through which the *Essay* is, today, variously viewed, came to be constructed.[1] I shall consider, in turn, the modernist crisis, subsequent interpretations of the *Essay* in Roman catholic theology before 1945, the 'views' of the *Essay* built up in England (and especially in anglican thought), and the various reassessments of the significance of the *Essay* in Roman catholic theology since the end of the second world war.

Until the closing years of the nineteenth century, the impact of the *Essay* on both Roman catholic and anglican theology had been slight. In a lecture delivered a few weeks before the publication of *Lamentabili*, Wilfrid Ward claimed that Newman was the 'embodiment' of the 'inductive temper of the nineteenth' century, 'restrained and tempered by Christianity' ([1908a] p 252). As such, his whole method of argument, his phenomenological approach to epistemological problems of belief, his view of the relationship of religious language to the mystery which it necessarily, but inadequately, attempts to articulate, his concern for historical detail, however idiosyncratically interpreted, made his thought impenetrable to the prevailing scholasticism. After the events of 1907, the *Essay* could no longer be ignored, but the complex and ambiguous relationship between it and the writings of the modernists ensured that no objective and dispassionate study of the *Essay* would be possible for several decades.

The enthusiastic summary and critique of the *Essay* which Loisy wrote in 1898[2] was lucid and balanced, and showed a grasp of Newman's mind superior to that of many subsequent commentators, both friendly and hostile.[3] There are many passages in the three 'little red books' which show the influence of the *Essay*, although explicit citations are rare.[4] To accuse Loisy of deliberately distorting Newman's thought, simply because his own concerns were significantly different, and because he only took over from Newman those aspects of his thought which seemed helpful to him, is unjust.[5] Loisy's respect for the man to whom, in 1896, he referred as 'le théologien le plus ouvert qui ait existé dans la sainte Eglise depuis Origène' (cited Vidler [1934] p 94). seems to have been sincere, and there is little reason to suppose, in his case, that he found Newman 'useful, not because he was by any means the most liberal, or progressive, or distinctively modern, theologian that the Roman Church produced in the nineteenth century, but because he had been more liberal than any other theologian whose name was held in honour in official circles'.[6] Not that, applied to others, this charge is without substance. During the weeks that followed the publication of *Pascendi*, 'The question of whether or not Newman had been condemned by the encyclical . . . was discussed with heat in the English press' (Barmann [1972] p 204). As *The Times* asserted in an editorial : 'It is idle to inquire whether the astute scholar who wrote what the Pope signed [ie, the encyclical *Pascendi*] was or was not thinking of Cardinal Newman. The important thing is that many Roman Catholics in our country feel that he was so thinking. They have received such intellectual stimulus from his teaching, their sense of security within the Roman fold risen so largely from the fact of Newman's having felt safe there, that to lay violent hands on him is like letting the wolves loose in their midst'.[7] Philip Sidney's claim that 'Newman's popular theory as to the development of dogma has been condemned by the reigning Pope' (*The Times*, 5 Nov 1907), drew forth affirmations of

Newman's orthodoxy some of which were so sweeping as irrevocably to compound confusion.[8]

So far as Tyrrell is concerned, the manner in which he handled his central distinction between 'revelation', 'theology' and 'devotion', shows signs of Newman's influence,[9] although he had harsh things to say about 'theories of development', because he wondered 'whether *in principle* Mr Ward (or Newman in the *Essay* of 1845) has really departed from the position of those whom he considers ultra-conservatives' ([1907] p 154). At the end of his life, he expressed the same worry more sharply, but did so in a manner which shows how little he understood the *Essay* which, he claimed, 'was undoubtedly written with one eye fixed on his scholastic critics, and with a view to dissemble the difference between their conception and his own as much as possible' ([1913] p 30). It needs to be borne in mind however that Tyrrell was directly combating not so much Newman himself as the position of those, such as Dublanchy who, energetically defending Newman against the charge of modernism, insisted on the 'substantial' immutability of christian doctrine, allowing only the occurrence in history of a 'Progrès accidentel dans la connaissance et la proposition des dogmes chrétiens' (Dublanchy [1924] cols 1606–1649).

Of all the major figures in the modernist crisis, the one whose thought comes closest to Newman's is surely Blondel. But, even if, as Nédoncelle showed, Blondel derived his concept of 'Tradition' from a study of Newman, the direct influence of the latter on Blondel's thought would, in general, seem to have been slight.[10]

Newman's 'theory of development' was not the only aspect of his thought to become the centre of a storm during the first decade of this century. The other focus of debate, especially in France, concerned the extent to which his analysis of faith was 'fideistic'. This charge was mounted, in its most sustained form, by Baudin : 'On peut donc se croire autorisé à rejeter la critique générale que Newman fait de la raison, et à considérer comme un echec son essai d'intuitionnisme et de fidéisme systématique'.[11] Bremond, whose stimulating and eccentric interpretation of Newman's thought, described by Tristram as a 'brilliant phantasy' ([1945d] p 241), was consistent with the enigmatic role he occupied throughout the modernist crisis, described Newman as 'this great despiser of reasoning' (Bremond [1907b] p 66). The debates be-

tween Bremond and Wilfrid Ward showed up the weaknesses in
the former's understanding of Newman but, unhappily, it was his
interpretation, rather than Ward's, which was to have by far the
greater influence : 'however numerous and careful have been the
studies inspired in France by the *Essay on Development*, I am not
sure that they have always detected its exact meaning' (Bouyer
[1945] p 182). Lebreton, while declining definitively to adjudicate
between Ward and Bremond, as interpreters of Newman, commented : 'on me permettre de dire que mes préférences vont à
l'école anglaise' (Lebreton [1907b] p 285). The debate was not
always conducted at a high level of scholarly objectivity. Bremond said of Ward : 'Il nous dit que le cardinal n'a jamais voulu
ériger de système, que l'impénétrable brouillard saxon défie nos
analyses latines' ([1908] p 341).

In England, the same charge of 'fideism' was not uncommon :
'Newman was concerned . . . with showing that faith moved in
a circle of its own, independent of and requiring no help from
reason'.[12] In 1925, White claimed that the *Essay* 'marks the sur-
render of his reason to his imagination' ([1925] p 128). We have
already seen that this form of the charge of irrationality against
Newman's thought in general, and the *Essay* in particular, has
managed to survive to our own day (*2.11*).

In view of the persistence of the charges of 'fideism' or 'anti-
intellectualism', must it not be conceded that there is some substance in them ? A global answer runs the risk of being as unsatisfactory as the global charge, and a detailed response lies outside the scope of this study. Nevertheless, it is possible to draw
attention to the fact that Newman's critics have usually ignored
the indications which he himself provided as to the senses in which
he used the term 'reason' (eg *US* pp ix–xvii). Moreover, one of
the reasons why the range of data regarded by Newman as relevant to the subject-matter of the *Essay* was so much wider than
has usually been the case with studies of doctrinal development
(see *3.3*) was that he habitually worked with a concept of rationality far broader, and richer, than that employed both in the
'rationalism' he deplored, and by many of his critics.[13]

As the dust settled after the storms of 1907, one question hung
over Newman's memory : Was he a modernist? Today, such a
question can be seen to be meaningless. It presupposes that 'modernism' was a coherent, unified conceptual system, and invites us

to test, against this postulated system, the rich, tentative and complex thought of a man whose acceptance, as central, of many of the problems with which the leading modernists attempted to deal lived in tension with an equally profound commitment to dimensions of truth which, at least in the heat of battle, they came to discount. Even Tyrrell's famous verdict that 'If a man is to be judged by what he is fundamentally, and in his dominant aims and sympathies, it is absurd to speak of Newman as a Modernist in any degree' ([1913] p 30), is less an acquittal than a regretful judgement that Newman did not recognise 'the intimate connection between methods and their results' (p 31). The question : Was Newman a modernist ? is anachronistic and in the last analysis lacking in intellectual seriousness. Nevertheless, it was asked, and for forty years the pattern of its answer dominated attempts by Roman catholic theologians to interpret Newman's thought.[14] Newman must be shown to be orthodox. If he was orthodox (that is, not a modernist), then he must, in some sense, have been a Thomist. The recurring attempts, between 1907 and 1945, at varying levels of sophistication, to demonstrate, for example, that 'Newman's theory [of knowledge] is in all essentials the same as that of the scholastics' (Brickel [1918] p 507), and that, therefore, he was not a modernist, bear striking witness to the narrow horizons within which the savage repression of modernism had restricted the perspectives of catholic theology.

As early as 1905, Bainvel defended the *Essay* against those who thought that 'Newman vero progressum vere vitalem admiserit, in assimilatione sc. elementorum extraneorum' by claiming that Newman's view of the problem did not significantly differ from that of Vincent of Lerins! ([1905] pp 123, 146–9; [1897] pp 179–80).

At the fourth session of the Malines Conversations, in 1925, Battifol's interventions in his debate with Gore on doctrinal development show the extent to which the 'scholasticisation' of Newman had been successful. Battifol, claiming that 'Newman estimait que les formules seules étaient neuves', could seriously maintain that 'Schultes se rapproche donc davantage de la pensée la plus stricte de Newman, tandis que Marin-Sola la dépasse'.[15]

Marin-Sola, whose study was 'perhaps the most influential thesis upon the theory of development written during the twentieth century' (Chadwick [1957] p 204), profoundly admired Newman, and made a genuine attempt to render more supple the categories within which the scholastic debate operated. But the inadequacy of his conception of revelation, his lack of a sense of history, and his assumption that doctrinal history proceeds primarily by rigorously syllogistic deduction, kept him firmly locked within the strait-jacket of the period. It is significant that, for all his respect for Newman, he should refer to the *Essay* as 'son livre génial . . . il a peut-être accordé trop d'importance au *sens*, à la *vie*, à l'*expérience*, à la *pratique*, comme moyens de développement du dogme catholique' ([1924] I p 310).

The obsession with modernism continued to frustrate any hopes that the *Essay* might be approached with greater objectivity. In 1929, Rivière affirmed that 'L'hétérodoxie de Newman n'est qu'un mythe créé par l'ignorance du cas et entretenu par les passions de la polémique' ([1929] p 84; cf Hayot [1938a], [1938b]; Philbin [1945]; Cavallera [1946] p 134). As late as 1945, Davis (whose more mature studies have placed all students of Newman in his debt) described Bremond's remark that, had Newman lived longer, he would have written, not the *University Sermons*, but *L'Action*, as 'an irresponsible and absurd libel'. He went on to say : 'Marin-Sola must be added to the group of sound modern Newman-interpreters, mainly in his own field of the evolution of dogma'.[16]

'It has been the misfortune of Cardinal Newman that Englishmen have not taken him seriously' (Burgum [1930] p 310). A number of factors have contributed to this situation which, at least until very recently, has remained the case.[17] In the first place, the weakness of English Roman catholic theology during the first half of the century, and the suspicion with which Newman's work, especially the *Essay*, was held after the modernist crisis, combined to restrict English catholic Newman studies, for the most part, to matters of historical and biographical detail. One effect of this was that Wilfrid Ward's work, which represented an approach to Newman study uncongenial to the French, tended to be somewhat neglected. I would wish to argue that Ward's value as an intelligent and not uncritical interpreter of Newman has been seriously underestimated. (All the studies by Ward listed in the bibliography are either directly concerned with Newman, or influenced by him.)

In the second place, so far as the *Essay* is concerned, the fact that it was Newman's personal *apologia* for leaving the church of England has led, not surprisingly, to its neglect, or reactive misinterpretation, in anglican theology. In particular, the survival in England of the view (which we have already noticed) that Newman's theology of faith was 'irrational' or 'fideist', reinforced the ancient suspicion that 'submission to Rome' entails the abandonment of intellectual integrity.[18] In this way, the reverence for church authority which so strongly marked Newman's temperament, together with the prominent role accorded in the *Essay*, for apologetic reasons, to the justification of one form of that authority, have created the presumption that there is little in the *Essay* which would be of interest to other than Roman catholic theologians. Thus, little is heard today of reactions such as that of Matthew Arnold, who considered that the *Essay* contained 'even a greater number of profound and valuable ideas than any other one' ([1870] pp 144–5; cf [1887]) of Newman's works. There is no discussion of the *Essay* in Rashdall [1898], nor in Caird [1893], and Orr's more conservative study only contained one explicit mention of it.[19] Quick acknowledged that 'It is a plain fact that Newman's *Essay on Development* is today in many ways more characteristically modern than anything which Liberal Protestantism has produced' ([1922] p 27), but his understanding of the *Essay* was superficial, eg 'Idea is opposed to fact as the basis of Christianity' (p 29).

In the third place, most English studies of Newman have concentrated on his role in the Oxford Movement. The effect has been to ignore the later development of his thought (with the exception of the *Grammar of Assent*), and to tend too uncritically to assume that, as a leader of the movement, he must have been a 'conservative'. An example of this tendency is Reardon's recent comprehensive study of ninetenth-century religious thought. He acknowledges that Newman 'is, probably, the outstanding religious figure of his century, with the sole exception of Kierkegaard' (Reardon [1971a] p 127), and that 'more, often, is to be learned from the process of his thinking, even when he is wrong, than from the acceptable conclusions of most others' (p 128). Nevertheless, very little space is devoted to his thought after 1845, and we are told that 'The ideas and ideals to which Newman dedicated himself throughout his long career, first as an Anglican and then as a Roman Catholic, were backward-looking and reactionery

even in his own times' (p 151). In this latter judgement, Reardon
is simply echoing Storr, for whom Newman 'was in spirit a medi-
evalist' ([1913] p 256; cf pp 254–7).

If Newman is ever to be treated, in England, with the serious-
nes—as a theologian—which he deserves, it will be necessary to
rely as little on received English views concerning the content
and direction of his thought as on the interpretations offered by
European Roman catholic scholars between the modernist crisis
and the end of the second world war. To summarise Newman's
thought is, notoriously, to distort it. As Sillem remarked, there is
simply no substitute for a close, patient, critical and sympathetic
attention to his own text ([1969] pp 15–22).

The effect of the suspicion which had, for so many years, clouded
Newman's reputation, can be seen in the fact that none of the
papers delivered to a Roman congress on doctrinal development
in 1951 contains any discussion of the *Essay*.[20] In France, however, the methodological revolution that came to be known as 'la
nouvelle théologie' (cf Schoof [1970] pp 108–15; 201–10), with
its abandonment of neo-scholastic categories in favour of a more
concrete, historical approach, and the recovery of a sense of
'living tradition', led to an increasing interest in Newman (fostered
by such studies as Davis [1958] and Laros [1958]), and a re-
appraisal of the significance of the *Essay*.[21] Both Congar and de
Lubac were strongly influenced by Blondel, and well read in
Newman.

Of particular importance was an article by de Lubac.[22] Although
he insisted that 'Nous n'avons voulu proposer aucune théorie'
([1948] p 158), he showed up the poverty of existing 'theories of
development,' and laid characteristic stress upon the notion of 'le
Tout de Dogme' (p 156; cf [1969a]), a notion strikingly reminiscent of Newman's insistence on the unity of christian doctrine,
although 'surprisingly enough it was apparently not derived
directly from him' (Schoof [1970] p 203).

By the late nineteen-fifties, it was widely acknowledged that
both the approaches to doctrinal development which had dominated the debate between the wars were thoroughly inadequate.[23]

Dramatic as were the shifts in method and concern which
marked the post-war period, catholic theology was still sufficiently
haunted by the fear of losing contact with the achievements of its
past to maintain an emphasis on conservation rather than on

creativity. So far as the problem of doctrinal development was concerned, the notion of 'homogeneous evolution' (see *4.3*), which had dominated the debate since Marin-Sola, remained the master-concept controlling even the fresh perspectives within which the problem was discussed.[24] As a result, the renewed interest in Newman's *Essay* led to an increasing tendency to isolate those features of his argument which were congenial to the concerns of the period, and to refer to the resulting oversimplified restatements as 'Newman's theory of development'. Thus, not the least significant thing about a remark such as the following is the assumption that the *Essay* embodies 'a solution' to the problem of doctrinal development. 'On peut dire que les théologiens d'aujourd'hui se rangent de plus en plus clairement du côté de la solution newmanienne'.[25]

In 1959, Abbot Butler claimed that 'The importance of Newman's theory in the present age of the Church emerges when we realise . . . that it does not only allow Christians to withstand the hostile attack of critical history; it encourages them to embrace and apply the methods and aims of historical criticism' (Butler, B. C. [1959] pp 344–5; cf *3.1*). During the last few years, the effects of just such an application have forced theologians to realise the inadequacy of even the most sophisticated theory of 'homogeneous evolution'. 'The problem of the evolution or development of dogma has been with us since the last century. Whereas Vatican I was hardly aware of it, Vatican II recognised it (*Dei Verbum*, art 8), but at a time when it had already been reformulated in the thinking of informed theologians . . . history was understood less as a continual process of "development", that is as a progress achieved through a gradual unfolding of what was already implicit, and more as a series of formulations of the one content of faith diversifying and finding expression in different cultural contexts'.[26]

The grounds of the 'reformulation' to which Congar refers are far from exclusively theological. In order to tackle the question of the abiding validity and usefulness of the thematic components of Newman's *Essay*, it would be necessary—on Newman's own principles—to take into account not only shifts in theological method, but also the bewildering complex of methodological questions that has emerged as a result of one discipline after another feeling the pressure on its procedures of the historicity of human existence, and of the forms of interpretation of that existence in words, symbols and institutions.

It would, however, be dangerous to assume that the abandonment, as inadequate, of theories of 'homogeneous evolution' justifies the assumption that Newman's *Essay* no longer has anything to teach us. I hope that it has become sufficiently clear, in the course of this study, that the complex, fugal patterns of argument in the *Essay*, the range of insights more or less successfully related one to another, above all the attitude towards religious truth and its necessary, but fragile embodiment in human statements and institutions, cannot legitimately be reduced to any single 'theory' or conceptual device for driving a smooth road through the rugged wilderness of christian history. Before dismissing the *Essay* as simply a pioneering achievement, or a brilliant exercise in apologetic rhetoric, theologians must surely ensure that it is the *Essay* itself, and not those 'views' of it which have built up under the pressure of subsequent debates, that they are evaluating.

Simply by way of illustration, one could mention two aspects of the *Essay* which are likely to prove of enduring significance. The first would be Newman's recognition of the inescapable tension between historical claims and the claims of christian belief, and that catholicity of concern which drove him always to keep in sight all aspects of any concrete problem. The second would be his insistence that the appropriate language in which to conduct the search for continuity in doctrinal history across cultural and linguistic change is not exclusively, or even primarily, the theoretical language of the theologian. It is, more basically, the concrete, symbolic language of creed and rite in the use of which the church seeks to preserve the memory of its origins, to articulate its present experience of the saving work of Christ, and proleptically to embody its hope in the fulfilment of that promise to which the scriptures bear witness.

In writing the *Essay on Development*, Newman was beginning a work which he did not, and could not, have completed. There is no reason to suppose that that work is finished yet : 'the *Development* will be consulted for its "hints and seeds of thought" during many years to come . . . Until its work is done, it cannot die' (Barry [1927] p 250). As Newman wrote in 1841, quoting a phrase which had been the text of the first sermon he ever wrote (cf *L&D* xxiv pp 170, 181–2), and which would be the text of 'The Parting of Friends' (*SD* pp 395–409): 'No man is given to see his work through. "Man goeth forth unto his work and to his labour until the evening", but the evening falls before it is done. There was One alone who began and finished and died' (*Ess* ii p 317).

Notes

1 The term 'historicity' is ambiguous. It has 'long been used in theological literature to designate an event which has been verified by historical research' (Kehm [1970] p xi). It is currently also used (and this is the sense in which I am using it in this chapter) as the equivalent of the German term *Geschichtlichkeit*. In the hope that any ambiguity will be reduced, or removed, by the context, I have preferred to risk using the one term 'historicity', rather than to employ such neologisms as 'historicness' or 'historicality' (cf Kehm [1970] pp x–xi).

2 So far as Roman catholic theology is concerned, the preference shown by the second Vatican Council's constitution *Lumen Gentium* for biblical, and thus eschatologically orientated imagery is of particular importance. The centrality accorded to the concept of the 'People of God', for instance, 'at once invites us to consider the Church inserted in a history dominated and defined by God's Plan for man' (Congar [1965] p 10). Speaking of the same constitution, another commentator noted : 'ici, ontologie est à peu prés synonyme d'historicité' (Gonzalez Hernandez [1966] p 188).

3 'The fundamental question facing theology in this age of ecumenical sensitivity is whether John Henry Newman or Adolf Harnack should be followed as the interpreter of Christianity's dogmatic past' (Capps [1966] p 486).

4 Hammans ([1965] p 41) estimated some sixty titles had been published.

5 'Even among those who are concerned with theological questions, there is little or no conception of the amount of interest which Newman *as a theologian* has aroused on the continent of Europe, still less of his influence on contemporary thinking' (Allchin [1965] p 66). For signs of this influence, in so far as the problem of doctrinal development is concerned, see Crowe [1964] p 20 (on Lonergan); Davis [1958] p 312; Rahner

[1969b] p 348; Schoof [1970] p 219 (on Schillebeeckx); Walgrave [1964b] p 11. These points will be filled out in 7.

CHAPTER TWO

1   The juxtaposition of 'evangelically' and 'apostolical' is intended simply to point to the problem which is discussed in Newsome [1967] pp 11–30, and Newsome [1970] pp 73–4. Cf Davies [1961] pp 244–52.

2   *Apo* pp 228–9 (this letter of 16 November 1844 was written to Manning: cf Purcell [1895] I pp 258–9); Ward, M. [1948] p 438 (letter of 8 January 1845). Cf *L&D* xxv p 160.

3   This is not easy to reconcile with the account, twenty years later, of his state of mind in 1841 : cf *Apo* p 148.

4   'Depend upon it, the strength of any party lies in its being *true to its theory*. Consistency is the life of a movement' (Letter of 8 April 1841, *Apo* p 187; cf *L&D* xi p 111; xiv p 46). The preoccupation with 'consistency', a theme on which the seven 'notes' of a true development are but variations, accounts in large measure for the long vigil at Littlemore. He was testing his *own* consistency just as much as that of the church of Rome : cf *L&D* xi p 60; *4.2.*

5   '. . . the *way* in which the book approaches the Catholic Church is by *phenomena*' (*L&D* xii p 171). See Boekraad [1955] pp 135–40; Pailin [1969] pp 172, 186–7; Sillem [1969] pp 127–39.

6   On Newman's concept of the 'philosophical', see Culler [1955] pp 182–5.

7   'Newman on the Development of Christian Doctrine' (anon) *The Dublin University Magazine* xxvii (1846) p 113; cf Butler, W. A. [1850] p 367.

8   *L&D* xvi p 122. Cf *1845* pp x–xi; *Apo* p 234; *L&D* xiii pp 328 (note of 1863), 373.

9   Sillem [1969] p 19. Sillem's comments (pp 17–18) on Bremond [1907b], [1908], Baudin [1906], Lebreton [1907a] and de Grandmaison [1907], are judicious and timely. See 7.

10   The assertion 'To be deep in history is to cease to be a Protestant (*Dev* Int 5) has autobiographical overtones. The first draft of it read : 'To strip himself of Protestantism was a necessary first condition of his writing effectively concerning the Church, at all' (*BOA* D.7.6).

11   When revising the *Essay* in 1877, Newman made several attempts to redraft that part of the argument which immediately follows the quotation from Chillingworth (*Dev* Int 4;

1845 p 4). One of these ran : 'This is a fair argument if it can be maintained : and I am not going to lose sight of it; however, what I propose to myself in this Essay is something more than to prove a negative, clause by clause, in answer to an objection which, however smart, is superficial. Rather, I shall attempt to bring forward a body of evidence on the contrary side of the controversy, sufficient to show that the Christianity of history does substantially fulfil those anticipations of unity and integrity in its character, its professions, and its drift (aim) with which it is reasonable at first sight to regard it' (*BOA* D.7.6).

12 This assertion will be substantiated, and where necessary qualified, in *4*. But the breakthrough can be clearly seen by comparing *Dev* Int 7–18 with the defence of 'Apostolical Tradition' against Blanco White and Hampden in Newman [1836b].

13 Bacchus [1924] p 107. 'Reason does not prove that Catholicism is *true*, as it proves that mathematical conclusions are true' (*L&D* xii p 289).

CHAPTER THREE

1 Chadwick [1957] p 100. Chadwick [1957] remains the most important historical study of the *Essay*. Those points, especially in this chapter, at which disagreement is expressed, stand against a far wider measure of agreement and indebtedness.

2 'Newman's ablest criticism of Gibbon' (McCloy [1933] p 272) occurs in the *Grammar* : *GA*, pp 457–65. The *Philosophical Notebooks* show that Newman had reached this assessment by 1865, when he said of Gibbon's 'five causes of christianity' : '*We* do not deny them—but only say that they are not *sufficient*' (*PN* p 151); this passage was quoted by Wilfrid Ward, in his defence of Newman against Abbott's *Philomythus* : see Ward, W. [1893c] p 150.

3 *Dev* 4.1.11. The history of Newman's opinions on the orthodoxy of the ante-Nicene Fathers (a question of some importance for his views on doctrinal development) can be traced through his shifting estimate of Bull and Pétau. He wrestled with the problem from 1833 (when *Arians* was first published) to 1890 (when he added a rather touchy note : *Ari* pp 420, 422). In 1845 he reversed his favourable judgement of 1836 concerning Bull's evaluation of the ante-Nicene teaching on the Trinity (see the passage from *Ess* i p 130, quoted in *Dev* Int 9, criticised in *Dev* Int 10; also *L&D* xi p 274).

4 This is the explanation of those passages in his early catholic

writings which made Acton believe that he 'drew in' his view of development during this period (see MacDougall [1962] pp 161–5). The strongest assertions of the deductive nature of theology are found in his Dublin lectures (eg *Idea* pp 223–4, 440–2); their tone may be partly due to the fact that he was here speaking 'in his official capacity as rector of a Catholic university' (Walgrave [1957] p 57).

5 See Ward, W. [1912] i pp 432–7. The observation that 'if we would solve new questions, it must be by consulting old answers' (*Idea* p 223), is in striking contrast to the assertion, thirty years later, that 'a new question needs a new answer' (*Insp* p 105).

6 Thus, if we make allowance for Newman's reluctance, for so long, to use the *term* 'theology' to describe his own work, we can agree with Willam that 'Newmans lebenslanges Anliegen ist es, dem induktiven Denken in der Theologie den ihm zukommenden Platz zu sichern' (Willam [1969] p 25).

7 The first of the *University Sermons*, which has 'une saveur nettement "noétique"' (Stern [1967] p 50), and is 'thoroughly out of character' (Culler [1955] p 234), is an exception.

8 In the previous section he had argued that, even in scientific matters, the non-scientist does in fact trust, or regard as antecedently probable, received scientific theory (cf *Dev* 3.1.2–3; *Ari* p 151).

9 *Dev* 3.2.3; cf *US* p 257; *GA* pp 317, 331–3; *SN* p 184 (a note hinting at the recovery, by 1863, of the flexible phenomenology of *US*, after some years of trying to force his language about 'faith' into the strait-jacket of scholastic terminology). In 1847, he noted : 'Accedit quod accuratissimae et praestantissimae investigationes, cum in materia scientiarum, tum in re theologica, vel ob ipsam pulchritudinem suam, vel subtilitatem, vel partium multiplicitatem, in logicas formas non facile cadunt' (*Theses* p 253).

10 *Dev* 4.0.2. Connolly, who regards this passage as making 'a crucial point' (Connolly [1963] p 113), says that 'To Newman, the war between the scientists and the theologians was not fought on rational issues but on imaginary ones' (p 115). He presumably means : on issues of the imagination, in which case he is surely correct.

11 Newman's lifelong attempts to grapple with the problem of the relationship between history and christian belief have led to estimates of his competence as an historian which range from the excessively generous verdict of Hughes ([1950] p 10) to : 'of historical evidence, as of the methods of historical inquiry, it may safely be affirmed that Newman knew nothing . . . Firmly

handled, the *Essay* . . . is nothing but a compost of sophistry and superstition' (Young, G. M. [1948] p 104; cf Smyth [1955] p 166). Recently, Young's judgement has been repeated almost verbatim : 'Of historical criticism the English divine, back in 1845, had known nothing and his essay takes no account of it' (Reardon [1970] p 22). A more judicious general assessment has been made by Holmes ([1969b]). So far as the *Essay* is concerned, see Chadwick [1957] pp 138–49.

12 Such as Manning, writing after the Vatican Council : 'The Church knows its own history, both by natural light and by supernatural illumination. It rejects and condemns those who appeal from its definitions to human history and human interpretations, precisely because it knows them to be false' (Manning [1888] p 78).

13 *Ess* II p 230. The phrase is crucial for understanding Newman's attitude towards 'The birth, the life, the death and resurrection of Christ' as 'the text' which the Indwelling Spirit 'has illuminated. He has made history to be doctrine' (*PS* II p 227). In this same early (1834) sermon, he spoke of the Spirit as 'the voice of Truth in the hearts of all rational beings' (*PS* II p 218).

14 Cf *Ess* II pp 196–7; *Ari* pp 354–5; *SD* pp 100, 310; Calkins [1969] p 360. In *Tract 85* (*DA* pp 109–253) he stretched his argument to the extent of claiming that the very unsystematic and haphazard (or very 'human') nature of scripture and biblical history was itself an argument that it was 'doctrinally divine'. Cf *DA* pp 150–1, where the inspiration which this type of argument owes to Butler is rather clear (see Butler, J. [1896] I pp 221–42; Guitton [1933] p 41). The more respectable form of the argument is to the effect that apparently random events may be providentially significant : cf the example, from Gibbon, of the death of Theodosius, in *Ess* II p 191, and *Dev* 1.2.2.

15 *Ess* II p 213. In *Dev* 2.2.10, Newman suggests that 'The revealed facts are special and singular . . . it is otherwise with the revealed principles; these are common to all the works of God'. Terminologically, this passage is difficult to reconcile with *Dev* 7.1.4 (an addition of *1878*) and the Milman article. For earlier formulations of the perspective of *Dev* 2.2.10, see *US* pp 32, 171.

16 Cf his criticisms of Milman's earlier *History of the Jews* in letters of 1830 and 1831 (in Culler [1955] pp 249, 313); also *Idea* pp 43–98. There are striking similarities between Blondel's critique of Loisy (cf Blondel [1964]; Dru [1964] p 213, on Blondel's *History and Dogma* and Newman's *Essay*), his reply to Venards (cf Blondel [1956]; Venards [1904]), and Newman's

critique of Milman. Those whose praise of Milman as an historian lead them to underestimate Newman's contribution to the debate perhaps overlook the extent to which that debate is still alive: cf Harvey [1967]; Roberts [1960]; Weiler [1970]. Above all, it is possible to detect a concern which is similar to Newman's in Pannenberg's rejection of an historical positivism that would close itself, on methodological grounds, to the problem of the presence and activity of God in history. This similarity of concern could be illustrated by a comparison between Newman's view of the relationship between 'antecedent probability' and 'evidence' (see 3.21), and Pannenberg's notion (partially derived from Collingwood) of the relationship between 'intuition' and historical cognisance of particular events. See Pannenberg [1970b].

17 *Dev* 2.1.2. Cf *Dev* 2.1.8–9 (where the echoes of the controversy with Milman are most apparent), 2.1.13, 2.1.17. In *1878*, the article on Milman is quoted at length in a different context: the discussion on the 'assimilative power' of the christian 'idea': *Dev* 8.2.12.

18 Sillem [1969] pp 120, 178; cf Boekraad [1955] p 198. Sillem misleadingly says that 'the term, "probability" refers to the conclusion of a *deductive* line of reasoning' (p 120; my stress). More often, it refers to the conclusions of those *inductive* patterns of argumentation many of the strands of which, as 'natural inferences', may be due to acquired or inherited assumptions, expectations and prejudices and, as such, may be 'altogether unconscious and implicit' (*GA* p 330). Newman regularly 'used the word "probable" in the sense defined by Dugald Stewart' (Dessain in *L&D* xi p 289; cf Sillem [1969] pp 178–9; Stewart [1814] ii pp 150, 203–43, esp p 240).

19 And, through Butler, from Locke (see Murphy [1963], pp 366–7, 381–5), although Locke had no direct influence on Newman at this point (see Sillem [1969] p 192). Undoubtedly, the most powerful personal influence here was that of Whately: cf Whately [1849] p 14.

20 See Whately [1849] pp 17–18, 35. Whately seems to distinguish between conclusions established by 'antecedent-probability' and those grounded on 'testimony' (Whately [1849] p 35), whereas Newman regards testimony as simply one of the grounds on which a case may be constructed for the antecedent probability that such-and-such is the case.

21 See Willam [1969] pp 36, 41. According to the *Apologia*, Newman first read Butler 'about' 1823 (*Apo* p 10). In fact, he 'began reading Butler's *Analogy* on 25 June 1825' (Sheridan [1967]

p 110; cf Sillem [1969] p 170). In the previous year, Newman spoke of 'the antecedent probabilities of [Cicero's] *Pro Milone*' (*HS* ɪ p 293). Cf Whately's use of 'presumption' in Whately [1830] p 188; also Hawkins' use of 'antecedent presumption' and 'prior presumption', in the context of an inductive, cumulative method of argument similar to Newman's : see Hawkins [1819] pp 2–6, 25; Hawkins [1840] p 204. The possibility of Davison's influence should not be ignored : 'Antecedently to a consideration of the proper Evidences of Revealed Religion, it cannot be said with any show of reason, that it is a thing improbable in itself that a divine Revelation should be made' (Davison [1861] p 1. On Davison and Newman, see *5.43*).

22   Thus the argument of *Dev* Int 1–3 takes the form of a general, provisional estimation of the facts. As he put it in 1836 (voicing sentiments that were then not entirely his own : cf *Apo* pp 108–10) : 'surely, there is such a religious *fact* as the existence of a great Catholic body' (*DA* p 5).

23   A similar concern played an influential role in Hawkins' *Dissertation* on tradition : perhaps 'men of superior learning, industry, and capacity' might 'make out from the Scriptures . . . many or most of the doctrines of our faith', but surely we might expect that 'the mode of acquiring' the 'truths of Christianity' should be level to the capacity of the 'great mass of Christians' (Hawkins [1819] pp 8–9).

24   *Dev* 3.2.4. Thus, although, when discussing our habitual trust of newspaper reports, Newman says that 'We do not call for evidence till antecedent probabilities fail' (*US* p 189), he firmly rejects the idea that we are entitled 'in argument to make any assumption we please . . . it seems fair to say that no testimony should be received, except such as comes from competent witnesses' (*GA* p 376). The witnesses may be cross-examined, but any objection in principle to the 'right of making assumptions' can be countered by demonstrating the impossibility of executing a programme of total scepticism : cf *US* p 213; Cameron [1962], pp 210–11.

25   Cf *Idea* p 52. Newman thought that the publication of a French edition of the last six *University Sermons* would be helpful 'in *preparing* for the Essay', because these sermons 'take in' one of the key principles of the *Essay*, 'that the main instrument of proof in matters of life is "antecedent probability"' (*L&D* xɪɪ p 5).

26   'Newman would have comprehended the distinction which . . . Stephen Toulmin draws between our working logic and the formal patterns of idealised logic, as well as Toulmin's project

of using the analogy of jurisprudence to show how we actually weigh the case in many instances of substantial argument' (Collins [1961] p 30). Toulmin's description of logic as 'generalised jurisprudence' ([1964] p 7) is similar to Newman's account of it as 'a sort of rhetoric' (*US* p xii), a phrase reminiscent of Whately : 'Rhetoric being in truth an off-shoot of logic' ([1849] p 6).

27   The image of the scissors is taken from Lonergan, whose own methodology is so heavily influenced by the *Grammar*, and who uses it to illustrate both the method of the positive sciences and that of a critical hermeneutics. See Lonergan [1957] pp 312–13, 522–3, 577–8, 586–7.

28   Cf *PS* II pp 81–2; *Idea* pp 94–5. Although Newman's treatment of miracles is sometimes notoriously unsatisfactory, his principle is that 'we must have recourse to the same kind of evidence as that by which we determine the truth of historical accounts in general' (*Mir* p 13; see Holmes [1966b] and [1966a] p 31). Cf *Apo* p 309; *Ess* II p 221; Ward, W. [1912] II pp 235, 297.

29   'For myself, I would simply confess that no doctrine of the Church can be rigorously proved by historical evidence : but at the same time that no doctrine can be simply disproved by it . . . in all cases there is a margin left for the exercise of faith in the word of the Church' (*Diff* II p 312; the closely reasoned argument runs from pp 311–14). Cf *US* p 227; *VM* I p 38.

30   Butler, J. [1896] I pp 303–4; cf pp 329–30, 347, 352. There is an echo of Butler's architectural analogy in the last *University Sermon* : cf *US* p 316; *L&D* xv p 498; *L&D* xix p 460; *PN* p 133; also Butler, J. [1896] II p 269; Davison [1861] pp 23–4; Ward, W. [1912] II p 495.

31   Such a use of 'view' is clearly metaphorical. As with the concept of 'imaging', Newman's preference for visual metaphors creates the most acute difficulties where it is the 'objects of faith' for which a 'view' or 'image' is being sought. Cf the analogy between the 'view' or 'idea' of the doctrine of the Trinity and 'an impression conveyed through the senses', in *US* pp 328–32 (extracts from which are quoted in *Dev* 1.2.9). Cf Price [1969] pp 340–8; Sillem [1969] p 23; Walgrave [1957] p 48.

32   Butterfield [1957] p 36; cf 37–8, 142, 149. On the indispensability of research in the attainment of a 'view', see *Ess* I pp 226–34; *Ess* II p 254; *VM* I p xx. Perhaps the fullest discussion of 'views' is found in *LG* : see pp 13, 16–19, 27, 34, 41, 65, 67–8, 70, 75, 127, 134–5, 137–8, 157, 163, 186, 190, 202, 209, 222, 225, 227, 235–6, 257, 279, 294, 303, 308, 327, 371, 380, 391.

33   The concepts of 'risk 'and 'venture' are central to Newman's

phenomenology of belief; this is liable to be overlooked if attention is paid too exclusively to the *Grammar*, where New-man was primarily concerned with the element of 'certitude' in belief. Cf *Jfc* p 271; *L&D* XI pp 60–1; *L&D* XII p 168; *LG* p 385; *PS* IV pp 295–306 ('The Ventures of Faith'); *PS* VI pp 114, 259; *US* pp 202–3, 215, 219, 224, 239, 249, 292–3.

34   Harvey [1967] p 119, following Troeltsch. However Finster-hölzl, discussing the 'principle of faith' in *Dev* 7, says: 'Die "Theologie der Hoffnung" hat diese von Newman erkannte Dimension neu ins Licht gehoben' (Finsterhölzl [1967] p 265).

35   As these terms are defined in *US* pp ix–xvii. The tenth of the *University Sermons*, a classic statement of this position, raises the problem of Newman's tendency 'to make the difference between the believer and the unbeliever in the end one between two temperaments, two psychological types' (Cameron [1962] p 211; cf Pailin [1969] pp 155–6; Walgrave [1957] pp 148–63). The distinction is foreshadowed in Butler, J. [1896] II p 289, in a manner that corresponds to Cameron's analysis rather than that of Boekraad, who refers it to 'the two-fold personality that is potentially present in the breast of every individual' (Boek-raad [1955] p 281; cf pp 226–81).

36   'When faith is said to be a religious principle, it is . . . the things believed, not the act of believing them, which is peculiar to religion' (*PS* I p 191). That statement of 1829 expresses New-man's more or less unwavering conviction that the battle be-tween 'faith' and 'reason' is a battle between conflicting intellec-tual ethics, rather than a specifically religious conflict : cf *PS* VI pp 330–1; *US* pp 188, 230. *US* p 179 points in the opposite direction. *US* p 193 is a nuanced statement which, while main-taining the general principle stated above, is sensitive to the specific characteristics of religious belief. The *University Ser-mons*, which Newman never repudiated, remain in many ways a more successful analysis than the *Grammar*, where a similar distinction tends to be unduly affected by scholastic termin-ology : cf, eg, *GA* p 99; Chadwick [1960] p 45.

37   The terminology is Coulson's, discussing Coleridge and Ben-tham : see Coulson [1970] p 4. He points out that 'The contrast in Wittgenstein's attitudes to language . . . between the *Trac-tatus* and the *Philosophical Investigations* is closely akin to that between the two traditions—analytic and fiduciary—which I have been describing' (*ibid* p 14). A similar distinction is drawn, by Trethowan, between the attitudes of Blondel and those of some English academic philsophers : see Trethowan [1964] p 86.

38 One element in Newman's justification of religious faith operat-
ing on weak evidence is the believer's love for 'the Word of
life . . . Because he has a love for it, his love being strong, though
the testimony is weak' (*US* pp 202–3). Cf *Apo* p 19; *PS* iv
307–18 ('Faith and Love'); *US* pp 193, 222–50.

39 The best known of such accusations is Huxley's comment
(which, in the context, was almost a compliment) that, from
a selection of Newman's works (including the *Essay*), he could
'compile a Primer of "Infidelity" ' (Huxley [1889] p 948). Wilfrid Ward was 'delighted' by Huxley's quip, because he believed that it showed how deeply Newman was able to enter
into states of mind which he did not personally share (see Ward,
J. [1918] p xxii). Newman's reply to Fairbairn (*SE* pp 69–107)
suggests that he failed to understand the latter's charge of 'philosophical scepticism'. Many of Fairbairn's shafts, in fact, strike
deep : 'In a certain sense, submission to Catholicism is the vic-
tory of unbelief; the man who accepts authority because he dare
not trust his intellect, lest it lead him into Atheism, is van-
quished by the Atheism he fears' (Fairbairn [1899] p 137; cf
pp 138, 205–34).

40 'I thank God that He has shielded me morally from what in-
tellectually might easily come on me—general scepticism'
(Letter of 14 March, 1845, to Pusey, quoted from Liddon
[1893] ii p 450. Acton duly noted this : see cul *Add* mss 4988,
nos 33, 84). Cf *L&D* xviii p 335—and refs there to *Ari* p 76 and
US pp 348–9; Butler, W. A. [1850] p 204; Chadwick [1960]
p 42; Chadwick [1970a] p 528; Cronin [1935] pp 75–82; Hort
[1896] ii pp 423–4.

41 Nevertheless, Nédoncelle believes that 'l'existentialisme contem-
porain est déjà contenu dans l'idée newmanienne que les
preuves métaphysiques ou théologiques ont un contexte psycho-
logique et qu'il faut prendre au sérieux la solitude du moi
en face de son Créateur' (Nédoncelle [1945] p 76). Cf Gorce
[1957].

42 Cf *Dev* Int 21, 3.2.1–2; *DA* p 295 (quoted *GA* p 95); *L&D*
xiv p 348; *Mir* pp 71–2; *Prepos* p 46; *PS* ii pp 15, 21; *PS* iv
pp 58–9; *PS* v p 45; *PS* vi p 336; *US* pp 179, 188; Vidler
[1966a] p 142 (the overtones of Newman which abound in this
note become explicit on p 144). On Newman's 'pragmatism',
see Ward, W. [1918a] pp 86–92.

43 Quoted *Dev* 1.2.8; notice the whole article, also *Dev* 2.2.3,
8.1.4. On Guizot's influence on Newman, see Kenny [1957]
p 92. For a similar analogy, see *Idea* pp 249–67.

44 Cf *SD* pp 218–36 ('The Christian Church an Imperial Power').

In 1871, Robertson Smith criticised this and the previous two sermons for claiming that the 'continuity of political existence is the necessary criterion of the identity of the promise and the people of the fulfilment' (Smith, W. R. [1912] p 279), and for anticipating 'a literal fulfilment in the present dispensation of the Old Testament hopes of theocratic glory' (*ibid* p 267). There is substance in this criticism although, as de Lubac has pointed out, these sermons were delivered 'against the pretense of a completely "spiritual" (that is to say, falsely spiritual) Christianity' (de Lubac [1969b] p 16). Cf also *L&D* xv pp 20, 58–9, 152–3; *VM* I pp 201, 202 (notes of 1877); Ward, W. [1912] II p 223.

45 On Newman's suspicion of democracy, see Kenny [1957]. However, in 1833, he wrote : 'I confess, Tory as I still am, theoretically and historically, I begin to be a Radical practically . . . I, of course, think that the most natural and becoming state of things is for the aristocratical power to be the upholder of the Church; yet I cannot deny the plain fact that in most ages the latter has been based on a popular power. It was so in its rise, in the days of Ambrose and in the days of Beckett, and it will be so again' (quoted Ward, M. [1948] p 225). In his early thinking about the Oratory, which he envisaged as 'in some sense . . . a return to the very first form of Christianity' (*OP* p 203), he wrote : 'I conceive that an Oratorian Congregation is in its external aspect a Democracy' (*OP* p 208). In December 1871, Newman wrote to Matthew Arnold : 'minute tokens . . . are showing themselves of the drawings of the Papal policy just now in the direction of democracy . . . it may be in the counsels of Providence that the Catholic Church may at length come out unexpectedly as a popular power' (quoted from De-Laura [1969] p 96).

46 'Its visible unity answers to the scriptural prophecy of a *kingdom*' (*L&D* XII p 336). See note 44 above. Coulson speaks of Newman's 'essentially *linguistic* conception of the Church as an institution' (Coulson [1970] p 206). But this is only half the story. Misner has shown how central to Newman's ecclesiology is 'the decisive idea . . . of the church as a kingdom, a single polity spread over the whole world' (Misner [1968] p 4; cf p 159). Moreover, in the move 'from the poetic anti-Romanism of the *Eve of St Bartholomew* to the full acceptance of the papacy in *Development* . . . the crucial point was the interpretation of Old Testament texts' concerning the kingdom, 'which were taken as prophecies of the Church' (*ibid* p 3).

47 For example, the reference to 'that intellectual action through

successive generations, which is the organ of development' (*Dev* 2.3.1). See *6.22*.

48 Even a preliminary restriction of the field of data to propositions admits of considerable variation in the range of the field, depending upon the emphasis placed upon scriptural, credal, conciliar or papal statements, the writings of theologians, and generalised expressions of the *sensus fidelium*. In modern times, the appeal to the *sensus fidelium* only seems to have been made as a last resort, when more favoured sources proved inadequate. (On the last point, one could consult the enormous volume of literature concerned with the dogmatic definition of the Assumption.)

49 Notice the range of the appeal in *Dev* 1.1.4–5. Also *Consulting* p 63; *VM* i p xxxvii. Mozley acknowledged the importance of this : see Mozley, J. B. [1847] pp 194–5.

50 On the inside front cover of the copy of *1845* which, in 1877, Newman used to prepare the revised version, he wrote : 'The argument seems to be this : Christianity is an objective fact, or supposed fact, and a very many sided multiform fertile productive fact.—Such extraordinary facts make a deep impression on the minds of those who come across them, which impression may be called the subjective idea of them—but from the vastness, richness etc. no individual mind more than partially embraces it, thus it makes a different impression or idea on different minds—the same indeed, but incomplete and therein different—also arranging differently and making different points the most important' (*BOA* D.7.6). Chadwick quoted this note, but for 'from the vastness, richness' he incorrectly read 'for the varying richness' (Chadwick [1957] p 245).

51 The references, in the *Essay*, to the 'Greeks', are casual and usually uncomplimentary : see *Dev* 4.1.10, 5.2.3, 5.7.3. As Mozley said of 'Mr Newman's line with respect to the Greek Church . . . His ordinary view supposes it not to exist' (Mozley, J. B. [1847] pp 204–5; cf Butler, W. A. [1850] pp 184–200; Middleton [1950] p 163).

CHAPTER FOUR

1 A detailed examination of the notion of the 'idea' in Newman's writings would entail discussion of a wide range of philosophical problems which lie outside the scope of this study. In general, so far as the sources of Newman's philosophy are concerned, we shall rely chiefly on Sillem [1969] pp 149–240. Boekraad [1961]

pp 14–31, Harrold [1940] and Pailin [1969] pp 87–92, are also useful. In particular, Coulson has demonstrated the 'remarkable . . . similarity between Newman's understanding of the term *idea* and its employment by Coleridge' (Coulson [1970] p 58). On Newman's philosophical method there is sharp divergence between the continental scholars (eg Boekraad [1955]; Boekraad [1961]; Walgrave [1957]) and some English philosophers (eg Cameron [1962]; Cameron [1967]; Coulson [1970]; Pailin [1969]). Sillem misunderstands the drift of Cameron's observations and excessively over-reacts to them : 'Newman . . . stood opposed to the whole tradition of British Empiricism' (Sillem [1969] p 193).

2 Although the *Essay* is a work of powerful originality, it is not surprising that Newman's concept of the 'idea' should have affinities with those employed by his contemporaries. We have already drawn attention to the similarity between Newman's notion and Coleridge's. Coulson's study of Coleridge and Newman ranges far wider than simply their notion of the 'idea' : he has persuasively argued that they share a common conception of religious language and, in many respects, of the church and its function in society : see Coulson [1970]; Davis [1945c]. Similarly, there are affinities between Newman's concept of the 'idea' and that implied in a passage such as the following, which Carlyle wrote in 1831 : 'Every Society, every Polity . . . is the embodiment, tentative and more or less complete, of an Idea' (quoted in Muirhead [1931] p 139). On Newman and Carlyle, see Cronin [1935] pp 23–4; Fletcher [1905]; Froude, J. A. [1883] pp 190–1; Tristram [1928] (the title of which was taken from Swinburne's poem on the two men).

3 Cf Chadwick [1957] p 149; Walgrave [1957] p 95. Guitton, exasperated, blames the vagueness and ambiguity of the English language : Guitton [1933] p 82; similarly, Nédoncelle [1946] p 229. The following passage, from a lecture of 1852, is both virtually a summary of *Dev* 1.1, and an indication of the impossibility of precisely defining Newman's terminology : 'An idea, a view, an invisible object, which does not admit of more or less, a form, which cannot coalesce with anything else, an intellectual principle, expanding into a consistent harmonious whole,—in short, Mind, in the true sense of the word' (*Campaign* p 250).

4 *Dev* 1.1.1; cf *US* p 207. A few lines earlier, the influence of the *Grammar* is detectable in the replacement of 'or fall under the general head of belief' (*1845* p 30) by 'or are prejudices, imaginations, or convictions'. Cf also the replacement of 'learn'

(*1845* p 30) by 'apprehend' (*Dev* 1.1.1), and 'seen' (*1845* p 32) by 'apprehended' (*Dev* 1.1.2).

5 *Dev* 1.1.4. It has been suggested (in Price [1969] pp 334–6) that Newman's analysis, in the *Grammar*, of the distinction between 'notional' and 'real' assent, in which the characteristic of the possible objects of real assent is their concrete particularity, makes it difficult to account for the 'passion for the theoretical' in, for example, the mathematician. It is therefore interesting to notice that, in *1878*, he modifies the statement that 'mathematical ideas, real as they are, cannot be called living' (*1845* p 35; cf *Dev* 1.1.4).

6 Cf *Apo* p 288; *DA* p 294; *GA* p 413. In *1878* Newman replaced the phrase : christianity 'is solemn, and it is cheerful' (*1845* p 35) by : 'it is esoteric and exoteric' (*Dev* 1.1.3; cf *VM* I p lii). This terminology, which occurs elsewhere in the *Essay*, in a quotation from Dewar (*Dev* 5.6.3; *1845* p 89), evokes the tractarian doctrine of 'economy'. Thus, the 'apologetic . . . function of the Alexandrian Church' is held to account for the fact that 'the writings of its theologians would partake largely of an exoteric character'; that is to say, they are marked by that 'reserve with which we are accustomed to address those who do not sympathise with us' (*Ari* p 42; Palmer, in his critique of the *Essay*, warned of the danger of 'insincerity' when the distinction 'between exoteric and esoteric doctrines' is, in practice, pressed too far : see Palmer [1846] p 38). As a result, unfortunately, 'their exoteric professions at times affected the purity of their esoteric doctrines' (*Ari* p 96). Underlying the distinction is Newman's conviction that only 'notional', not 'real' apprehensions are communicable : 'Hence it is that an intellectual school will always have something of an esoteric character; for it is an assemblage of minds that think' (*GA* p 309; cf *PN* pp 27, 89).

7 To define an 'aspect' simply in terms of the object of which it is an aspect, and to omit any reference to the 'observer' (as we might be inclined to do in contemporary English usage) would not do justice to Newman's usage, in which there are strong overtones of the term's etymological origins. Perhaps we can say that, for Newman, the notion of an 'aspect' includes a noetic, and not merely a noematic component.

8 *Dev* 1.1.5 The phrase 'under their various aspects' is an addition in *1878* : cf *1845* p 37. The seeds were sown in Butler's *Analogy* : 'Length of time, then, proper scope and opportunities, for reason to exert itself, may be absolutely necessary to its prevailing over brute force' (Butler, J. [1896] I p 82; cf p 84).

9   In 1871, he said that 'the doctrine may rather be said to use the minds of Christians, than to be used by them' (*US* p 317). The previous edition was less explicit : 'the doctrine may rather be said to employ the minds of Christians than to occupy them' (Newman [1844] p 316).

10 The passage is worth quoting in full : 'it would be absurd to suppose that the first and divinely assisted teachers of a divine revelation would not have at least as full a view of it as the unassisted mind of man could enjoy, that is to say, at least as full a view as any future disciples could hope to attain. If then the doctrines of Christianity were clearly laid down at its commencement, and if we have any reason to suppose that they were afterwards sullied and polluted by human inventions, there would seem to be only one method of ascertaining the justice of our suspicions, and of attempting the restoration of the doctrines to their native and genuine form. If the stream has contracted impurities in its course, we must recur to the fountain head for pure and unsullied water. We must recur for truth and light, first to Scripture, and then if difficulties or doubts occur as to its interpretation, to those Christian writers who lived at the outset of the Christian system' (Rose [1825] p 27).

11 See 5.2. In 1837 he had described the Roman view of 'tradition' : 'It is latent, but it lives. It is silent, like the rapids of a river, before the rocks intercept it' (*VM* I p 32).

12 *Dev* 1.1.4 : in *1845*, 'only the adequate representation of the original idea . . . its exact image' (pp 36–7). The notion of 'representation' in *Dev* 1.1 is ambiguous. In *Dev* 1.1.4, as in *Dev* 1.1.3, it refers to the relationship between language and the reality it attempts to express; in *Dev* 1.1.2, it refers rather to the relationship between the 'idea' and the 'object'.

13 *Dev* 2.3.5; in *1845*, for 'he would take to be his own' read 'they would mistake for their own' (p 138). Cf *Diff* I pp 364, 367–8, 395–6; *Diff* II p 198; *Ess* II p 9; *HS* I p 402; *KC* p 219; *L&D* XI p 110; XII p 332; XIII pp 78, 295; XIV pp 351, 378; XV p 42; XX p 55; *LG* p 365; *SD* p 393; *VM* II p 392.

14 CUL *Add* MSS 5463. In similar mood, Acton reflected on the closing paragraph of the *Essay*'s Introduction : 'He tested his development on few topics, leaving the rest, as he said, to those who have time. This was his view—he said—and it seemed to him defensible. Whether it was also true, was a question for specialists. Therefore it was no more than a hypothesis—and therefore Newman never conducted you further than the threshold (CUL *Add* MSS 4987.14).

15   Mozley, J. B. [1847] p 265. Mozley continued : 'He professes a theory, but admits, as circumstances require, into it, things which contradict it, and things which it does not account for. He has a theory on paper and none in fact : he begins with philosophical simplicity, and ends in arbitrary mixture'. Mozley's verdict of confusion is, in fact, less an indictment of the *Essay* than a witness to the methodological gulf which separates him from Newman.

16   More generally, 'Victorian thought was dominated by the idea of history as a sequence of events in time . . . This temporal, historical, linear habit of thought was on the whole shared by optimists and pessimists alike : it was common to religious thinkers and scientists, used by Newman in his *Development of Christian Doctrine* and by Jowett interpreting the Bible, as much as by Huxley defending Darwin' (House [1966a] pp 71–2).

17   Cf *Apo* pp 208–9, 244; *Consulting* p 63; *DA* pp 239–42; *Diff* I pp 216, 276; *Jfc* pp 315–6; *PS* v p 14; vi p 263; *SD* p 115; *US* pp 17, 23–7.

18   See *4.1.* Hence the contrast between the 'unreality' of the 'Via Media' and the 'reality' of Roman catholicism, as he had now come to view it : cf *Dev* 2.3.4; *Apo* pp 68–72; *Diff* I pp 5, 38; *GA* p 57; *VM* I p 16.

19   Cf *Ari* p 221; *Campaign* p 253; *Consulting* p 61; *Ess* I p 47; *Jfc* p 314; *PS* vii p 190. For the inadequacy cf *Apo* p 27; *Ari* p 145 (on the 'antirationalisme' of *Arians*, see Stern [1967] p 95); *BOA* 30.11 (quoted in Pailin [1969] p 84); *US* pp 84–5 (on which, see Cameron [1962] p 205). In 1859, discussing the introduction of the term 'person' into Trinitarian theology, he noted : 'We knew, eg before we used it, that the Son was God yet was not the Father but differing in sonship from Him; the word Person tells us nothing in addition to this. It is only the symbol of the mystery; the symbol, that is, of our ignorance' (*PN* p 105; cf *L&D* xix p 533). The same apophatic tendency is present in the last essay that Newman wrote : 'nor is punishment *therefore* infinite, because it is without end. What we know about the eternal state is negative, that there is no future when it will not be' (*SE* p 85).

20   Newman never fully reconciled the tension between the historian's recognition that doctrinal formulas were, to some extent, 'arbitrary' (*Ari* p 181; cf *TT* pp 336–9), and the theologian's claim that they were, quite simply, true.

21   Artz credits Newman with introducing the *concept* of *Geschichtlichkeit* into catholic theology independently of the

Tübingen school : Artz [1968], p 193. So far as the *term* is concerned, there is no exact English equivalent : see *1*, note 1.

22 See *7*. Thus de Grandmaison : 'le virus de l'hégélianisme est éliminé de la notion d'évolution adoptée par Newman' (de Grandmaison [1907] p 474). For a good study of Newman and Hegel, see Brunner [1957].

23 In 1858, Newman distinguished 'Science', which expresses 'not mere thoughts, but things', from 'literature', which 'expresses, not objective truth, as it is called, but subjective; not things, but thoughts' (*Idea* p 274). Thus, later in the same lecture : 'the beginning of St John's Gospel' and 'the Creed' are said to be 'of the nature of Science . . . passages such as these are the mere enunciation of eternal things, without (so to say) the medium of any human mind transmitting them . . . they are in no sense Literature . . . and therefore they are easy to apprehend, and easy to translate' (*Idea* p 290). This attempt to safeguard the objectivity of revealed truth by immunising certain propositions from cultural relativity is the trace of a view of scripture which he held, as an evangelical, as early as 1820 (cf *AW* p 163), and which anticipates certain features of the distinction between 'notional' and 'real assent' in the *Grammar* : cf *GA* pp 75, 98, 124–7. The same approach to 'objectivity' is apparent in *Tract 73* : cf *Ess* i pp 34–5, 40–1; also *DA* p 233. See Stern [1967] p 38; *4.31*; *4.32*; *5.2*; *6.21*.

24 Cf *Ath* ii pp 94, 146, 161–72, 293–303; *Ess* i pp 74, 87; *L&D* xi pp 135, 240; xiii p 3; xv pp 56–8; *PS* iii p 129. As Brilioth observed, in the 'zeal for maintaining the complete Divinity in Newman and Pusey', there is 'concealed a kind of refined Docetism' (Brilioth [1925] p 223).

25 'The term "evolution" is sometimes used to describe any form of orderly change . . . The term "development" is, of course, much older than that of evolution and independent of it. Development is a process whereby that which exists "potentially" becomes actual . . . Neither development nor evolution is the same as progress. Progress is development or evolution in a direction which satisfies rational criteria of value' (Ginsberg [1968] pp 100–1). Newman's concept of 'development' is wider than that indicated by Ginsberg : it is as broad as the latter's notion of 'evolution'.

26 Chadwick [1957] p 97. 'Newman's view of history was apocalyptic . . . he did not view it as a linear forward movement towards light and truth' (Willey [1969] p 95). Guitton, who refers to Hegel's thought as 'ce *totalitarisme* historique . . . d'un progrès nécessaire' (Guitton [1957] p 93), observes that 'Newman

n'a jamais parlé de Hegel, ni de Spencer, ni du *devenir* hégélien, ni de l'*évolution* spencérienne. Mais, s'il avait connu le *devenir* et l'*évolution*, il les aurait rejetés également' (*ibid* p 90); cf *6.1*. It was a similarly 'progressive' concept of evolution that Fairbairn had in mind when he said that the thesis of the *Essay*, 'far from being the equivalent of evolution, is its antithesis and contradiction' (Fairbairn [1899] p 303).

27 In his anglican writings, the corollary of the insistence that faith is safeguarded by loving obedience (cf *DA* p 201; *PS* II p 153; III p 81; VIII p 107; *US* pp 61, 80–1, 225, 250) is the recognition that there is a wisdom, or 'instinctive moral perception which the practice of virtue ensures' (*Ari* p 110). Cf Chadwick [1960] pp 35–6. This correlation between growth in truth and growth in virtue appears, in a different form, in the 'Tamworth Reading-Room' (*DA* pp 254–305). Newman was, of course, by no means opposed to the spread of scientific education, but the expectations of some of its proponents seemed to him ridiculous : 'to have recourse to physics to *make* men religious is like recommending a canonry as a cure for the gout' (*DA* p 299). In our own day, Ginsberg has said that : 'modern psychological theories . . . expose the *naïveté* of the assumption which earlier theories had taken for granted that intellectual advance will be necessarily reflected in improved human relations' (Ginsberg [1968] pp 72–3).

28 'if developments of additional truth were vouchsafed as the Church grew older, it would be at once a proof of her increased holiness and purity . . . and men that lived since the times of the Tridentine Council might, nay must, be holier than the saints from Augustine to Bernard . . . which we saw that our author denied in another place' (*Quondam* [1846] p 19).

29 'It has been much the fashion at various times, to speak as if Christianity was becoming better and better understood as time went on, and its professors more enlightened and more virtuous . . . [today some] assume it as an axiom in all their reasonings . . . that the nineteenth century (ie *because* the nineteenth) is superior to the first and second' (Newman [1836c] p 216). That was in 1836. In the following year : 'Century after century the Church Catholic has become more and more disunited, discordant, and corrupt' (*VM* I p 209; cf pp 354–5). In 1849 : 'how *weary* the angels must get of the *history* of the world' (*SN* p 9). In 1874, cf *SN* pp 252–3. Cf *Idea* p 73; *PS* I pp 85, 136; II p 82; IV pp 154–6; VI p 239; VII pp 247–8; *SD* p 71; *US* pp 40, 97, 102.

30 'What he felt deeply was the power of error and sin, the failure

of the Church. Believes that truth prevails, but slowly, because man is corrupt . . . Therefore intellect advances and morality stands still' (Acton, CUL *Add* MSS 4987.8). Cf *DA* p 299, 304; *GA* p 416; *Idea* pp 120–1; *PS* I p 85; VII pp 245–6; *US* pp 55, 58–9.

31   The antidote to rationalising tendencies is 'realisation' (see *4.12*). However, in Newman's early catholic writings, the attempt to adapt his thought to that of the Roman schools led him to employ a static, intellectualist notion of faith from the standpoint of which even 'realisation' seems to be a merely epistemological achievement not necessarily entailing an enhanced 'religious' or moral sensitivity : cf eg *Diff* I pp 269, 276.

32   *Dev* 2.2.3; cf 4.3.1–7. Or, more depressingly : 'Such is the history of society : it begins in the poet, and ends in the policeman' (*HS* III p 77). Such passages echo the mood of *Arians*, described by Wilfrid Ward : 'He regarded the crystallisation of portions of the early creed into definite *formulae* as a protection gradually called for—much as in a civil polity laws are passed to prevent infringements on the rules necessary for social life' (Ward, W. [1912] I p 48).

33   In the years following the modernist crisis, the appeal to 'homogeneity' was defensive : the adversary was a 'hegelian' model of historical process, understood to be 'transformist' in the sense that it allowed the possibility that christian doctrine should have undergone a *metabasis eis allo genos*, under the influence of 'heterogeneous' elements. This is the force of de Grandmaison's claim that 'le virus de l'hégélianisme est éliminé de la notion d'évolution adoptée par Newman' (de Grandmaison [1907] p747). According to Loisy, Harnack had maintained that 'le fait ecclésiastique est comme étranger, hétérogène, adventice au fait évangélique', whereas he himself 'a vouloue montrer que les deux faits sont connexes, homogènes, intimement liés, ou plutôt qu'ils sont le même fait dans son unité durable' (Loisy [1903] p 12).

The assumption that 'Once the dogma has evolved, the task theology has [is that] of showing its homogeneity with the deposit' (Pozo [1968] p 101), is expressed, in one form or another, in : Congar [1968] p 56; Dhanis [1953] p 197; Dupuy [1970] p 23; Rahner [1961] p 41; Schutz [1968] p 35. Other studies, which show an awareness that the problematic which generated theories of 'homogeneous evolution' has been, or is in urgent need of being, transcended, include : Congar [1970d] p 611; Jossua [1968]; Rahner [1969c]. Leuba, however, has pointed out that, so far as official church pronouncements are concerned, neither the Montreal *Faith and Order* conference of 1963, nor the constitution *Dei Verbum* of Vatican II, has answered the question : 'Comment ainsi la tradition apostolique n'est-elle pas engagée dans une évolution noétique dont rien n'assure qu'elle ne soit pas une *metabasis eis allo genos?*' (Leuba [1968] p 488). See Lash [1971d].

34   Marin-Sola [1924]. He explicitly offered the concept of 'évolution homogène' in contrast to 'évolution . . . transformiste', which he understood to be the heart of modernist thinking (*ibid* I p 1) : 'Ainsi donc la conservation ou la non-conservation de la *même nature* spécifique constitue le trait distinctif entre l'évolution homogène et l'évolution transformiste dans les êtres matériels' (*ibid* I p 21).

35   In 1903, Loisy claimed that during the previous few years, 'il choisit pour guide le Cardinal Newman, et reprit son idée du développement chrétien, pour l'opposer aux systèmes de MM. Harnack et A. Sabatier' (Loisy [1903] p 7). There is irony, however, in the fact, that as we saw in note 33, Loisy's own intention was to argue for the homogeneity of doctrinal history. This intention is reaffirmed in the form taken by one of the echoes of Newman's *Essay* in *L'Evangile et l'Eglise* : 'L'enseignement et l'apparition même de Jésus ont dû être interprétés. Toute la question est de savoir si le commentaire est homogène ou hétérogène au texte' (Loisy [1902] p 128; see *5.11*).

36   'The new truth which is promulgated, if it is to be called new, must be at least homogeneous, cognate, implicit, viewed relatively to the old truth' (*Apo* p 253); 'every department of thought has its own principles, homogeneous with itself, and necessary for reasoning justly in it' (*US* p 54; a note of 1871). I have not found any use of the term, by Newman, before 1864 (it occurs in the 1881 version of 'Apostolical Tradition' [see *Ess* I p 129], but not in the original version of 1836 : cf Newman [1836b] p 193). In 1862, in a letter to Acton, he appealed to Vincent of Lerins, who 'says it is a false development "si humana species in aliquam deinceps *non sui generis* vertatur effigiem" ' (*L&D* xx p 231, Newman's stress).

Newman did use the term 'heterogeneous' as early as 1832 : cf *US* p 78; *Ari* p 147; *Diff* I p 35. Coleridge's use of the two terms has some similarities with Newman's early use of 'heterogeneous' : see Coleridge [1848] pp 43, 67–8; also Wiseman [1839] p 160. Spencer's conception of 'progress' as 'an advance from homogeneity of structure to heterogeneity of structure' (Spencer [1966] p 154), in which he was partly influenced by Coleridge (Duncan [1908] p 541), represents a line of thought completely different from that which found expression in the use made of the terms in later catholic theology; nor does there seem to be any evidence that Newman knew, or was influenced by, Spencer's terminology.

37   The term 'heterogeneous' did occur in *1845* : 'throwing off from itself what is utterly heterogeneous in them' (p 37); cf *Dev* 1.1.5 : 'whatever in them it cannot assimilate'. When preparing the revision, Newman pencilled against the passage on *1845* p 154, which was to become the second part of *Dev* 2.3.2 : 'They are just what developments wd be—not heterogeneous but of one family' (*BOA* D.7.6).

38   *Dev* 7.6.2. This is almost the reverse of the argument which, in 1834, he put in the mouth of a tractarian clergyman : 'Can you point to any period of Church history, during which doctrine remained for any time uncorrupted?' (*VM* II p 23).

39   According to Moeller, up to Trent and, to some extent, even to our own day, 'la "théologie positive" a travaillé selon les cadres d'une psychologie qu'on a fort justement nommé "psychologie du cylindre". . . à quelque moment que l'on fasse "une coupe" dans ce cylindre "homogène", on retrouverait, de manière quasi explicite, la même "quantité" de vérités' (Moeller [1952] p 352).

40   *Dev* Int 21; 1.1.7 ('and expanded' has been added : cf *1845* p 38); 2.1.1 (where *1845* has 'develope' instead of 'expand' p 94); 2.1.9; 5.3.1.

41   *Dev* 2.3.1. (an addition in *1878*); 3.1.7; 5.1.1 (where the quotation from Vincent of Lerins is significantly extended : cf *1845* p 58); 5.7.1; 6.0.1 (where the relevant second paragraph is new material in *1878* : cf *1845* p 204). Cf *Ess* I pp 285, 288; *SD* p 259. In 1835, Froude pertinently asked : 'You lug in the Apostles' Creed and talk about expansions. What is the end of expansions? Will not the Romanists say that their whole system is an expansion of the Holy Catholic Church and the Communion of Saints?' (*Moz* II p 127).

42   Or 'a circle ever enlarging' (*DA* p 49); cf the image of the 'telescope or magnifier' in *Apo* p 196.

43   *Dev* 5.1.1, quoting Vincent of Lerins. The *Commonitorium* is quoted again in *Dev* 11.0.1. Notice also the use of terms such as 'age', 'youth', 'maturity', in *Dev* 6.0.1; 7.0.1. Stephenson rightly objects to Newman's use of Vincent in *Dev* 11.0.1. But his generalisation that 'The role in [the *Commonitorium*] of the biological metaphors and analogies seems to be the opposite of their role in the *Essay*' ([1966] p 476) goes too far. In *Dev* 5.1.1, Newman cannot even be accused of originality : the phrases he there quotes from Vincent were used, in the same

sense, by Albert Pigge in 1538. (For the use of organic analogies, inspired by Vincent, by Pigge and other Catholic controversialists of the sixteenth century, see Tavard [1959] pp 149, 234). Cf *Ess* II pp 43–4; *PS* VI p 98; *VM* I pp 82, 224; Ward, W. [1912] I pp 639–40.

44 *Dev* 6.3.3.23, quoting *Apo* p 196. Cf *Dev* 5.2.1; 5.7.1; *US* p 317. On the eucharist, cf *PS* VI p 141. On the Virgin : cf *Diff* I p 395; II p 26 (where, as in *L&D* XVI p 341, he allows an increase in 'devotion towards the Blessed Virgin', but not a 'growth' in 'doctrine').

45 Gore [1926b] p 835. In fact, Mozley exaggerated. It is not true that Newman's definition of corruption 'simply omits the whole notion of corruption by excess' (Mozley [1847] p 139) : cf *Dev* 5.6.1.

46 Thus, for example, Congar observes that, so far as ecclesiology is concerned, in the seventeenth century, 'Le *De Ecclesia* a été ainsi attiré dans le contexte de l'autorité du magistère . . . [that] On a par le fait même, risqué de négliger les aspects sacramentels, l'insertion de l'Eglise dans un plan de grâce englobant toute l'Histoire humaine et même l'eschatologie' (Congar [1970c] p 379). More generally, it may have been customary to consider doctrinal development 'as a kind of *expansion* of elements that were entrusted to the Church from the beginning . . . But "development" can take another form which has generally been overlooked. Instead of being an expansion, the fructifying of a scriptural plant, it can on the contrary be the *pruning* of some too vigorous growth' (Bévenot [1968] p 407).

47 *Apo* p 196; cf *Dev* 1.1.4; *US* pp 316–7. Notice the claim that, in Bellarmine, 'we find the whole series of doctrines carefully drawn out . . . and exactly analysed one by one' (*Dev* 5.4.3). The acknowledgement, in principle, of the importance of the concept of 'harmony' is common, not only to Newman and Mozley, but also to Milman ([1846] p 455) and W. G. Ward ([1844] p 268).

48 *Dev* 3.2.12. After Vatican I, he explicitly rejects the possibility of 'reversal', preferring to speak of the need for 'explanation' or 'completion' : cf *Diff* II p 307; *L&D* XXV pp 310, 322, 330.

49 'What the Catholic Church once has had, she never has lost. She has never wept over, or been angry with, time gone and over' (*HS* II p 368). So rhetorical a passage should not, perhaps, be taken too literally, but it does invite Inge's reply to Emerson. The latter had claimed that 'One accent of the Holy Ghost The careless world has never lost'; Inge retorted : 'I should like to know how Emerson obtained this information' ([1922] p 181).

50   *Dev* 5.6.2; cf 11.0.1. Cf *GA* pp 247, 251, 395–6; *L&D* xi p 191;
     xiv p 46. In 1879 he wrote : 'I had begun the movement with
     vague incomplete views, which cleared as I went on, but were
     not definite and consistent till I joined the Catholic Church'
     (Newman [1879] p xvi).

51   Chadwick [1957] p 143. In 1871, Newman wrote : 'Certainly we
     all hold the "Quod semper, quod ubique", etc, as much as we
     ever did, as much as Anglicans do' (*L&D* xxv p 298).

52   Compare the remarks on Mediterranean civilisation in *Idea*
     p 253. In 1842, Newman went so far as to say that 'externals
     cannot destroy identity, if it exists, which is something inward'
     (*SD* p 190; cf *US* p 303). He illustrated this with the analogy
     (taken from Butler : see Butler, J. [1896] i p 21) of 'worms of
     the earth [that] at length gain wings, yet are the same' (*SD*
     p 191), which reappears in a letter to Mivart in 1873 (quoted
     in de Achaval [1964] p 246) and, in a slightly different form, in
     Dev 5.1.4.

53   'from the very time of the Apostles, in every successive age,
     there had been in the teaching of the Church, a prima facie ap-
     pearance (though, for my part, I did not believe it to be more
     than an appearance), of a change or accession of doctrine . . .
     I could have written its subject on its title page, viz "The diff-
     erences and additions in doctrinal teaching observable in the
     history of the Church are but apparent, being the necessary
     phenomena incident to deep intellectual ideas" ' (*L&D* xv pp
     372, 374).

54   Walgrave's psychological and philosophical preoccupations led
     him to overestimate the extent to which the field of data which
     Newman regards as relevant to a study of the history of an 'idea'
     can be subsumed under the category of 'social psychology'. Some
     years earlier, in an influential article, Simonin had described
     the standpoint of the *Essay* as 'à la fois psychologique et apolo-
     gétique' (Simonin [1937] p 129).

55   Davis [1967a] p 186. Nevertheless, while organic analogies play
     a large part in the first (for discussion of *Dev* 5.1.1, see *4.3*),
     third and seventh notes, they do so only to break down in the
     sixth (see below), and are almost entirely absent from the sec-
     ond, fourth (except in *Dev* 5.4.1) and fifth. Guitton may be
     correct in suggesting that Newman's selection of *seven* 'notes'
     was influenced by Whately's list of seven marks of corruption
     in the Roman catholic church (cf Whately [1830] pp 10–11;
     Guitton [1933] pp 93–4) but, in so far as the latter's letter of
     1825 is concerned, Guitton misleads by reducing Whately's list
     of eight classes of error to seven : cf *Moz* i p 100.

56 '. . . the whole natural world and government of it is a scheme or system; not a fixed, but a progressive one : a scheme, in which the operation of various means takes up a great length of time, before the ends they tend to can be attained . . . the very history of a flower, is an instance of this : and so is human life. Thus vegetable bodies, and those of animals, though possibly formed at once, yet grow up by degrees to a mature state . . . Thus, in the daily course of natural providence, God operates in the very same manner, as in the dispensation of Christianity' (Butler, J. [1896] I p 251). The analogy of plant growth was the theme of a sermon which Wiseman preached in 1839, of which Wilfrid Ward said, not without exaggeration, that it was 'a close anticipation of the main argument of Newman's *Essay*' (Ward, W. [1897] I p 314). Vidler accepted Ward's judgement without qualification : cf Vidler [1934] p 57.

57 'The life of a plant is not the same as the life of an animated being, and the life of the body is not the same as the life of the intellect; nor is the life of the intellect the same in kind as the life of grace; nor is the life of the Church the same as the life of the State' (*Diff* I p 44).

58 See *4.1*. The passages in which the concept of 'growth' occurs should be read with this in mind : eg *Dev* Int 20; 1.1.4–7; 2.1.3; 2.1.9; 2.1.16; 2.3.1; 4.3.8; 5.0.2–4; 5.1.1; 5.3.1–2; 5.3.5; 5.4.1; 5.6.1; 5.7.1–3; 8.1.3; 11.0.1; 12.1–2; 12.8–9. The characteristic claim, in 1875, that 'a growth in its creed is a law of its life' (*Diff* II p 356) is in striking contrast to the peremptory affirmation, in 1851, that 'The Catholic Church has never grown' (*SN* p 86).

59 *SD* pp 308–80. On these sermons, see *Apo* pp 152–5; *Diff* I pp 73–8; *KC* pp 246–7; *L&D* XI p 101; XIII p 296; *OS* p 47; Stern [1967] p 165.

60 *PS* IV p 170. Cf *DA* p 379; *Ess* I pp 162, 333; *GA* p 464; *Jfc* pp 53, 198; *PS* II p 288; IV pp 173, 175, 315; V pp 41, 93; VII pp 208–9; *US* pp 28–9, 88, 291; *VM* II p 54. On the 'idea' as 'form', see *Diff* I p 101, quoted in Walgrave [1957] pp 171–2.

61 Thus 'the Truth, to which they were to bear witness, . . . a something definite, and formal, and independent of themselves' (*Dev* 7.5.3), is later said to be 'Grace, and . . . Truth' (*Dev* 8.0.2). In a famous passage, written in 1838, Newman contrasted the 'Anglican' view of revealed truth, 'entirely objective and detached' (the image is that of a Calvary, with the church represented by the figures of Mary and John), with the 'Roman' view of that truth as being 'hid in the bosom of the Church as if one with her' (the image is that of a Madonna and child : *Ess*

ɪ pp 209–10; cf *Apo* p 112; *Diff* ɪ p 394; Stern [1967] p 141). The charge against the Roman church was that it acted with a spontaneity in doctrinal matters which, while proper in the early church, is dangerous at a time when the church has lost that original innocence, to which Newman looked back with nostalgia : 'when confessions do not exist, the mysteries of divine truth, instead of being exposed to the gaze of the profane and uninstructed, are kept hidden in the bosom of the church, far more faithfully than is otherwise possible' (*Ari* p 37). It is clear from the *Essay* that Williams was wrong to assume that Newman eventually abandoned his 'Anglican' for his 'Roman' view (cf Williams, W. J. [1906] pp 95–6). There is undoubtedly a shift in emphasis, corresponding to Newman's changing views on the theology of tradition (see *6.21*), but he constantly attempted to synthesise the two and, even as early as 1834, later articles of faith are said to be 'hidden . . . in the Church's bosom from the first' (*VM* ɪɪ p 40; contrast *DA* p 233; *Ess* ɪ pp 69–70).

62   *Jfc* p 189; the passage goes on immediately to speak of the 'Living Presence' of Christ. Cf *SD* p 101. In *1878*, the 'order of succession' in the 'separate stages' of the development of an idea is said to be 'variable' (*Dev* 1.1.6); in *1845* it was said to be 'irregular' (p 38).

63   Cf *PS* ɪᴠ p 337 ('rose again vigorously . . . having loosed the pains of death'; cf 'recurrence to the former state of vigour', *Dev* 12.9; *1845* had 'recurrence to such a state', p 452); *PS* ᴠ p 124; *US* p 317. In *Dev* 12.9, the explicit analogy is that of waking from sleep, another image of the resurrection which Newman uses elsewhere : cf *Ess* ɪɪ p 53; *L&D* xɪᴠ p 141 (defending the language used in the sermon in *OS*); *OS* p 137; *PS* ɪᴠ p 321 (notice the juxtaposition of 'awake out of sleep', Rom 3 : 11, and 'be strong', 1 Cor 16 : 13).

64   The passage covers sections 19–29 (*US* pp 329–37); *1845* quoted the whole of sections 20–23 (*US* pp 329–32; *1845*, pp 54–7), whereas *1878* omitted some of this material, notably 'the strong passage . . . about the propositions being inadequate to the idea' (Chadwick [1957] p 248).

65   *US* p 333. Cf *DA* pp 241–2; *Ess* ɪ p 182; *GA* p 98 (but notice the awkward passage in which he denies that it is possible to give real assent to the mystery of the Trinity 'when it is viewed, *per modum unius*, as one whole', *GA* p 129; cf pp 122–41); *VM* ɪ p 116.

66   There is no 1877 disclaimer to the passage in the *Via Media* which affirms that 'A Romanist then cannot really argue in defence of the Roman doctrines; he has too firm a confidence

in their truth . . . to adjust the due weight to be given to this or that evidence' (*VM* I pp 68–9). This passage was quoted in that part of the section on 'Parallel Instances' which was omitted in *1878* (cf *1845* p 186; *3.11*; Chadwick [1957] pp 145–7).

67 'three centuries and more were necessary for the infant Church to attain her mature and perfect form, and due stature' (*DA* p 24). Cf *Ari* p 55; *GA* p 144; *TT* p 335; *6.21*.

68 The Oxford Movement, 'though dogmatic, was not dogmatic simply because it possessed or shared a particular theory of dogma. It always saw dogma in relation to worship, to the numinous, to the movement of the heart . . . so that without this attention to worship or the moral need, dogma could not be apprehended rightly' (Chadwick [1960] p 11). Cf *Ari* p 146; *Campaign* p 253; *GA* p 121; *Jfc* pp 314–16; *PS* II p 29.

CHAPTER FIVE

1 As with so many features of Newman's method, this one has suffered from being developed in isolation from those other principles which, in his hands, check and balance it. In reaction against Loisy's 'historicism' and Harnack's reductionism, Gardeil appealed to the *Essay* (Gardeil [1903c] p 446) in elaborating his eccentrically systematic 'méthode régressive' (Gardeil [1903a]).

2 If 'it is from the tradition that we receive the necessary prior understanding, then only as the matter of the text has had time to work in the tradition can we approach that text with an appropriate prior understanding' (Jenson [1969] p 182). Cf Bloch [1954] pp 39–47, esp p 45.

3 'Luther has taken on himself to explain St Augustine . . . without persuading the world that [he has] a claim to do so' (*Dev* 3.1.3). In 1866, this restriction of the boundaries of the 'world' is made explicit : 'Of course we must define the orbis terrarum. I mean by it that rounded, circumscribed definitely distinct body, which has one polity, one organisation, one government, one administration' (*BOA* B.7.4, quoted from Biemer [1967] p 107).

4 Hawkins insisted that his argument 'claims *no independent authority* for the traditions conveyed to us by the Church' (Hawkins [1819] p 20; cf Sheridan [1967] p 79); hence the title of his address : 'A Dissertation upon the use and importance

of unauthoritative Tradition'. In his *Bampton Lectures*, he charged the tractarians with 'an indiscreet endeavour to bring into one and the same definition both the Test of sound doctrine, which is Holy Scripture, and one of the Means of ascertaining the true sense of Scripture' (Hawkins [1840] pp 29–30).

5   Hawkins [1819] p 11, quoted—except for the final clause—in Stern [1967] p 63. Cf *Apo* p 9; *Ari* p 50; Biemer [1967] p 37. For the general problem of Newman's view of scripture, see Seynaeve [1953]; the weakest features of Seynaeve's study have been pointed out in Holmes [1967b] pp 3, 18–19, and uncritically adopted in Burtchaell [1969] p 79. Stern [1967] is excellent on the historical development of Newman's views on scripture and tradition before 1845 (especially on Newman's relationships with Hawkins, pp 58–66, and Jager, pp 111–36; on the latter, see Tristram [1945c] and Stern [1964]). Biemer [1967] is useful on the general question, though he tends to smooth out the difficulties, and to overstress the continuity in Newman's thought.

6   Even this tone of voice he had inherited from Hawkins : 'how is [scripture] complete for *teaching*, when daily experience shows the frequent need of other aid . . . [and] that for teaching the faith it scarcely is sufficient' (Hawkins [1819] p 33).

7   Cf *DA* p 133; *Ess* I pp 112, 120–1. In 1877, he conceded that the debate as to whether 'Scripture, or Scripture and Tradition is the record and rule of faith . . . is, as between Catholics and Anglicans, of a verbal character' (*VM* I p 288, where he quotes *Diff* II pp 12–3). According to Chadwick, 'an appeal to the Fathers as interpreters of Scripture' was 'fundamental to the mind of the Oxford Movement' (Chadwick [1960] p 18).

8   Biemer [1967] p 162. This was 'a view for which he found abundant confirmation in the Fathers' (Biemer [1967] p 161). In *1845* he regarded Palmer's opinion 'that it is not determined by the Council of Trent, whether the whole of the Revelation is in Scripture or not' as 'untenable' (*1845* p 320; cf *Prepos* p 317). In *1878* the qualifying sentence : 'Though this position be untenable, at least it is a remarkable testimony on the part of the opponents to the Church's reverence for the written word' was omitted (cf *Dev* 7.4.2; *GA* pp 379–80).

9   Nevertheless, a passage in which he described the differences between patristic and modern uses of scripture has won the approval of Congar and de Lubac : cf *Ess* I p 286; Congar [1966] p 81; de Lubac [1969b] p 66. Seynaeve, however, admits that, 'historically speaking, we cannot help thinking that Newman, during his Anglican period and for several years even

during his Catholic career, was inclined to overestimate the prominence of the mystical interpretation in patristic and later times' (Seynaeve [1953] p 320).

10   Cf *Dev* 9.4.7. In 1837, Newman argued that some reason had to be found for the 'universal and apparently Apostolical custom of praying for the dead', and that the 'distressing doctrine' of Purgatory was invented, as an interpretation of certain obscure biblical texts, to meet this need (*VM* i p 180). This, and the previous paragraph, were incorporated into *1845* (p 421) and dropped from *1878* (cf *Dev* 9.4.6; *VM* i p 179). In 1837, Newman went on to suggest that 'there was no definite Catholic Tradition for Purgatory in early times, and that, instead of it, certain texts of Scripture, in the first instance interpreted by individuals, were put forward as the proof of the doctrine' (*VM* i p 180). This paragraph was never taken into the *Essay*. The two interpretations of the same evidence are not mutually incompatible, but they neatly illustrate the shift in perspective between the *Via Media* and the *Essay*.

11   Cf the quotation from à Lapide in *Dev* 7.4.4. A similar passage, *Dev* 2.1.4, contains an important hint of the severe limitations imposed upon theological deductions from scripture by the paradoxical status of the 'premise'; but the hint is not followed up. See *3.12*.

12   *Dev* 7.4.1. In *1845* Newman claimed that, 'on turning to primitive controversy, we find this method of interpretation to be the very basis of proof of the Catholic doctrine of the Holy Trinity' (pp 323–4). In 1871, when he constructed an Appendix to *Arians*, on 'The Syrian School of Theology', out of materials from the *Essay*, he altered this to 'In the early centuries we find this method of interpretation to be the very ground for receiving as revealed the doctrine of the Holy Trinity' (*Ari* p 404). The significance of the change is unclear, and it was not incorporated into *1878*.

13   'Theodore was bent on ascertaining the literal sense, an object with which no fault could be found' (*Dev* 6.3.2.4); he is gentle with the early Antiochenes : what higher praise could there be for Theodoret than that he 'abounds in modes of thinking and reasoning which without any great impropriety may be called English' (*Dev* 6.3.2.3)!

14   '. . . though allegory can be made an instrument for evading Scripture doctrine, criticism may more readily be turned to the destruction of doctrine and Scripture together' (*Dev* 6.3.2.4). The same imbalance had been evident in Ward's *Ideal* : 'the superficial meaning of the New Testament (the meaning, that

is, which may be obtained from it by principles of criticism)' (Ward, W. G. [1844] p 37).

15   '. . . words which are not human but divine' (*Dev* 3.1.6). Newman is using a favourite argument against 'the critical commentator' who claims that 'the sacred text *need not* mean more than the letter' (*Dev* 3.1.6; cf *Jfc* p 122; *PS* III p 280). In 1865, he wrote : 'The great question then always is, What did the sacred writer *mean? not*, what does the bare letter say?' (*L&D* XXI p 433).

16   Haag [1969] p 221. The history of the theory of a *sensus plenior* has been studied by Raymond Brown : see Brown, R. E. [1953] and [1963]. That Newman's treatment of the senses of scripture left its mark is indicated by the fact that Coppens, in 1952, offered 'Newman's solution' as one of three possible answers to 'the question of the hagiographer's awareness of the fuller sense' (Brown, R. E. [1953] p 160). For a detailed discussion of Newman's views on 'The different meanings of Holy Scripture', see Seynaeve [1953] pp 307–48, 390–3.

17   Because he needs to emphasise the importance of the 'mystical sense' for the purpose of his argument in the *Essay*, his treatment is less balanced than in many of his other writings : cf *Ari* pp 59–63; *HS* II pp 288–9; *Insp* p 116; *VM* I p 257. One of his best treatments of the question dates from 1838 : 'Words stand for one idea, not two . . . We must not then interpret the terms used in Scripture by our scholastic theories' (*Jfc* p 119); 'Our business is . . . to get through and beyond the letter into the spirit' (*ibid* p 121).

18   Schlink [1967] p 54. There is an echo of Newman's distinction between 'natural' and 'formal' inference in the observation that : 'There is a difference between thought-progression and its subsequent inductive and deductive arrangement and verbal expression' p 55).

19   *Idea* pp 45, 59, 67, 73, 456; *DA* p 49. In 1835, in a passage reminiscent of Butler, he contrasted the extrapolation possible in the sciences (*Ex pede Herculem, Ess* I p 38) with the unpredictability of salvation history. In 1870, the rationality of extrapolating *ex pede Herculem* is grounded in the unity of the world : 'if we may justly regard the universe . . . as one whole' (*GA* p 260; cf *Ess* I p 337). Shortly before, in 1868, he had argued that the *Depositum* of faith 'is a large philosophy; all parts of which are connected together . . . so that he who really knows one part, may be said to know all, as ex pede Herculem' (*Flanagan* p 594).

20   Chadwick [1957] p 195. Stephenson's similar conclusions

(Stephenson [1966] pp 465, 484–5) are partly due to his acceptance of an 'objective-subjective' distinction similar to that which created difficulties for Newman (see *4.12*; Stephenson [1966] pp 463, 465). Misner locates Chadwick's objection in the tradition of anglican reactions to the *Essay* (Misner [1970] pp 32–5). There are certainly striking similarities (especially in regard to the critic's own apparently assumed notion of revelation) between Chadwick's criticism and one strand in Mozley's argument: cf Mozley, J. B. [1847] pp 171–211. The more important of the anglican works in question are listed in Chadwick [1957] p 236, Guitton [1933] pp 222–7; some of them are discussed in Brown, C. G. [1971], and Nicholls [1965].

21 *Dev* 2.2.10. Cf *US* pp 27, 32. In a letter of June 1864 he remarked that while 'the Scriptures constitute one of [the] channels' of revelation, there are other 'organs of that Divine Authority', such as 'a Greek poem or philosophical treatise . . . nay even the Koran' (*L&D* xxi p 122).

22 The strongest expressions of this claim are usually found in his early catholic writings: eg *HS* iii p 164; *Idea* pp 223–4, 255–6, 440–1; *SN* pp 317–8; *TT* p 333. By 1859, when he was beginning to stress the creative, and not merely the conservative function of theology, he describes the task of reasserting 'what is old with a luminousness of explanation which is new', as 'a gift inferior only to that of revelation itself' (*HS* ii p 476; cf Ward, W. [1912] i pp 432–7). But cf *Diff* ii p 327.

23 Paradoxically, both the ultramontane and the conservative anglican demanded a straight-forward affirmation that the whole of revealed truth has been present to the mind of the church 'from the beginning'. Newman satisfied neither, for different reasons. Thus, in 1869, the strand of historical and epistemological agnosticism, or at least caution, in Newman worried W. G. Ward, who said of *US* p 331 (quoted in *Dev* 1.2.9): 'Most truly and most nobly said, but at the same time most inconsistent with what has been said before' ([1869] p 55).

24 See *4.12*, note 19. The term 'extrinsicism' is used in the sense in which it was originally applied to these problems by Blondel, and has been taken up by Rahner: cf Blondel [1964] pp 225–31; Rahner [1966g], p 10; Misner [1970] p 40.

25 Misner [1970] p 42. Misner is correct in saying that this does not come through sufficiently clearly in Newman's writings, but he insufficiently appreciates the unity of 'object' and 'idea' (cf *4.1*), with the result that he speaks of 'ideas which represent their (*absent*) objects' (p 44, my stress). However, while the stress on the abiding presence of 'the revealed *reality*' (p 43), which

Misner inherits from Kasper, Rahner and Lehmann, is both a necessary corrective to excessively intellectualist views of revelation, and in harmony with much that Newman, in his description of a 'living, real idea' was trying to say, it would seem that the concept of divine self-communication is not without its difficulties. The same could be said of the contemporary stress on tradition as the communication of 'reality', which is a closely related problem: cf Congar [1966] p 287; de Lubac [1948] p 157; Lengsfeld [1969a] p 66.

26 *Dev* 5.4.3. Cf *L&D* xv p 374; *Flanagan* pp 594–5. At least Newman was always more guarded than Marin-Sola, who claimed that: 'Tous les dogmes que l'Eglise a déjà définis ou définira à l'avenir, se trouvaient donc dans l'intelligence des Apôtres . . . d'une façon immédiate, formelle, explicite' (Marin-Sola [1924] I pp 56–7; on which see de Lubac [1948] p 152).

27 Misner [1968] p 214. Cf *OS* pp 191–2; *TT* p 147; Ward, W. [1912] II pp 378–9. But as far back as 1837 Newman had described the history of christianity as 'that of a certain principle of universal empire, repressed and thwarted by circumstances' (*SD* p 100; cf *Ess* I p 370).

28 Misner [1968] p 215. In 1877, Newman made the uncharacteristically unguarded assertion that 'It seems to me plain from history that the Popes from the first considered themselves to have a universal jurisdiction' (*VM* I p 180). On the other hand, in 1880 he said 'it was impossible that the promises and commands of our Lord during the forty days should come into execution at once . . . It was not a question at first of the structure of the Church, but of the existence of it . . . And again, if we take the case of the Episcopacy, of the bishops, why, it is acknowledged that they did not—though they existed at a certain date—exist quite from the beginning' (Newman [1880] pp 23–4).

29 Rome, in 1847, reminded him of Oxford '16 or 17 years ago . . . There is a deep suspicion of *change,* with a perfect incapacity to create anything *positive* for the wants of the times' (*L&D* xii pp 103–4).

30 *DA* p 237, quoted, with insignificant alterations, in *Dev* 4.1.3. The use of the notion of 'tending towards', in the description of the state of historical evidence before a decision by ecclesiastical authority, is the same as his use of the notion when describing the assessment of 'motives of credibility' before that individual decision which is the act of faith. Cf Thesis 7 of the twelve *Theses de Fide* of 1847 : *Theses* p 232.

31 *PN* p 35. Notice that while he admits, in *Dev* 3.2.1, that the

'facts' of history 'are not present', he recommends that we handle the mediating witnesses, such as 'traditions . . . analogies, parallel cases . . . and the like . . . *like the evidence from the senses*' (my stress). The argument is similar to that employed by Marc Bloch, who argues that much of the historian's knowledge is as direct as that of the scientist in his laboratory : 'knowledge of all human activities in the past, as well as of the greater part of those in the present, is . . . a knowledge of their traces' (Bloch [1954] pp 54–5). As memory is the making 'present' of the past, so 'Religious faith is . . . the making present of what is future' (*Jfc* p 252).

32 Sillem [1969] p 215; cf pp 204–20. Of particular interest are the descriptions of the relationship between 'faith' and 'sight' in *Idea* p 400, and the comments (using similar imagery) on the function of arguments in natural theology in *GA* p 315.

33 Ward, W. [1912] II p 591 (my stress). However, Allies' criticism of *1845* p 10 (*Dev* Int 9), written while he was still an anglican, would today be more acceptable to many Roman catholic historians than would Newman's account : 'Now these words of Mr Newman seem to imply that the expressions of Fathers, or the decrees of Councils, *look towards* this presumed Catholic truth, *tend to it*, and finally admit it, as a truth which they had been all along implicitly holding, or unconsciously living upon . . . On the contrary, to my apprehension, they hold another view about the See of Rome, and express it again and again . . . the Fathers generally express a view about other Bishops which is utterly incompatible with [the Papal] theory as now received, which by no process of development can be made to agree with it' (Allies [1846] p 169, my stress). Mozley reviewed Allies' book with considerable enthusiasm : see Mozley, J. B. [1846b].

34 Cf *DA* pp 126, 184; *Diff* II p 312; *VM* I pp 38, 139. Davison's analogy concerning 'several lines' which 'tend we know not whether to a common centre, yet if when viewed from some one point their tendency to it is apparent, that point must be concluded to be the true locus of their direction and concourse' (Davison [1861] p 289), is strikingly similar (On Davison and Newman, see *5.43*, note 42).

35 See the discussion of 'views' in *3.22*. Occasionally, Newman's 'perspectivism' gets him into trouble : Cameron speaks of his 'desperate resort on occasion to Pascal's expedient of supposing that . . . *il faut parier*' (Cameron [1962] p 240; cf *PS* II p 21; VI p 259; *US* p 194).

36 *Dev* 8.1.6. That passage is the more interesting in that it dates

from 1845. Cf *Dev* 1.1.7; 4.3.4; 7.5.6; *Apo* p 259; *Ath* II p 143; *HS* III pp 192–4; *L&D* XIX p 179. Nowhere is Newman's appreciation of the positive role of error in the search for truth more eloquently expressed than in his 1855 lecture on 'Christianity and Scientific Investigation' (*Idea* pp 456–79), which Wilfrid Ward described as 'almost a Magna Charta of the freedom demanded by secular science in a Catholic University' [1912] I p 402).

37 *Dev* 7.1.2–5; the first half of 7.2.3; 7.3.1–3; and the last paragraph of 7.5.6, are all additions. The only other chapter to include extensive additions was chapter 4 : 4.0.1; the last paragraph of 4.0.2; the middle section of 4.1.3; 4.1.4; the first half of 4.1.5; the discussion of Ambrose and Jerome in 4.1.6; and 4.1.7, are new material.

38 This qualification accounts for an apparent hesitation in *1878*. Originally, Newman had written : 'doctrines develope, and principles do not' (*1845* p 70); he altered this to : 'doctrines develope, and principles at first sight do not' (*Dev* 5.2.1; cf 4.1.8; 5.2.3).

39 *Dev* 5.2.1. 'Doctrine is the *voice* of a religious body; its principles are of its *substance*' (*L&D* XXIII p 107). One of the few places, outside the *Essay*, in which Newman explicitly discussed the relationship between 'principles' and 'doctrines', was his *British Critic* article of 1842 on Davison (the date is significant) : *Ess* II pp 408–9. Notice the characteristic reference to 'animating' or 'actuating' principles in *Mix* pp 2, 4, 72.

40 Cf *Ess* I p 288. In 1864, Newman denied having written all of this essay (*Apo* p 94). In 1871, he reversed this judgement (*Ess* I p 308). The 1871 note (*Ess* I p 288) is puzzling since, so far as the relationship of 'principles' to 'doctrines' is concerned, the original text (eg pp 284–7) seems to go no further than *Dev* 5.3.5.

41 *Dev* 5.2.3. The importance of this observation is not nullified by the fact that, in context, it is an attack on protestantism which, 'viewed in its more Catholic aspect, is doctrine without active principle'.

42 *Dev* 2.1.10. Cf Davison [1861] p 35. Newman once described Davison as 'our greatest light' (at Oriel), 'more so than Whately, Arnold, Keble, Pusey, or Copleston' (*L&D* XVII p 161); although he is only once quoted in the *Essay* (in *Dev* 3.1.9), there are signs of his influence throughout. The advocacy of cumulative methods of argument is as characteristic of Davison's *Discourses on Prophecy* as it is of the *Essay*. That this is no coincidence is clear from a reference of Newman's, in 1868, to

'what Mr Davison calls a *cumulative* argument, that is, an argument lying in a cumulation of propositions' (*L&D* xxiv pp 145–6). Moreover, the concept of 'enlargement' (see *4.3*) plays a similar role in the argument of both books, and there is the same recommendation that the 'evidences' of religion should be handled no more suspiciously than other 'alleged facts . . . as come to us with a fair presumption in their favour' (*Dev* 3.1.2 : cf 'come before us with the presumption in their favour', Davison [1861] p 4). On 'the Seed of the woman' and 'till Shiloh came' (*Dev* 2.1.9; cf *Dev* 4.3.9; *LG* p 303; *SD* p 219; *VM* I p 340 [note of 1877]), see Davison [1861] pp 53–5, 78. Davison went to great lengths to show that, in 'the history of the Church and See of Rome' was to be found the fulfilment of those prophecies which describe 'the corruptions of some reigning power in the Christian Church' (Davison [1861] p 313; cf pp 312–31). Already in 1842, Newman directly confronted this objection : *SD* p 235.

43 *Dev* 7.4.1; cf 4.3.9; *Ari* p 58; *L&D* xi pp 238–9. 'That cannot be the true sense of Scripture, which never has been fulfilled . . . God's word shall not return unto Him void' (*PS* vi p 271; preached in 1836).

44 *Dev* 2.1.14. In the first two editions of the *University Sermons*, the same passage from Butler was quoted at length in a note, and followed by a comment which should be compared with the last sentence of *Dev* 2.1.14 : 'This view of Butler's differs from the remark in the text so far as this, that Butler is speaking of the *discovery* of *new* truths in passages of Scripture, and the text speaks of a *further insight* into the *primitive* and *received* sense of Scripture passages, gained by meditating upon them, and bringing out their one idea more completely' (Newman [1844] p 318). Cf *GA* p 498 (note of 1880).

45 Cf *Dev* 2.1.1. The statement 'We must distinguish between a revelation and a reception of it, not between its earlier and later stages' (*Dev* 2.2.8), is not a tacit admission that 'new revelation' occurs in the 'later stages'. Newman is considering the objection that an 'infallible authority' is antecedently improbable, as 'precluding the exercise of faith' (*Dev* 2.2.8). His answer is to the effect that the existence of a divinely accredited interpretation of revelation would no more inhibit freedom of response than did 'A revelation, in itself divine, and guaranteed as such' (*Dev* 2.2.8).

46 The year after the Vatican Council, he republished his essay on the 'Fall of De La Mennais', in which he had said, in 1837, that 'the Papacy, too, may be a human and rebellious work,

and yet, in the divine counsels, a centre of unity may have been intended for the Church in process of time . . . one is forced in this day to speak of the Papal power as an evil, yet not a pure evil, as in itself human, yet, relatively to the world, divine' (*Ess* I p 150; cf Trevor [1969] pp 157–9; *3.13*).

47   *Dev* 4.3.7; see *3.23*. One favourite form of argument is : 'If the primitive Church can be proved to be anti-papal, it can as easily (*I* should say as sophistically) be proved to be Arian' (*L&D* XI p 238).

CHAPTER SIX

1   A 'good' theory will, of course, remain tentative, because an exhaustive theory is impossible within the historical process : cf Rahner [1961] p 41.

2   As Davis acknowledged : 'Newman's theory . . . is not a yard-stick whereby the individual can judge of the lawfulness of in-dividual developments' ([1958] p 315). He seems later to have qualified this, in claiming that the 'tests . . . could also be used as a true test for any doctrine not yet defined by the Church but defended by her theologians' (Davis [1967a] p 186). See *3.21*, at end.

3   The most influential interpretation of the *Essay* to reveal, by its ascription of a major difference of aim and standpoint to the two parts, a misunderstanding of the *Essay*, is Walgrave's : [1957] pp 10, 26, 51–2, 242–3, 259; [1964b] p 15. (Among the more recent studies uncritically to adopt Walgrave's account, see Hunt [1967] pp 75–6). Cf Dupuy [1961] pp 151–2; Lash [1969] p 340; Stern [1967] pp 204–5.

4   *Dev* 5.0.1, my stress. This and the following article are largely new material in *1878*. In the passage which, in *1845*, most closely corresponds to them, Newman preemptively declared that the 'logical' continuity was as undeniable as the 'historical' (*1845* p 203) but, in doing so, he was using the term 'logical' in an even wider sense, to cover 'sound logic or fallacious', 'corrupt' developments and 'legitimate' ones. The argument in *1878* is more carefully formulated.

5   *Dev* 5.0.1. It hardly needs pointing out that Newman's insis-tence on 'logic' or rationality as a criterion of 'true' develop-ment has little in common with the perspectives adopted by twentieth-century 'logical' theories of doctrinal development. Newman's concept of rationality is broad enough to allow for 'capricious and irregular' development (*Dev* 1.2.2, stronger

than *1845*, which had 'capricious and intricate', p 46; cf *Dev* 1.2.3).

6   The extent to which Newman's standpoint differs from such theories may be gathered by comparing the *Essay* with, for example, Charlier [1938] (placed on the Index in 1942).

7   Butler, W. A. [1850] p 81. (When, at the time of the Modernist crisis, however, de Grandmaison levelled this charge against Loisy, he insisted that the latter was here being unfaithful to Newman's *Essay*: de Grandmaison [1903] pp 155–8; [1907] p 747). Mozley assumed, from the signs which he detected of this tendency (cf Mozley, J. B. [1847] pp 139, 142, 193–4) that, in practice, 'The doctrine of the Papal Infallibility comes out as the keystone of Mr Newman's whole argument' (p 171), although he admits that 'No reader would find out, from the way in which it comes, the absolutely fundamental place which it holds in the discussion' (p 172). See *6.21*. We have seen in *2.2* how strongly Newman denied this.

8   This may sound paradoxical. However, the more uncritical the trust in the 'privileged axis', the stronger the assumption that the past may not exercise normative control over the present point on that axis, because were it to do so the axis would have lost its privileged status.

9   Cf Inge [1919] p 144; Irons [1846] p 59; Moberley [1846] p xix; Palmer [1846] p 110. This is the ground of Mozley's charge that what Newman had done in the *Essay* was 'to assert the old ultra-liberal theory of Christianity; and to join the Church of Rome' (Mozley, J. B. [1847] p 265). Obviously, if it could be established that, from this point of view, Newman had jettisoned tradition, it would a fortiori be the case that, criteriologically, he had jettisoned scripture. A blemish in Greenfield's excellent study is his tendency to oversimplify Newman's thought in this direction. Thus he says of *Tract 85* that 'In order to provide a firmer basis for dogmatic Christianity, he divorced it from the necessity of being derived from Scripture at all' (Greenfield [1956] p 231). What he means here by 'derivation' is clear from passages such as that in which he charges Ward, Oakeley and (implicitly) Newman with formulating 'a completely new theory . . . which *abandoned the appeal to Antiquity* and looked to contemporary Rome as normative' (*ibid* p iv, my stress; cf p 274).

10   *L&D* xi p 101, note of 16 Feb 1876. Cf xi p 87; xiii p 86; xvii p 205. Mozley's article has been widely acclaimed as 'The ablest answer, brilliant as the essay itself' (Gore [1926b] p 830). Cf Chadwick [1957] p 96; Davis [1967a] p 187; Middleton [1950]

p 229. It is, however, as one of Dean Church's biographers observed, 'marked by certain traces of ill-temper' (Smith, B. A. [1958] p 50).

11 *Dev* 5.0.2. The article is new material in *1878*, except for the phrase 'the causes which stimulate the growth of ideas may also disturb and deform them'; cf 'the causes which stimulate may also distort its growth' (*1845*, pp 57–8).

12 The 'fidelity' of 'the development of an idea' can only be discerned, even in principle, by applying all seven 'notes', including the sixth : 'the protection which its later [phases] extend to its earlier' (*Dev* 5.7.4). In practice, however, it is doubtful whether Newman's tests could be effectively applied so as to ensure that any significant impoverishment, distortion or suppression would be detected. See *5.3*.

13 The recent literature on the problem is enormous. There is useful bibliographical material in Congar [1966] and Dupuy [1968b]. The ecumenical convergence in the theology of tradition is witnessed to, from protestant standpoints, in the following studies of the constitution *Dei Verbum* : Berkouwer [1965]; Leuba [1968]; Lindbeck [1970]; Schlink [1968]; Schutz [1968]; Widmer [1969]; see Lash [1973].

14 To concentrate on Newman's use of the *term* 'tradition', as Biemer [1967] tends to do, somewhat obscures the extent to which the *Essay* may be regarded as a contribution, within the limits imposed by its apologetic nature, to the theology of tradition.

15 Thus, while recognising that the constitution *Dei Verbum* of Vatican II, and the *Report on Tradition* of the fourth World Conference on Faith and Order represent 'une convergence de base extrêmement frappante', Leuba also admits that 'En somme, le Rapport, par son silence' on the question of *magisterium*, 'et la Constitution, par ses déclarations, ne me paraissent pas avoir fait autre chose que de mettre en évidence la difficulté la plus tangible du problème de la Tradition' (Leuba [1968] pp 478, 494–5).

16 'Function', rather than 'functionaries', in order to avoid, at this point, some complex historical problems : cf Murray, R. [1970] pp 115–6; Lash [1973] pp 73–80.

17 Byrne, in a useful study of Newman's thinking on development between 1825 and 1845, distinguished three 'distinct' but 'not mutually exclusive' theories : 'the development of our knowledge of Sacred Scripture . . . the development of the Creed . . . and finally the development of the idea' ([1937] p 231). The first of these is taught by Newman all through the period; the

second appears in *Arians* and 'grows into its full form in the *Via Media*'; the third appears in 1843 and 'is completed and perfected in the *Essay*'.

18 *Ari* p 47. Newman will later say, of this discussion of the *Disciplina Arcani* (pp 42–56), that the 'whole passage . . . is founded on the hypothesis of Apostolical Tradition co-ordinate with Scripture' (letter to Froude, 24 December 1835, *Moz* II p 148).

19 *DA* pp 1–43. Although not published until 1836 in the *British Magazine* (as 'Home Thoughts Abroad') a copy was sent to Froude in August 1833 : cf *Moz* I p 444.

20 Cf Biemer [1967] p 43; Stern [1967] p 117. The second and third categories correspond fairly closely to the distinction, at Trent, between 'apostolic' and 'ecclesiastical' *traditiones* : cf Bévenot [1963]; Murray, R. [1967] p 53; Ratzinger [1966] p 26; Ratzinger [1969] p 157.

21 Letter to Froude of 9 August 1835, *Moz* II p 123. This point will be of some importance when we come to consider the *Essay*.

22 Newman [1836b]. In fact, only pp 166–71 are so headed. The remaining pages are headed 'Apostolical Tradition', as is the revised version which was introduced into the fifth (1881) edition of *Ess* I pp 102–37. I have followed the 1836 version, because Newman later so heavily rewrote it (cf *Ess* I p 137) that hardly more than one third of the original text survived.

23 Newman [1836b] p 182. Both here and in Newman [1836e] Newman's interpretation of Hampden was misleading and 'one-sided' (Chadwick [1970a] p 116) and gave no indication of the methodological insights contained in the latter's Bampton lectures. Phrases such as the following could easily be paralleled in Newman's writings : historically, we observe the 'continued struggle in the Latin Church, between the advocates of Reason and the advocates of Authority' (Hampden [1833] p 36); on the early Fathers : were we 'to form a system of divinity out of these writers, it would be found necessary to explain away many of their positions and expressions, in order to bring them into accordance with the admitted truths of Scripture' (p 359); 'even the most sacred articles of the Trinity, and of the Incarnation, only *gradually* reached their perfect dogmatic expression' (p 369); 'the speculations of "heresy",—in other language, the conclusions of human reason,—forced the Church into successive adoptions of additional doctrinal statements' (pp 369–70).

24 Newman [1836b] p 181. At Nicea, it was the Arians who 'did but profess to argue from Scripture' (p 191), whereas the ortho-

dox party appealed to 'a fixed and recognised doctrine . . . formally committed to the guardianship of every bishop everywhere, and by him made over to his successor' (p 192).

25   Cf Newman [1836b] pp 187, 193–4. Biemer's claim that the distinction *does* feature in the essay appears to be based on a passage in the 1881 version : cf *Ess* ɪ p 130; Biemer [1967] p 46.

26   According to Newman, 'The Church Catholic may be truly said almost infallibly to interpret Scripture aright'; however, in practice, 'possession of past tradition' has deprived the church of the need, and 'the divisions of the time present' of the opportunity, for exercising this power (*VM* ɪ p 158).

27   The same is true of a passage in his essay on 'Vincentius of Lerins', which dates from the same period : *HS* ɪ p 381. Also *Apo* p 288.

28   Stern, noticing the stress in the sermon on the *unity* of the 'Object' of faith, says : 'ainsi se trouve renversé le système des "articles fondamentaux", bâti sur l'hypothèse d'une Révélation composée d'un certain nombre de vérités distinctes les unes des autres' (Stern [1967] p 185). I find no evidence that the system of 'fundamentals' was built on this hypothesis.

29   *Dev* 4.3.1–4. It should not be assumed that because, in the *Essay*, problems previously discussed in reference to 'Episcopal Tradition' are now discussed in reference to the papacy, Newman was, in principle, abandoning a 'collegial' for a monolithically papal ecclesiology. On the status of some of these arguments, see *3.23*.

30   *Dev* 2.2.2. The combined effect of the apologetic stress on the normative significance of the decisions of present authority, and the recommendation to 'accept the whole' or 'reject the whole', is that the implications of this distinction between the 'essentials' and 'non-essentials' are not adequately spelt out in the *Essay*, giving the impression that the distinction is neglected. See *2.2*.

31   Cf *Dev* 2.2.1–4; 2.2.11. Although the terminology may vary, the same ideas are at work in other passages : for example, the claim that 'Truth', if it is to be unitive and not divisive, must be 'a something definite, and formal, and independent' of the individual members of the church (*Dev* 7.5.3). In 1881, Newman wrote to Bloxam : '. . . personal experience of the power of the Gospel is our great, or our only defence from scepticism . . . Beyond this internal evidence, an Infallible Church is the main external safeguard' (cited in Middleton [1947] p 235).

32   This is borne out, for example, by the fact that the key passage from *VM* ɪ is quoted in the previous article : *Dev* 2.2.2; cf 2.2.4.

33   See *Perrone*. The two concepts are defined on pp 404, 407. The importance of this paper consists in the fact that it was an attempt to summarise, for Perrone, the main features of the argument of the *Essay*.

34   Biemer's claim that the Flanagan paper represents 'his final views on tradition' (Biemer [1967] p 59; cf p 63), is curious. Neither the letter to Norfolk (see *6.22*), nor the 1877 edition of the *Via Media* can be neglected in this context. Although the Flanagan paper is not without interest, it is hardly 'the most illuminating of all Newman's treatments of the subject' (Dessain [1964] p 184); and if it is 'Newman's clearest explanation of the matter' (Dessain [1958] p 324), this clarity is a weakness rather than a strength (especially in so far as the account of the Apostles' grasp of the *revelatum* is concerned).

35   In the notes to the 1877 edition of the *Via Media*, Newman indicated that the doctrine of 'fundamentals' still played a part in his thinking, and he did so in a way which implies a correction to the language of the *Essay*. He observed that not all 'revealed truths' are 'subjects of primary instruction' (*VM* I p 232). The latter are embodied in the creed, which he now claims does not admit of material expansion : 'The Apostles' Creed is rudimental; the so-called Creed of Pope Pius is controversial, and in this point of view is parallel to the Thirty-nine Articles, which no one would call a creed. We may call it Pope Pius's Creed improperly, as we call the Hymn *Quicunque* the Athanasian "Creed", because it contains what is necessary for salvation, but there can be but one rudimental and catechetical formula, and that is the Creed, Apostolic or Nicene' (*VM* I p 230; cf pp 232, 233). The distinction drawn here is similar to that which he made, as an Anglican, between the Prayer Book and the Articles, on the grounds that 'the Liturgy is the repository of the Apostles' complete teaching, whereas the Articles are no more than protests against certain errors and their authority correspondingly limited' (Härdelin [1965] p 52).

36   *VM* I p 90. In 1877, although he objected to the *use* which, in 1837, he had made of this observation, he nevertheless commented : 'All this is true' (*ibid*).

37   This question has sometimes been thought to have been settled by Vatican I's assertion that papal dogmatic definitions are irreformable 'ex sese, non autem ex consensu Ecclesiae' (but cf Caffrey [1970]; Groot [1966] p 816; Lash [1973] pp 76–9; Murray, R. [1968]; Thils [1969] pp 167–75). There is still work to be done on this problem of 'reception' : 'C'est une réalité diffi-

cile à manier. Il n'existait à peu près rien sur elle jusqu'à ce jour' (Congar [1970d] p 616).

38 *Dev* 7.3.2. The objection, clearly with untramontane attitudes in mind, to that 'lightness of mind' which is shown by 'a readiness to receive any number of dogmas at a minute's warning' (*Dev* 7.3.2), echoes his remark, shortly after the Vatican Council, that 'A German who hesitates may have more of the real spirit of faith than an Italian who swallows' (*L&D* xxv p 430).

39 *L&D* xxv p 330. 'Every exercise of Infallibility is brought out into act by an intense and varied operation of the Reason, both as its ally and as its opponent, and provokes again, when it has done its work, a re-action of Reason against it' (*Apo* p 252).

40 Cf *Diff* ii p 303; *L&D* xxv pp 71, 165, 172, 215, 219–20, 235, 316. In a note added in the following year (1875), he only qualified this to the extent of observing that 'subsequent reception' did not enter into the necessary conditions of a '*de fide* decision' (*Diff* ii p 372). This letter to Norfolk contains other remarks on the regulative function of theology : cf *Diff* ii pp 176, 279–80, 294, 307.

41 See *4.32*. According to Congar, 'L'idée d'infaillibilité de l'ensemble des fidèles n'est soutenable que si on les considère dans leur totalité et selon une durée de temps suffisante' (Congar [1970d] p 606). But how long is sufficient time ?

42 'Here, then, is the aboriginal germ—a Religion without a priesthood, or any provision for it' ([1899] p 169). Williams saw that Fairbairn's regret that Newman did not clearly state what the 'germ' was, rested on a fundamental misunderstanding of the *Essay* : Williams, W. J. [1906] pp 102–53; cf Kenny [1957] pp 54–5. Williams' own enthusiasm for the *Essay* is partly due to the fact that he only recognised in it those features of Newman's argument which were congenial to the evolutionary optimism of the modernist. In the light of subsequent events, Wilfrid Ward's highly commendatory review of Williams' book ('the work of a man who has got a deep and absorbing hold on the more profound qualities of Newman's mind'), published in the same month as *Lamentabili*, is interesting : Ward, W. [1907] p 13.

43 Fawkes [1903] p 67. Poulat's comparison of Harnack and Loisy is more judicious : 'On appauvrirait leur pensée en y voyant soit une condamnation radicale, soit une justification *a priori* du développement doctrinale. Pour l'historien allemand, ce développement, inéluctable, n'a de valeur que dans la mesure où il éclaire l'intuition centrale du christianisme; pour l'exégète

français, il manifeste progressivement une intentionalité riche initialement de significations multiples' (Poulat [1962] p 96).

44   However, Loisy's judgement, at an early stage in his development, when he had just come under the influence of the *Essay*, is worth recording : '*L'Histoire des dogmes* de M. Harnack est plus érudite que l'*Essai sur le développement de la doctrine chrétienne*; mais combien elle lui est inférieure pour l'intelligence générale du christianisme et de sa vie multiple, du rapport intime qui existe entre toutes les formes et toutes les phases de cette vie' (Loisy [1898] p 20).

45   *Dev* 7.1.3; cf 1.1.3; 1.2.10. The reference to the centrality of the incarnation, in all three passages, is new material in *1878*. See *4.1, 4.11, 5.42*.

46   *Dev* 7.1.4. In his early years as a Roman catholic, in which he set the interdenominational contrasts in the starkest relief, he went so far as to say that the catholic church and the church of England 'cannot unite, because they proceed on different *ideas*' (*L&D* xii p 234, his stress). 'Pagans may have, heretics cannot have, the same principles as Catholics' (*Dev* 5.2.3); cf Boekraad [1955] pp 281–3; Walgrave [1957] pp 166–7.

47   As a young man, he sometimes adopted a more explicitly soteriological perspective : 'The leading doctrine to be discussed would be (I think) that of regeneration; for it is at the very root of the whole system' (*Moz* i p 143).

48   *Dev* 7.1.4, his stress. See *2.1*. The interpenetration of doctrinal and epistemological considerations comes through clearly in the beautiful passage in the *Grammar* in which Newman describes the 'Image' of God in Christ as 'a principle of association, and a real bond of those subjects one with another, who are thus united to the body by being united to that Image' (*GA* p 464).

49   The first draft of *Dev* 7.1.3, made on 24 August 1877, began : 'The central doctrine which for convenience I will take as the leading idea of the Revealed Dispensation—but only for convenience not as presuming to master and analyse what comes to us from the infinite heavens above, is the Incarnation' (*BOA* D.7.6).

50   Thus Finsterhölzl, commenting on the passages with which this section is concerned, suggests that, today, we would prefer to place the focal emphasis on the paschal mystery, rather than on the incarnation as such (Finsterhölzl [1967] p 264). For Newman, however, the notion of incarnation is wider than that implied by Finsterhölzl's comment, and is focused on the redemptive work of Christ. Thus, when preparing the revision of

the *Essay*, Newman scribbled at *1845*, p 66 (*Dev* 5.1.3): 'Surely the leading idea of the Gospel is the Redemption "Xt crucified". There are other ideas subordinated to this—eg Call no man yr master' (*BOA* D.7.6).

51 *Dev* 1.1.3; in *1845* he merely said 'For Christianity has many aspects', p 35. The following phrase, in *1878*: 'Christianity is dogmatical, devotional, practical all at once', echoes the ecclesiology of the 1877 Preface to the *Via Media* (but the same pattern was already hinted at by the reference, in *1845*, to the 'philosophical . . . ethical . . . political' aspects of christianity). Finally, the phrase 'it is esoteric and exoteric' (*Dev* 1.1.3, replacing 'it is solemn, and it is cheerful', *1845* p 35), is an evocation of the tractarian doctrine of 'economy': cf *Dev* 5.6.3; *Ari* pp 42–3, 96; *GA* p 309; *PN* pp 27, 89; *VM* ɪ p lii; Palmer [1846] p 38.

52 Dumont, who sees 'orthopraxie' as one of the 'trois dimensions retrouvées en théologie' today, comments: 'Voilà des années que le thème de l'Action se dessine comme en filigrane dans la pensée chrétienne. Spontanément, on en attribue l'origine à Maurice Blondel. Mais il serait sans doute intéressant de remonter plus haut, à la recherche d'un courant dont on retrouverait les traces chez Gratry ou Lacordaire, chez Newman et dans l'école de Tubingue' (Dumont [1970] p 574). Notice the use of the phrase 'right practice' in the sermon on 'Knowledge of God's Will without Obedience' (*PS* ɪ p 33). In the same sermon, that very Victorian virtue of 'earnestness' is described as one of the 'two foundations of true Christian faith' (*PS* ɪ p 40).

53 See *4.32*, note 68; *5.4*. '. . . it will be seen how ineffectual all attempts ever will be to secure doctrine by mere general language. It may be readily granted that the intellectual representation should ever be subordinate to the cultivation of the religious affections . . . considering the doctrine as given us as a practical direction for our worship and obedience' (*Ari* pp 145, 159). Forty years later, the same concern is expressed in the distinction, in the *Grammar*, between 'religion' and 'theology': 'Theology, as such, always is notional, as being scientific: religion, as being personal, should be real' (*GA* p 55; cf pp 57, 73, 79, 98, 121, 216). The grace of revelation 'is given, not that we may know more, but that we may do better' (*PS* ɪ p 203); 'That a thing is true is no reason that it should be said, but that it should be done' (*PS* ᴠ p 45); 'knowledge is a call to action: an insight into the way of perfection is a call to perfection' (*PS* ᴠɪɪɪ p 30; cf *L&D* xɪɪɪ p 373).

54 Christopher Butler, describing the shift, in the second Vatican

Council's treatment of revelation, from a neo-scholastic conception of christian truth to one that, as more authentically biblical, includes a personalist dimension, invokes Newman's motto : 'Cor ad cor loquitur' (Butler, B. C. [1967] p 30).

55 *VM* I p 87. The formulation is unguarded : he would have done better to say that action is *a* criterion of true faith. A man might merely act, as on the Pascalian wager, 'as if' the state of affairs implied in the claims of belief were true. Newman's rather puzzling note, of 1877, to this passage, shows that he is aware of this. See *4.2*, note 31.

56 *Dev* 2.1.16. In 1833, he had observed that 'there are truths' which are 'the peculiar discoveries of the improved moral sense (or what Scripture terms "*the Spirit*")'—*Ari* p 33; cf pp 136–7. Cf *GA* p 314; *Moz* II p 409–10; 'obedience to God is the way to know and believe in Christ' (*PS* VIII p 204).

57 Tyrrell sometimes tended to argue in the latter direction : Tyrrell [1903] pp 169, 209. On Newman and 'fruitfulness' as a 'badge' of truth, see *Dev* 5.2.2–3; *US* p 318.

CHAPTER SEVEN

1 For a discussion of the influence of the *Essay*, cf Artz [1968] pp 167–98; Dupuy [1964]. For the history of catholic theories of doctrinal development in this century, cf Hammans [1965]; Hammans [1967]; Schoof [1970].

2 Loisy [1898]. In the five articles that followed, which were a sustained attack on Harnack and (especially) Auguste Sabatier, Loisy rarely referred explicitly to Newman, but there are several traces of the influence of the *Essay* : eg Loisy [1899a] pp 204–5, 213–14; Loisy [1900a] pp 250, 258, 270; Loisy [1900b] pp 134–5.

3 An exception was his paraphrase of *Dev* 1.1.7 : 'Ici-bas vivre c'est changer, et ce qui est devenu parfait ne l'a été qu'après bien des *transformations*' (Loisy [1898] p 6, my stress). But this misrepresentation, which did not distort the main lines of his presentation of Newman's thought, was probably due to the quality of the translation with which he was working : cf Bremond [1906] pp xxi–xxiv. Poulat says of the *Essay* that, prior to the appearance of this article, 'on ne peut dire qu'il ait trouvé beaucoup d'écho' (Poulat [1962] pp 74–5; cf Dupuy [1964] pp 148–9).

4 Thus, for example, in *L'Evangile et l'Eglise*, Newman is first explicitly mentioned only on p 161, and quoted only three

times : *1845* p 154 is quoted on p 194 (cf *Dev* 2.3.2); *1845* p 358 on p 231 (cf *Dev* 8.2.5); the article on Milman on p 213.

5 For instance, Loisy can hardly be blamed for asserting, of Proposition 25 of *Lamentabili* ('Assensus fidei ultimo innititur in congerie probabilitatum', Dz 2025), that 'C'était la doctrine de Newman' (Loisy [1908] p 64). This assertion is, at worst, an oversimplification : cf Thils [1956]. De Grandmaison, the one theologian, as Loisy later remarked, 'avec lequel j'aurais pu discuter' (cited in Poulat [1962] p 119), only asked whether, in *L'Evangile et l'Eglise*, Loisy had not 'fait quelque peu devier les idées de Newman à ce sujet' (de Grandmaison [1903] p 155).

6 Vidler [1934] p 51. Any broader discussion of the exceedingly complex question of Loisy's 'sincerity' at this period lies outside the scope of the present study. On this topic, as on several others, Loome [1973], while acting as a welcome and scholarly corrective to the work of Barmann and Vidler, seems to me to raise as many questions as it answers.

7 Editorial in *The Times*, 2 November 1907. In the same issue, W. T. Williams wrote of the 'evil that, while one Pope has implied a direct approval of the writings of an English Catholic by making him a Cardinal, his successor should reverse the decision by condemning every characteristic proposition for which that writer made himself responsible' (the initials 'W. T.' would seem to be a misprint for 'W. J.'). This claim was dealt with, with the severity it deserved, by Bremond : Bremond [1908] pp 343–6. On Williams' letter and, in similar vein, Tyrrell's article in *The Guardian* of 20 November ('The Condemnation of Newman'), see Gougaud [1909] pp 560–1.

8 'I am enabled to state on information received today from the highest authority that the "genuine doctrine and spirit of Newman's Catholic teaching are not hit by the Encyclical, but the theories of many who wrongly seek refuge under a great name are obviously censured" ' (Letter of Fr Norris to *The Times*, 4 November 1907). That was cautious, but the following day Abbot Gasquet wrote to *The Times* claiming that 'we know on the highest authority that no theory, no idea, no opinion even, put forward by the great Cardinal has been either implicitly or indirectly set aside, let alone condemned by the late Encyclical'. The following year, Paul Sabatier wrote : 'Que la bulle n'ait pas visé Newman, j'en suis très sûr, pour la bonne raison que ses rédacteurs ignoraient Newman. Ques ses idées ne soient pas atteintes par les condamnations, le dise qui veut, le dise qui peut' [1909] p 44). On Wilfrid Ward's worries on this score, see Ward, M. [1937] pp 254–5, 559; Barmann [1972] pp 204–6.

9   Eg 'Devotion tends . . . to run into puerilities and superstitions. Philosophical theology tends . . . to the other extreme of excessive abstraction' (Tyrrell [1907] p 95); 'Devotion and religion existed before theology, in the way that art existed before art-criticism; reasoning, before logic' (p 105).

10 Nédoncelle [1964] p 106; cf Dru [1964] p 213. On Newman's influence on Blondel generally, cf Bremond [1908] p 359. Bremond's judgement that 'le père de la Barre, et M. Blondel, et M. Loisy, tous, chacun à sa façon, s'inspirent de Newman ou se rencontrent avec lui' ([1906] p xxvii), is judiciously guarded.

11 Baudin [1906] p 54. Baudin's account was adopted by de Grandmaison : de Grandmaison [1907] pp 45–58, 722, 743. For a similar judgement, see de Blic [1948] p 141.

12 Storr [1913] p 278. Storr took up Fairbairn's charge of 'intellectual scepticism' : 'Newman was at heart a thorough-going sceptic' (p 284; see 3.22). He acknowledged that the Essay 'raised by anticipation many of the problems which are so prominent in discussion at the present time' (p 295), but the value of his testimony is reduced by the fact that he seriously misunderstood the Essay. On his account, the tension between static and dynamic theological perspectives in the Essay is a 'confused' mélange of 'logical' and 'biological' conceptions of development (pp 301–9; see 4.31).

13 'L'un des mérites incontestables des Sermons universitaires aura été d'élargir la notion d'intelligence, trop étroitement définie par le rationalisme classique' (Nédoncelle [1945] p 75).

14 In France, up until 1935, scholars tended to lose interest in the Essay 'in the general reaction against modernism' (Dupuy [1967] p 148).

15 de Bivort de la Saudée [1949] p 142, 145. Batiffol seems, however, to have had a more profound sense of historicity than Gore. In spite of Newman's devastating critique of the adequacy of the Vincentian canon, Gore still attempted to stand by it. Batiffol responded : 'Dans la perspective du développement . . . aucun des articles de la foi des conciles oecuméniques ne s'ajuste strictement à la règle de Vincent' (ibid p 148).

16 Davis [1945a] 49–50. In the same year : 'Marin-Sola's work has been recognised as a clear and complete vindication of Newman's Essay' (Benard [1945] p 96).

17 The year after Burgum's article, Tristram wrote : 'L'Angleterre n'apporte guère de contribution à l'étude de la philosophie et de la théologie de Newman' (Tristram [1931] col 398). Cf Boekraad [1957] p 110; Davis [1967c]. As late as 1965, Coulson could complain : 'many of the most formative continental theo-

logians—Louis Bouyer, Yves Congar, Peter Fransen, Hans Küng—are thoroughly versed in Newman studies . . . What then has been done for Newman in the country of his birth? Most of his works are out of print . . . and his work and character are still liable to misrepresentations as gross as those which precipitated the *Apologia* itself' (Coulson [1965] p 5). Recently, with the publication of Coulson [1970]; Pailin [1969]; Sillem [1969], there are signs that the balance is being redressed.

18　In the climate of opinion in which the *Essay* was written, it is not surprising to come across passages such as : 'I see not how any Romanist can stop short of the unavoidable inference, that, the Pope, as Christ's vicar upon earth, has all the power which the most ardent ultramontane would ascribe to him' (Alford [1846] p 30). Less excusable is Inge's comment that Newman's 'theory [of development] marks . . . the complete and final apotheosis of the Pope and the hierarchy' (Inge [1919] p 144). More generally, it is regrettable that, as recently as 1966, we can be told that 'The new theologians' of doctrinal development are 'wildly unorthodox' (Nicholls [1966] p 284, referring specifically to Karl Rahner), and that, on the basis of their speculations, 'We are handed over to an authority which is not merely infallible, but practically inspired, an oracle whose scope for defining dogmas is unlimited' (p 292).

19　Orr [1901] p 20. There are some phrases in the book, however, which suggest the influence of the *Essay* : eg 'all systems equally appeal to Scripture, and there would still seem to be the need of a tribunal to decide on this appeal' (p 15; cf *Dev* 2.1.3); 'it is only in the light of the later doctrines that the wealth and range of the earlier are fully discovered' (p 23).

20　Balic [1952]; Bea [1952]; Boyer [1952]; Dhanis [1953] (which mentions the *Essay* once : p 222); Filograssi [1952]; Flick [1952]; Rambaldi [1952]; Spiazzi [1952]. Blondel was also completely ignored.

21　The shift in method is hinted at in Dhanis' remark that the 'definibility' of truths 'qui sont reliées à la doctrine primitive par une inférence non pas *demonstrative*, mais plus ou moins *persuasive* . . . Impliquée dans *l'Essai sur le développement de la doctrine chrétienne* de Newman, elle s'est de plus en plus imposée au théologiens à la suite des progrès réalisés par l'histoire des dogmes' (Dhanis [1953]; my stress). Of Germany, 'one cannot say that the renewal of Catholic theology in Germany in the 1920s took Newman as its pattern' (Becker [1967] p 181). There, also, it was after 1945 that 'The greatest and most effective Newman renaissance' (p 182) took place.

22 De Lubac [1948]. He showed his appreciation of those, such as Bainvel, de Grandmaison, Lebreton, Marin–Sola and Simonin, who had attempted, in different ways, to widen the problematic of doctrinal development. He was defended by Baumgartner, who in turn appealed to the authority of Newman : Baumgartner [1953]; [1956]. The following year saw the publication of a sensitive article by Taymans [1949], who also appealed to Newman and Blondel.

23 Approaches often referred to as 'logical' (or 'dialectical') and 'theological'. The latter, because of its tendency to lay considerable emphasis on the charism for 'penetrating and distinguishing the truth' which it attributed to the holders of apostolic office in the church, was rightly described by Hammans as encouraging 'theological agnosticism' (Hammans [1967] p 60). On the inadequacy of the pre-war problematic, see Leonard [1958] (an article review of Walgrave [1957]) and Moeller [1952]; both of them appealed to Newman. See also Lash [1973] pp 119–27.

24 The more important of the studies which began to break new ground at this period, such as those by Lonergan, Rahner and Schillebeeckx, still tended to pay insufficient attention not only to problems of historicity but, more fundamentally, to developments in new testament exegesis and hermeneutics. Cf Lonergan [1959], pp 28–41; Rahner [1961]; Rahner [1966a]; Richard [1963]; Richard [1964]; Schillebeeckx [1967b]. See Lash [1973] pp 128–40.

25 Walgrave [1964b] pp 47–8. Even more recently, the survival of similarly oversimplified views of the *Essay* is evident in phrases such as : 'the evolutionary ecclesiology of John Henry Newman' (Hoffman [1968] p 196); 'According to Newman, therefore, there is a homogeneous or linear development in Christian doctrine' (Bent [1969] p 14); 'The linear, organic view that has been so prevalent since Möhler and Newman' (Echlin [1970] p 10). Again, in relation to the second Vatican Council : 'Au niveau de développement doctrinal, les attaches entre Newman et la constitution *Dei Verbum* sont presque littérales' (Van der Plancke [1969] p 234); the relevant sentence in article 8 of *Dei Verbum* is described as 'practically a précis of Newman's theory of the development of doctrine' (Butler, B.C. [1967] p 40).

26 Congar [1970b] p 87. In a note he refers to Baum [1968]; Jossua [1968]. Jossua's analysis was anticipated (as he himself acknowledged) by Bouillard, whose tentative reflections in 1944 pointed in the same direction as the position more recently taken up in

Wiles [1967] : cf Bouillard [1944] pp 216–20. It is important to remember Bouillard's debt to Blondel : cf Bouillard [1949]. The significance of cultural and linguistic pluralism for the problem of doctrinal change and continuity, at which Congar hints in that passage, has recently been stressed in Lonergan [1967a]; [1967b]; [1968]; [1971]; Rahner [1969c]; [1969d]. See also Lash [1973] pp 143–82.

Appendix

THE SECOND (1846) EDITION
The following changes were introduced by Newman into the text of the second (1846) edition of the *Essay*:

1. *1845*, p 1, line 7: 'It may legitimately'
   1846, p 1, line 7: 'It may indeed legitimately'
2. *1845*, p 27, lines 24–5: 'teachers could'
   1846, p 27, line 25: 'teachers, could'
3. *1845*, p 28, lines 25–6: 'different, I am obliged to say, in a more hopeful position, as'
   1846, p 28, lines 25–6: 'different,—I am obliged to say in a more hopeful position,—as'
4. *1845*, pp 61–2: 'difference can seem wider'
   1846, pp 61–2: 'difference seems wider'
5. *1845*, p 85; *1846*, p 85: the order of the two footnotes is reversed in *1846*: but this is simply a correction.
6. *1845*, p 92, lines 11–12: 'perhaps they go'
   1846, p 92, line 12: 'perhaps, they go'
7. *1845*, p 114, line 5: 'that, to be'
   1846, p 114, line 6: 'that to be'
8. *1845*, p 119, line 2 from bottom: 'as it is in this passage'
   1846, p 119, line 2 from bottom: 'as is intended in this passage'
9. *1845*, p 124, lines 4–5: 'we henceforth argue for a standing authority in matters of faith, on the analogy'
   1846, p 124, lines 4–6: 'and henceforth our argument for a standing authority in matters of faith proceeds on the analogy'
   For the third version of this passage, see *Dev* 2.2.10.
10. *1845*, p 136, line 2: 'reconciling it with'
    1846, p 136, line 2: 'reconciling that theology with'
11. *1845*, p 136, line 7: 'that this is really the case'
    1846, p 136, lines 6–7: 'of the truth of this representation'
12. *1845*, p 165, lines 28–31: 'there was need neither of Bishop nor Pope; their power was dormant, or exercised by Apostles. In course of time, first the power of the Bishop awoke'
    1846, p 165, lines 28–31: 'there was the display neither of Bishop nor Pope; their power had no prominence, as being exercised by Apostles. In course of time, first the power of the Bishop displayed itself'
    Cf *Dev* 4.3.2
13. *1845*, p 166, lines 5–4 from bottom: 'for it never had been operative'

P

1846, p 166, lines 5–4 from bottom: 'for they never had been carried into effect'
Cf *Dev* 4.3.3.

14. *1845*, p 167, lines 7–8: 'first local disturbances gave rise to Bishops, and next ecumenical disturbances gave rise to Popes'
1846, p 167, lines 7–9: 'first local disturbances gave exercise to Bishops, and next ecumenical disturbances gave exercise to Popes'
Cf *Dev* 4.3.4.

15. *1845*, p 167, line 2 from bottom: 'should rise'
1846, p 167, line 2 from bottom: 'should display itself'
Cf *Dev* 4.3.5.

16. *1845*, p 169, lines 5–4 from bottom: 'first instance necessarily dormant'
1846, p 169, lines 5–4 from bottom: 'first instance more or less dormant'
Cf *Dev* 4.3.6.

17. *1845*, p 171, line 22: 'the Head of Christendom'
1846, p 171, line 22: 'the Sovereign Head of Christendom'
Cf *Dev* 4.3.8.

18. *1845*, p 289, line 21: 'of saints'
1846, p 289, line 21: 'of Saints'

No further changes were introduced into the text beyond this point.

Select Bibliography

Reference is made to the bibliography in the text and notes, by surname (initials) and date of the edition used, which comes first in the entry. (Apart from Newman references, for which a special system is used.) Where there is possible ambiguity (eg several publications in one year) the abbreviation used is the last item. In the bibliography itself abbreviations are used for some frequently occuring journals, as indicated below, and for five collections noted in the bibliography under the first word as indicated below.

DR	Downside Review
DuR	Dublin Review
ETL	Ephemerides Theologicae Lovanienses
HJ	Heythrop Journal
JES	Journal of Ecumenical Studies
NRT	Nouvelle Revue Théologique
RSPT	Revue des Sciences Philosophiques et Théologiques
RSR	Recherches de Science Religieuse
TS	Theological Studies
Id	*Ideas*
Inf	*Infallibility*
JHN	*John* (see p 227)
MS	*Mysterium*
NS	*Newman*

1. *SELECTED LIST OF NEWMAN'S WORKS*

The date given in square brackets, after that of the edition used, is that of the original edition (which, in some instances, means the first occasion on which the contents were gathered into one volume). In the case of those works which were included in the standard (1868–1881) edition, the date at which the work was first included in the standard edition is also given, in round brackets. In cases where the original edition was that first included in the standard edition, only round brackets are used.

Apologia pro Vita Sua: being a History of his Religious Opinions. London 1885 [1864] (1873). Cf Svaglic [1967]. *Apo.*

The Arians of the Fourth Century. London 1897 [1833] (1871). *Ari.*

'The Brothers Controversy: Apostolical Tradition', *The British Critic, Quarterly Theological Review, and Ecclesiastical Record*, xx (1836) 166–99. Newman [1836b].

'Burton's History of the Christian Church', *The British Critic, Quarterly Theological Review, and Ecclesiastical Record*, xx (1836) 209–31. Newman [1836c].

Callista. A Tale of the Third Century. London, 1898 [1855] (1876). *Call.*

'Cardinal Newman's Theses de Fide and his Proposed Introduction to the French Translation of the University Sermons', ed Henry Tristram, *Gregorianum*, xviii (1937) 219–60. *Theses.*

Catholic Sermons of Cardinal Newman. Ed at the Birmingham Oratory. London 1957. *Cath Ser.*

Certain Difficulties Felt by Anglicans in Catholic Teaching. 2 vols, i, London 1918 [1850] (1879). ii, London 1920 (1876). *Diff* i, ii.

Correspondence of John Henry Newman with John Keble and Others, 1839–1845. Ed at the Birmingham Oratory. London 1917. *KC.*

Discourses Addressed to Mixed Congregations. London 1902 [1849] (1871). *Mix.*

Discussions and Arguments on Various Subjects. London 1873 (1872). *DA.*

'Dr Wiseman's Lectures on the Catholic Church', *The British Critic, Quarterly Theological Review, and Ecclesiastical Record*, xx (1836) 373–403. Newman [1836d].

Elucidations of Dr Hampden's Theological Statements. Oxford 1836. Newman [1836e].

An Essay in Aid of a Grammar of Assent. London 1889 (1870). *GA.*

An Essay on the Development of Christian Doctrine. London 1890 [1845] (1878). Cf Artz [1969]; Bremond [1906]; Walgrave [1964b]. *Dev.*

Essays Critical and Historical. 2 vols, London 1919 (1871). *Ess* i, ii.

Fifteen Sermons Preached before the University of Oxford. London 1892 [1843] (1871). (The second edition is listed separately, as *Sermons, chiefly on . . .*). *US.*

Historical Sketches. 3 vols, London 1876 (1872). *HS* i, ii, iii.

The Idea of a University Defined and Illustrated. London 1875 (1873). *Idea.*

John Henry Newman. Autobiographical Writings. Ed Henry Tristram. London 1956. *AW.*

'Le Bas' Life of Archbishop Laud', *The British Critic, Quarterly Theological Review, and Ecclesiastical Record,* xix (1836) 354–80. Newman [1836a].

Lectures on the Doctrine of Justification. London 1892 [1838] (1874). *Jfc.*

Lectures on the Present Position of Catholics in England. London 1913 [1851] (1872). *Prepos.*

Letters and Correspondence of John Henry Newman during his Life in the English Church. Ed Anne Mozley. 2 vols, London 1891. *Moz* I, II.

The Letters and Diaries of John Henry Newman. Ed Charles Stephen Dessain. 18 vols (XI–XXVIII) to date. London 1961–1975. *L&D* XI–XXVIII.

Loss and Gain. The Story of a Convert. London 1900 [1848] (1874). *LG.*

Meditations and Devotions of the Late Cardinal Newman. London 1893. *MD.*

'Mr Taylor versus Nicolas Ferrar', *The British Critic and Quarterly Theological Review,* xxvi (1839) 440–57. Newman [1839].

My Campaign in Ireland. Part I. Aberdeen (printed for private circulation) 1896. *Campaign.*

Newman the Oratorian. His Unpublished Oratory Papers. Ed Placid Murray. Dublin 1969. *OP.*

'The Newman-Perrone Paper on Development', ed T. Lynch, *Gregorianum,* xvi (1935) 402–47. *Perrone.*

On Consulting the Faithful in Matters of Doctrine. Ed John Coulson. London 1961. *Consulting.*

On the Inspiration of Scripture. Ed. J. Derek Holmes and Robert Murray. London 1967. *Insp.*

Parochial and Plain Sermons. 8 vols, London 1868 [1834–43] (1868). *PS* I–VIII.

The Philosophical Notebook of John Henry Newman. Ed Edward Sillem. 2 vols; II, *The Text*, revised A. J. Boekraad. Louvain 1970. *PN*.

'Preface' to *The Anglican Ministry. Its Nature and Value in Relation to the Catholic Priesthood*, by Arthur Wollaston Hutton. London 1879. Newman [1879].

'Preface' to *The Life of George Bull, DD, Sometime Bishop of St David's*, by Robert Nelson. Oxford 1840. Newman [1840].

'Preface' to *Notes of a Visit to the Russian Church in the Years 1840, 1841*, by the late William Palmer, MA, formerly Fellow of Magdalen College, Oxford, selected and arranged by Cardinal Newman. London 1882. Newman [1882].

Select Treatises of St Athanasius in Controversy with the Arians. Freely translated by John Henry Cardinal Newman. 2 vols, London 1881 [1841, 1844] (1881). *Ath* I, II.

Sermon Notes of John Henry Cardinal Newman. 1849–78. Ed by Fathers of the Birmingham Oratory. London 1913. *SN*.

Sermons Bearing on Subjects of the Day. London 1869 [1843] (1869). *SD*.

Sermons Chiefly on the Theory of Religious Belief, Preached Before the University of Oxford. Oxford 1844 [1843]. (For the third, revised edition, which included an extra sermon, 'Evangelical Sanctity the Completion of Natural Virtue', see above, *Fifteen Sermons . . .*). Newman [1844].

Sermons Preached on Various Occasions. London 1900 [1857] (1870). *OS*.

Stray Essays on Controversial Points, Variously Illustrated. Privately printed 1890. *SE*.

Tracts Theological and Ecclesiastical. London 1902 (1874). *TT*.

Two Essays on Biblical and on Ecclesiastical Miracles. London 1890 (1870). *Mir*.

Two Sermons Preached in the Church of S. Aloysius, Oxford, by H. E. Cardinal Newman, on Trinity Sunday, 1880. Privately printed 1880. Newman [1880].

The Via Media of the Anglican Church. Illustrated in Lectures, Letters, and Tracts Written Between 1830 and 1841. 2 vols, London 1891. I [1837] (1877). II (1877). *VM* I, II.

Verses on Various Occasions. London, 1890 [1867] (1874). *VV*.

2. SELECTED LIST OF OTHER WORKS CONSULTED

Abbott, Edwin Abbott. *The Kernel and the Husk. Letters on Spiritual Christianity.* By the author of 'Philochristus' and 'Onesimus'. London 1886.

de Achaval, Hugo M. 'An Unpublished Paper by Cardinal Newman on the Development of Doctrine', *Gregorianum*, xxxix (1958) 585–96. (The text of Newman's letter is referred to as *Flanagan*). Cf Dessain [1958].
'Newman und Mivart', trans Inge Schrader, in *NS* [1964] 227–49.

Acton, John Emerich Edward Dalberg. *Lectures on the French Revolution.* Ed John Neville Figgis and Reginald Vere Laurence. London 1932. (First published 1910.)
'Inaugural Lecture on the Study of History', *Essays in the Liberal Interpretation of History.* Ed William H. McNeill. Chicago 1967. (Reprinted from *Lectures on Modern History.* London 1906).

Ahern, Barnabas. 'The Permanence of Tradition', *The Future of Belief Debate*, 19–28. Ed Gregory Baum. New York 1967.

Alford, Henry. *An Earnest Dissuasive from Joining the Communion of the Church of Rome. Addressed to the Younger Members of the Church of England, and Especially to Students in the Universities.* London 1846.

Allchin, A. M. 'The *Via Media*—an Anglican Revaluation', in Coulson [1965] 62–111.
'The Theological Vision of the Oxford Movement', in Coulson [1967] 50–75.

Allen, Louis. 'The Idea of Doctrinal Development', *The Tablet*, ccxi (1958) 326–7.

Allies, Thomas William. *The Church of England Cleared from the Charge of Schism, upon the Testimony of Councils and Fathers of the First Six Centuries.* London 1846.

Alston, George. *The Development of Divine Instruction, as Exemplified in the Several Revelations made to Man, Briefly Considered.* London 1846.

Altholz, Josef. *The Liberal Catholic Movement in England.* London, 1962.
'Some Observations on Victorian Religious Biography: Newman and Manning', *Worship*, xliii (1969) 407–15.

Anglican Priest, An. *A Few Words Addressed to the Author of 'An Essay on the Development of Christian Doctrine'.* London 1846.

Arnold, Matthew. *St Paul and Protestantism. With an Essay on Puritanism and the Church of England.* London 1870.
Literature and Dogma. London 1887. (First published 1873).

Arnold, Thomas. 'The Oxford Malignants and Dr Hampden', *The Edinburgh Review or Critical Journal*, lxiii (1836) 225–39.

Artz, Johannes. 'Newman and Intuition', *Philosophy Today*, i (1957) 10–15.

'Entstehung und Auswirkung von Newmans Theorie der Dogmenentwicklung', *Tübinger Theologische Quartalschrift*, cxlviii (1968) 63–104, 167–98.

ed. *Uber die Entwicklung der Glaubenslehre*. By John Henry Newman. Trans Theodor Haecker. Mainz 1969.

Ashwell, A. R. *The Life of the Right Reverend Samuel Wilberforce, D.D.* 3 vols, London 1880, 1881, 1882.

Atkins, Anselm. 'Religious Assertions and Doctrinal Development', *TS* xxvii (1966) 523–52.

Bacchus, Francis. 'Newman's Oxford University Sermons', *The Month*, cxxxix (1922) 1–12.

'How to Read the "Grammar of Assent" ', *The Month*, cxl (1924) 106–15.

cf Tristram [1931].

Bainvel, Jean V. 'L'Eglise. Histoire du Dogme. L'Evolution des idées', *Etudes*, lxx (1897) 5–16, 175–94.

'Histoire d'un Dogme', *Etudes*, ci (1904) 612–32.

De Magisterio Vivo et Traditione. Paris 1905.

Bakker, Leo. 'Man's Place in Divine Revelation', *Concilium*, i, 3 (1967) 11–19.

Balic, Carlo. 'Il Senso Cristiano e il Progresso del Dogma', *Gregorianum*, xxxiii (1952) 106–34.

Baraúna, Guilherme and Y. M.-J. Congar, eds *L'Eglise de Vatican* ii: *Etudes autour de la Constitution Conciliaire sur l'Eglise, Unam Sanctam* 51, Paris 1966. Baraúna [1966].

Barmann, Laurence. 'Newman and the Theory of Doctrinal Development', *American Ecclesiastical Review*, cxliii (1960) 121–9.

Baron Friedrich von Hügel and the Modernist Crisis in England. Cambridge 1972.

Barry, William. *Cardinal Newman*. London 1927. (First published 1904).

Barter, William Brudenell. *The English Church not in Schism. Or, a Few Words on the Supremacy of the Pope, and the Progress of Antichrist*. London 1845.

Barter, William Brudenell. *A Postscript to The English Church not in Schism. Containing a Few Words on Mr Newman's Essay on Development*. London 1846.

Bastable, James D. 'The Germination of Belief within Probability according to Newman', *Philosophical Studies*, xi (1961–2) 81–111.

Baudin, Emil. 'La Philosophie de la Foi chez Newman', *Revue de Philosophie*, viii (1906) 571–98; ix (1906) 20–55, 253–85, 373–90.

Baum, Gregory. 'Doctrinal Renewal', *JES*, ii (1965) 365–81.

'Foreword' to Femiano [1967] Baum [1967a].

Baum, Gregory—*continued*.
'The Magisterium in a Changing Church', *Concilium*, i, 3 (1967) 34–42. Baum [1967b].
'Orthodoxy Recast', *The Future of Belief Debate*, 103–8. Ed Gregory Baum. New York 1967. Baum [1967c].
'Vatican II's Constitution on Revelation: History and Interpretation', *TS*, xxviii (1967) 51–75. Baum [1967d].
The Credibility of the Church Today. A Reply to Charles Davis. London 1968.

Baumgartner, C. 'Tradition et Magistère', *Recherches de Science Religieuse*, xli (1953) 161–87.
'Du Concile du Vatican au Développement du Dogme', *RSR*, xliv (1956) 573–5.

Bea, Augustin. 'Il Progresso nell'interpretazione della Sacra Scrittura', *Gregorianum*, xxxiii (1952) 85–105.

Becker, Werner. 'Newman's Influence in Germany', in Coulson [1967] 174–89.

Benard, E. D. *A Preface to Newman's Theology*. London 1945.

Bennett, W. J. E. *The Schism of Certain Priests and Others, Lately in Communion with the Church. A Sermon*. London 1845.

Bent, Charles N. *Interpreting the Doctrine of God*. New York 1969.

Bergeron, Richard. *Les Abus de l'Eglise d'après Newman*. Tournai 1971.

Berkouwer, G. C. *The Second Vatican Council and the New Catholicism*. Grand Rapids 1965.

Best, Geoffrey. 'Evangelicalism and the Victorians', in Symondson [1970] 37–56.

Bévenot, Maurice. 'Tradition, Church, and Dogma', *HJ*, i (1960) 34–47.
' "Faith and Morals" in the Councils of Trent and Vatican I', *HJ*, iii (1962) 15–30.
'*Traditiones* in the Council of Trent', *HJ*, iv (1963) 333–47.
'Primacy and Development', *HJ*, ix (1968) 400–13.

Biemer, Günter. 'The Anglican Response to Newman?', *Philosophical Studies*, viii (1958) 64–70.
Newman on Tradition. Trans and ed Kevin Smyth. London 1967. (Revised version of *Uberlieferung und Offenbarung. Die Lehre von der Tradition nach John Henry Newman*. Freiburg 1961).

de Bivort de la Saudée, J. *Anglicans et Catholiques: le Problème de l'Union Anglo-Romaine (1833–1933)*. Brussels 1949.

Blehl, Vincent F. 'Newman, the Fathers and Education', *Thought*, xlv (1970) 196–212.

Blenkinsopp, Joseph. *Celibacy, Ministry, Church*. London 1969.

de Blic, J. 'L'analyse de la Foi chez Newman', *ETL*, xxiv (1948) 136–45.

Bloch, Marc. *The Historian's Craft*. Manchester 1954.

Blondel, Maurice. 'Fidelité Conservée par la Croissance même de la Tradition', *Revue Thomiste*, (1935) 611–26.

'De la Valeur Historique du Dogme', *Les Premiers Ecrits de Maurice Blondel: Lettre sur les Exigences de la Pensée Contemporaine en Matière d'Apologétique; Histoire et Dogme*, 229–45. Paris 1956. (Reprinted from *Bulletin de Littérature Ecclésiastique de Toulouse*, [1905] 61–77).

'History and Dogma', in Dru [1964] 221–87. (First published as articles in *La Quinzaine*, lvi [1904] 145–67, 349–73, 433–58).

Boekraad, Adrian J. *The Personal Conquest of Truth According to J. H. Newman*. Louvain 1955.

'Continental Newman Literature', *Philosophical Studies*, vii (1957) 110–16.

'Cardinal Newman Studien III', *ibid* viii (1958) 140–5.

and Tristram, Henry. *The Argument from Conscience to the Existence of God According to J. H. Newman*. Louvain 1961.

'Aristotelische Erkenntnislehre bei Whately und Newman', *Philosophical Studies*, xi (1961–2) 174–8.

Bokenkotter, Thomas S. *Cardinal Newman as an Historian*. Louvain 1959.

Bony, Paul. 'La Parole de Dieu dans l'Ecriture et dans l'Evénement', *La Maison-Dieu*, xcix (1969) 94–111.

Bouillard, Henri. *Conversion et Grâce chez Saint Thomas d'Aquin*. Paris 1944.

'L'intention Fondamentale de Maurice Blondel et la Théologie', *RSR*, xxxvi (1949) 321–402.

Bouyer, Louis. 'Newman et le Platonisme de l'âme Anglaise', *Revue de Philosophie*, vi (1936) 285–305. (Also available in English as 'Newman and English Platonism', *Monastic Studies*, i [1963] 111–31).

'Newman's Influence in France', *Du R*, ccxvii (1945) 182–8.

Newman. His Life and Spirituality. Trans J. Lewis May. London 1958. (First published as *Newman: sa Vie; sa Spiritualité*. Paris 1952).

Boyer, Charles. 'Relazione tra il Progresso Filosofico, Teologico, Dogmatico', *Gregorianum*, xxxiii (1952) 168–82.

Braaten, Carl E. 'The Limits of Pluralism in Doctrine and Worship', in Pannenberg [1970e] 73–88.

Brekelmans, Antonius. 'Origin and Function of Creeds in the Early Church', *Concilium*, i, 6 (1970) 33–42.

Bremond, Henri, ed *Newman. Le Développement du Dogme Chrétien*. Paris 1906. (Partial French ed of *Dev*).

'Apologie pour les Newmanistes Français', *Revue Pratique d'Apologétique*, iii (1907) 655–66. Bremond [1907a].

The Mystery of Newman. Trans H. C. Corrance. London 1907. Bremond [1907b].

'Autour de Newman', *Annales de Philosophie Chrétienne*, v (1908) 337–69.

Brickel, A. G. 'Cardinal Newman's Theory of Knowledge', *American Catholic Quarterly Review*, xliii (1918) 507–18, 645–53.
'Newman's Criteria of Historical Evolution', *ibid*, xliv (1919) 588–94.

Brilioth, Yngve. *The Anglican Revival. Studies in the Oxford Movement.* London 1925.

Brown, C. G. 'Newman's Minor Critics', *DR*, lxxxix (1971) 13–21.

Brown, Raymond E. 'The History and Development of the Theory of a *Sensus Plenior*', *Catholic Biblical Quarterly*, xv (1953) 141–62.
'The *Sensus Plenior* in the Last Ten Years', *ibid*, xxv (1963) 262–85.

Brown. R. K. 'Newman and von Hügel. A Record of an Early Meeting', *The Month*, ccxii (1961) 24–32.

Brunner, August. 'Idee und Entwicklung bei Hegel und Newman', *Scholastik*, xxxii (1957) 1–26.

Burgum, E. B. 'Cardinal Newman and the Complexity of Truth', *Sewanee Review*, xxxviii (1930), 310–27.

Burke, W. P. 'The Beauty ever Ancient, ever New', *American Essays for the Newman Centennial*, 189–207. Ed J. K. Ryan and E. D. Benard. Washington 1947. (First published as 'The Ancient Newness of Dogma', *American Ecclesiastical Review*, cxv [1946] 169–85).

Burtchaell, James Tunstead. *Catholic Theories of Biblical Inspiration since 1810: a Review and Critique.* Cambridge 1969.

Butler, Basil Christopher. 'The Significance of Newman Today: The Theory of Development', *Du R*, ccxxxiii (1959) 337–46.
The Theology of Vatican II. London 1967.

Butler, Joseph. *The Works of Joseph Butler, DCL.* Ed W. E. Gladstone. 2 vols, Oxford 1896.

Butler, William Archer. *Letters on the Development of Christian Doctrine, in Reply to Mr Newman's Essay.* Ed Thomas Woodward. Dublin 1850.

Butterfield, Herbert. *Christianity and History.* London 1957. (First published 1949).

Byrne, J. J. 'The Notion of Doctrinal Development in the Anglican Writings of J. H. Newman', *ETL*, xiv (1937) 230–86.

Caffrey, Thomas A. 'Consensus and Infallibility: the Mind of Vatican I', *DR*, lxxxviii (1970) 107–31.

Caird, Edward. *The Evolution of Religion.* 2 vols, Glasgow 1893.

Calkins, Arthur Burton. 'John Henry Newman on Conscience and the Magisterium', *DR*, lxxxvii (1969) 358–69.

Cameron, James M. *The Night Battle.* London 1962.
'Newman and the Empiricist Tradition', in Coulson [1967] 76–96.

Capes, J. M. 'A Parallel and a Contrast', *The Gentleman's Magazine*, ix (1872) 33–44.
To Rome and Back. London 1873.

Capps, Walter H. 'Harnack and Ecumenical Discussion', *JES*, iii (1966) 486–502.

Cavallera, F. 'Le Document Newman-Perrone et le Développement du Dogme', *Bulletin de Littérature Ecclésiastique*, xlvii (1946) 132–42, 208-25.

Chadwick, Owen. *From Bossuet to Newman: The Idea of Doctrinal Development*. Cambridge 1957.
ed. *The Mind of the Oxford Movement*. London 1960.
The Victorian Church. Part i. ²London 1970. Chadwick [1970a].
The Victorian Church. Part ii. London 1970. Chadwick [1970b].

Charlier, L. *Essai sur le Problème Théologique*. Thuillies 1938.

Chavasse, A. 'L'Ecclésiologie au Concile du Vatican. L'Infaillibilité de l'Eglise', *L'Ecclésiologie au* xixe *Siècle*, 233–45. Unam Sanctam 34. Paris 1960.

Chevalier, J. 'Newman et la Notion de Développement', *Trois Conférences d'Oxford*, 81–118. ²Paris 1933.

Church, Richard William. *The Oxford Movement. Twelve Years: 1833–1845*. London 1891.
Occasional Papers. 2 vols, London 1897.

Cognet, Louis. *Newman ou la Recherche de la Vérité*. Tournai 1966.

Coleridge, Samuel Taylor. *On the Constitution of Church and State According to the Idea of Each*. Ed H. N. Coleridge. London 1839.
Hints Towards the Formation of a More Comprehensive Theory of Life. Ed Seth B. Watson. London 1848.

Collin, W. E. 'Cardinal Newman and Recent French Thought', *Transactions of the Royal Society of Canada*, xxxi, section 2 (1937) 33–43.

Collingwood, R. G. *The Idea of History*. [Ed T. M. Knox]. Oxford 1966.

Collins, James, ed. *Philosophical Readings in Cardinal Newman*. Chicago 1961.

Concilium General Secretariat, eds. 'The Creed in the Melting Pot', *Concilium*, i, 6 (1970) 131–53.

Congar, Yves. 'Dogme Christologique et Ecclésiologie. Vérité et Limites d'un Parallèle', *Das Konzil von Chalkedon. Geschichte und Gegenwart. Bd* iii. *Chalkedon Heute*, 239–68. Ed Aloys Grillmeier and Heinrich Bacht. Wurzburg 1954.
'Tradition et Vie Ecclésiale. La Tradition, Mode Original de Communication', *Istina*, viii (1961–2) 411–36.
Tradition and the Life of the Church. London 1964. (First published as *La Tradition et la Vie de l'Eglise*. Paris 1963).
'The Church: the People of God', *Concilium*, i, 1 (1965) 7–19.
Tradition and Traditions. Trans Michael Naseby and Thomas Rainborough. London 1966. (First published as *La Tradition et les Traditions*. 2 vols, Paris 1960, 1963).

Congar, Yves—*continued*.

'Theology's Task after Vatican II', *Theology of Renewal. Vol I, Renewal of Religious Thought*, 47–65. Ed L. K. Shook. New York 1968.

'Bulletin d'Ecclésiologie', *RSPT*, liv (1970) 95–127. Congar [1970a].

'Church History as a Branch of Theology', *Concilium*, vii, 6 (1970) 85–96. Congar [1970b].

L'Eglise: de Saint Augustin à l'Epoque Moderne. Paris 1970. Congar [1970c].

'Infaillibilité et Indéfectibilité', *RSPT*, liv (1970) 601–18. Congar [1970d].

Connelly, P. *Cardinal Newman versus the Apostles' Creed*. London 1880.

Connolly, F. X. 'Newman and Science', *Thought*, xxxviii (1963) 107–21.

Coppens, Joseph. 'La Définibilité de l'Assomption', *ETL*, xxiii (1947) 5–35.

'Les Harmonies des Deux Testaments en Etudiant les Divers Sens des Ecritures. II Les Apports du Sens Plenier', *NRT*, lxxi (1949) 3–38.

Coulson, John, ed. *On Consulting the Faithful in Matters of Doctrine*. By John Henry Newman. London 1961.

Coulson, John, A. M. Allchin, and Meriol Trevor. *Newman: a Portrait Restored*. London 1965. Coulson [1965].

Coulson, John, and A. M. Allchin, eds. *The Rediscovery of Newman: an Oxford Symposium*. London 1967. Coulson [1967].

Coulson, John. 'Newman on the Church—his Final View, its Origin and Influence', in Coulson [1967] 123–43.

Newman and the Common Tradition: a Study in the Language of Church and Society. Oxford 1970.

Cronin, J. F. *Cardinal Newman: His Theory of Knowledge*. Washington 1935.

Cross, F. L. *John Henry Newman. With a Set of Unpublished Letters*. London 1933.

'Newman and the Doctrine of Development', *Church Quarterly Review*, cxv (1933) 245–57.

Crowe, Frederick E. 'Development of Doctrine and the Ecumenical Problem', *TS*, xxiii (1962) 27–46.

'The Exigent Mind: Bernard Lonergan's Intellectualism', *Spirit as Inquiry. Studies in Honor of Bernard Lonergan*, 16–33. Ed Frederick E. Crowe. *Continuum*, ii, 3 (1964).

'Development of Doctrine', *American Ecclesiastical Record*, clix (1968) 233–47.

'Dogma versus the Self-correcting Process of Learning', *TS*, xxxi (1970) 605–24.

Culler, A. Dwight. *The Imperial Intellect: a Study of Newman's Educational Ideal*. London 1955.

Cunningham, William. 'Newman on Development', *North British Review*, v (1846) 418–53.

Daniélou, Jean. 'Ecriture et Tradition', *RSR*, li (1963) 550–7.

Darlap, Adolf. 'Théologie Fondamentale de l'Histoire du Salut', in *MS* 1 [1969] 42–206.

Davies, Horton. *Worship and Theology in England.* III. *From Watts and Wesley to Maurice. 1690–1850.* Princeton 1961.
ibid IV. *From Newman to Martineau. 1850–1900.* Princeton 1962.

Davis, Henry Francis. 'The Catholicism of Cardinal Newman' in *JHN* [1945] 36–54. Davis [1945a].
'Newman and the Psychology of the Development of Doctrine', *Du R*, ccxvi (1945) 97–107. Davis [1945b].
'Was Newman a Disciple of Coleridge?', *Du R*, ccxvii (1945), 165–72. Davis [1945c].
'Newman and Thomism', in *NS* [1957] 157–69.
'Is Newman's Theory of Development Catholic?', *Blackfriars*, xxxix (1958) 310–21.
'Le Rôle et l'Apostolat de la Hiérarchie et du Laïcat dans la Théologie de l'Eglise chez Newman', *L'Ecclésiologie au XIXe Siècle*, 329–49. *Unam Sanctam* 34. Paris 1960.
'Newman and the Theology of the Living Word', in *NS* [1964] 167–77.
'Doctrine, Development of', *A Catholic Dictionary of Theology.* II. *Catechism—Heaven*, 177–89. London 1967. Davis [1967a].
'Foreword' to *Newman on Tradition.* By Günter Biemer. London 1967. Davis [1967b].
'Newman's Influence in England', in Coulson [1967] 216–32. Davis [1967c].

Davison, John. *Discourses on Prophecy, in Which are Considered its Structure, Use, and Inspiration.* ⁷Oxford 1861. (First published 1824).

Dawson, Christopher. *The Spirit of the Oxford Movement.* London 1933.

Decanus. *Whose is the Loss, or Whose the Gain, by the Secession of the Rev Mr Newman, and Others? Considered in a Letter to the Archbishop of Dublin.* London 1846.

Dejaifve, Georges. 'Bible, Tradition, Magistère dans la Théologie Catholique', *NRT*, lxxviii (1956) 135–51.
'Diversité Dogmatique et Unité de la Révélation', *NRT*, lxxxix (1967) 16–25.

DeLaura, David J. *Hebrew and Hellene in Victorian England.* London 1969.

Dell, Robert Edward. 'A Liberal Catholic View of the Case of Dr Mivart', *The Nineteenth Century*, xlvii (1900), 669–84.

Denziger, H. and Karl Rahner, eds. *Enchiridion Symbolorum Definitionum et Declarationum de Rebus Fidei et Morum.* ³¹Rome 1957. Dz.

Dessain, Charles Stephen. 'Cardinal Newman on the Theory and Practice of Knowledge. The Purpose of the Grammar of Assent', *DR*, lxxv (1957) 1–23. Dessain [1957a].
'The Newman-Archives at Birmingham', in *NS* [1957] 269–73 Dessain [1957b].

Dessain, Charles Stephen—*continued.*
'An Unpublished Paper by Cardinal Newman on the Development of Doctrine', *Journal of Theological Studies*, ix (1958) 324–35.
'The Reception Among Catholics of Newman's Doctrine of Development', in *NS* [1964] 179–91.
'Cardinal Newman and Ecumenism', *Clergy Review*, 1 (1965) 119–37, 189–206.
John Henry Newman. London 1966.
'The Biblical Basis of Newman's Ecumenical Theology', in Coulson [1967] 100–22. London 1967.
'Cardinal Newman Considered as a Prophet', *Concilium*, vii, 4 (1968) 41–50. Dessain [1968a].
'Infallibility: What Newman Taught in Manning's Church', in *Inf* [1968] 59–80. Dessain [1968b].

Dhanis, E. 'Révélation Explicite et Implicite', *Gregorianum*, xxxiv (1953) 187–237.

Dibble, Romuald A. *John Henry Newman: The Concept of Infallible Doctrinal Authority.* Washington 1955.

Donnelly, P. J. 'Theological Opinion on the Development of Dogma', *TS*, viii (1947) 659–99.

Dru, Alexander. 'The Importance of Maurice Blondel', *DR*, lxxx (1962) 118–29.

Dru, Alexander and Illtyd Trethowan, eds *Maurice Blondel: The Letter on Apologetics and History and Dogma.* London 1964.

Dublanchy, E. 'Dogme', *Dictionnaire de Théologie Catholique*, iv, cols 1574–1650. Paris 1924. (First published 1911).

Dulles, Avery. 'The Theology of Revelation', *TS*, xxv (1964) 43–58.
'The Constitution on Divine Revelation in Ecumenical Perspective', *American Ecclesiastical Review*, cliv (1966) 217–31.
'Dogma as an Ecumenical Problem', *TS*, xxix (1968) 397–416.
'Authority and Reason in the Assent of Faith', in Pannenberg [1970e] 32–50. Dulles [1970a].
'Official Church Teaching and Historical Relativity', *ibid* 51–72 Dulles [1970b].
Revelation Theology. London 1970. Dulles [1970c].

Dumont, C. 'De Trois Dimensions Retrouvées en Théologie: Eschatologie—Orthopraxie—Hermeneutique', *NRT*, xcii (1970) 561–91.

Duncan, David. *The Life and Letters of Herbert Spencer.* London 1908.

Dupuy, Bernard-D. 'Bulletin d'Histoire des Doctrines: Newman', *RSPT*, xlv (1961) 125–76.
'L'Influence de Newman sur la Théologie Catholique du Développement Dogmatique', in *NS* [1964] 143–65.
'Newman's Influence in France', in Coulson [1967] 147–73.
'Historique de la Constitution', in Dupuy [1968b] 61–117. Dupuy [1968a].

Dupuy, Bernard-D.—*continued.*
  ed *Vatican* II: *La Révélation Divine.* 2 vols, *Unam Sanctam* 70a–b. Paris 1968. Dupuy [1968b].
  'Lignes de Force de la Constitution "Dei Verbum" de Vatican II', *Irénikon,* xliii (1970) 7–37.

Echlin, E. P. 'Foreword' to Pannenberg [1970e].

Egan, Harvey. 'Towards a Theology of the Development of Dogma', *Canadian Journal of Theology,* xv (1969) 227–39.

Egner, G. *Apologia pro Charles Kingsley.* London 1969.

Elbert, J. A. *Evolution of Newman's Conception of Faith.* Philadelphia 1932.

Eliot, George 'The Influence of Rationalism', *Fortnightly Review,* i (1865) 43–55.

Eliot, T. S. *Four Quartets.* London 1944.

English Churchman, An. *A Review of Mr Newman's Essay on the Development of Christian Doctrine.* London 1846.

Faber, Geoffrey. *Oxford Apostles: A Character Study of the Oxford Movement.* London 1933.

Faber, G. S. *Letters on Tractarian Secession to Popery: with Remarks on Mr Newman's Principle of Development, Dr Moehler's Symbolism, and the Adduced Evidence in Favour of the Romish Practice of Mariolatry.* London 1846.

Fairbairn, Andrew Martin. *The Place of Christ in Modern Theology.* London 1893.
  Catholicism: Roman and Anglican. London 1899.

Farrer, Austin M. 'Infallibility and Historical Revelation', in *Inf* [1968] 9–23.

Fawkes, Alfred. 'Recent Theories of Development in Theology', *Edinburgh Review,* cxcviii (1903) 52–81.

Feiner, J. 'Révélation et Eglise: Eglise et Révélation', in *MS* 3 [1969] 11–69.

Femiano, Samuel D. *Infallibility of the Laity: the Legacy of Newman.* New York 1967.

Fenton, J. C. 'Newman and Papal Infallibility', *American Essays for the Newman Centennial,* 163–85. Ed J. K. Ryan and E. D. Benard. Washington 1947. (First published as 'John Henry Newman and the Vatican Definition of Papal Infallibility', *American Ecclesiastical Review,* cxiii [1945] 300–20).

Filograssi, G. 'Tradizione Divino-Apostolica e Magisterio della Chiesa', *Gregorianum,* xxxiii (1952) 135–67.

Finsterhölzl, Johann. 'Newmans Kriterien Echter Lehrentwicklung und Die Heutige Theologie', in *NS* [1967] 261–79.

Flanagan, Philip. *Newman, Faith and the Believer.* London 1946.

Fletcher, Jefferson B. 'Newman and Carlyle: An Unrecognised Affinity', *Atlantic Monthly*, xcv (1905) 669–79.

Flick, Maurice. 'Il Problema dello Sviluppo del Dogma nella Teologia Contemporanea', *Gregorianum*, xxxiii (1952) 5–23.

Fothergill, Brian. *Nicholas Wiseman*. London 1963.

Fransen, Piet F. 'Unity and Confessional Statements: Historical and Theological Inquiry of RC Traditional Conceptions', *Bijdragen*, xxx (1972) 2–38.

Frieden, Pierre. 'Pascal et Newman: la Drame de l'Homme Libre', in *NS* [1957] 170–202.

Fries, Heinrich. 'Die Dogmengeschichte des Fünften Jahrhunderts im Theologischen Werdegang von John Henry Newman', in *NS* [1954] 67–99.
'La Révélation', in *MS* 1 [1969] 209–95.

Froude, James Anthony. 'Father Newman on "The Grammar of Assent"', *Short Studies on Great Subjects. Second Series*, 101–45. London 1874.
'The Oxford Counter-Reformation', *Short Studies on Great Subjects. Fourth Series*, 163–253. London 1883.

Froude, Richard Hurrell. 'Mr Blanco White, Heresy and Orthodoxy', *The British Critic, Quarterly Theological Review, and Ecclesiastical Record*, xix (1836) 204–25.
'Remarks on the Grounds of Orthodox Belief', *Remains of the Late Reverend Richard Hurrell Froude, MA, Fellow of Oriel College, Oxford*, Part II, Vol I, 315–56. Derby, 1839. (Same study as Froude, R. H. [1836], slightly edited by J. H. Newman).

Fuchs, J. 'Origines d'une Trilogie Ecclésiologique à l'Epoque Rationaliste de la Théologie', *RSPT*, liii (1969) 186–211.

Galvin, John J. 'A Critical Survey of Modern Conceptions of Doctrinal Development', *Proceedings of the Catholic Theological Society of America*, (1950) 45–63.

Gardeil, A. 'La Réforme de la Théologie Catholique: Idée d'une Méthode Régressive. La Documentation de Saint Thomas. Les Procédés Exégétiques de Saint Thomas', *Review Thomiste*, xi (1903) 5–19, 197–215, 428–57. Gardeil [1903a, b, c].

Gardiner, Patrick. *The Nature of Historical Explanation*. Oxford 1961. (First published 1952).

Ginsberg, Morris. 'The Idea of Progress: a Revaluation', *Essays in Sociology and Social Philosophy*, 71–128. London 1968.

Godet, P. 'J. H. Newman', *Revue du Clergé Français*, xxvi (1901) 113–43.

Gonzalez Hernandez, Olegario. 'La Nouvelle Conscience de l'Eglise et ses Présupposés Historico-Théologiques', in Baraúna [1966] ii, 175–209.

Q

Gorce, Denys. *Newman et les Pères. La Secret de sa Conversion.* Juvisy 1934.

'Newman Existentialiste?', in *NS* [1957] 203–24.

Gore, Charles, ed *Lux Mundi: a Series of Studies in the Religion of the Incarnation.* [15]London 1904. (First published 1889).
Can We Then Believe? London 1926. Gore [1926a].
The Reconstruction of Belief. London 1926. Gore [1926b].

Gornall, Thomas. 'Newman on Catholicism', *HJ*, v (1964) 436–9.

Gougaud, L. 'Le Mouvement Intellectuel Religieux dans les Pays de Langue Anglaise: le Modernisme', *Revue du Clergé Français*, lvii (1909) 541–65.

Grabinski, Joseph. *La Renaissance Catholique en Angleterre et le Cardinal Newman. D'après une Etude du Cardinal Capecelatro.* Lyon 1893.

Graef, Hilda. *God and Myself: the Spirituality of John Henry Newman.* London 1967.

de Grandmaison, Léonce. 'L'Evangile et l'Eglise', *Etudes*, xciv (1903) 145–74.

'John Henry Newman Considéré comme Maître', *Etudes*, cix (1906) 721–50; cx (1907) 39–69.

Le Dogme Chrétien, sa Nature, ses Formules, son Développement. Paris 1928.

Greenfield, R. 'The Attitude of the Tractarians to the Roman Catholic Church'. Unpublished Dissertation, Oxford 1956.

Gregory, T. S. 'Newman and Liberalism', in Tierney [1945] 85–115.

Groot, J. C. 'Aspects Horizontaux de la Collégialité', in Baraúna [1966] iii, 805–28.

Guibert, J. *Le Réveil du Catholicisme en Angleterre.* Paris 1907.

Guitton, Jean. *La Philosophie de Newman: Essai sur l'Idée de Développement.* Paris 1933.

La Pensée Moderne et le Catholicisme. Parallèles: Renan et Newman. Aix 1938.

'La Théorie du Développement et son Actualité', in *NS* [1957] 77–98.

Gundersen, B. *Cardinal Newman and Apologetics.* Oslo 1952.

Gwynn, Aubrey. 'Newman and the Catholic Historian', in Tierney [1945] 279–306.

Gwynn, Denis. 'John Henry Newman, 1801–1890', in *JHN* [1945] 16–35.

Haag, Herbert. 'De la Parole de Dieu au Livre de l'Ecriture Sainte', in *MS* 2 [1969] 73–262.

Hamer, Jerome. 'Les Maîtres de xixe Siècle. Möhler, Newman, Scheeben', *RSPT*, xliii (1959) 331–6.

Hammans, Herbert. *Die Neueren Katholischen Erklärungen der Dogmenentwicklung.* Essen 1965.

Hammans, Herbert—*continued.*
'Recent Catholic Views on the Development of Dogma', *Concilium*, i, 3 (1967) 53–63.

Hampden, Renn Dickson. *The Scholastic Philosophy Considered in its Relation to Christian Theology.* Oxford 1833

Hanson, R. P. C. *Tradition in the Early Church.* London 1962.

Härdelin, Alf. *The Tractarian Understanding of the Eucharist.* Uppsala 1965.

Harnack, Adolf. *What is Christianity?* Trans T. Bailey Saunders. London 1901. (First published as *Das Wesen des Christentums,* 1900).

Harper, Gordon Huntington, ed. *Cardinal Newman and William Froude, FRS, A Correspondence.* Baltimore 1933.

Harrold, Charles Frederick. 'John Henry Newman and the Alexandrian Platonists', *Modern Philology*, xxxvii (1940) 279–91.
John Henry Newman: an Expository and Critical Study of his Mind, Thought and Art. London 1945.

Harvey, Van Austin. *The Historian and the Believer.* London 1967.

Hawkins, Edward. *A Dissertation Upon the Use and Importance of Unauthoritative Tradition, as an Introduction to the Christian Doctrines; Including the Substance of a Sermon, Preached Before the University of Oxford, May 31, 1818, Upon 2 Thess ii. 15.* Oxford 1819.
An Inquiry into the Connected Uses of the Principal Means of Attaining Christian Truth. Oxford 1840.

Hayen, A. 'Hegel et Blondel: à propos d'un Livre Récent', *Revue Philosophique de Louvain,* lvii (1959) 342–50.
'La Philosophie Catholique de Maurice Blondel au Temps de la Première "Action" ', *ibid,* lix (1961) 249–314.

Hayot, M. 'Bremond et Newman. La Pensée et l'Oeuvre d'H. Bremond au Début du Siècle. I. Le Problème de la Foi', *Revue Apologétique,* lxvii (1938) 321–33. Hayot [1938a].
ibid 'II. La question du Dogme', 449–60. Hayot [1938b]

Heaney, J. J. *The Modernist Crisis: von Hügel.* Washington 1968.

Hick, John. *Faith and Knowledge.* ²London 1967.

Hoffmann, Manfred. 'Church and History in Vatican II's Constitution on the Church: a Protestant Perspective', *TS,* xxix (1968) 191–214.

Hogan, Jeremiah J. 'Tractarian Oxford', in Tierney [1945] 27–56.

Hollis, Christopher. 'Cardinal Newman and Dean Church', in *JHN* [1945] 68–91.
Newman and the Modern World. London 1967.

Holloway, John. *The Victorian Sage.* London 1953.

Holmes, J. Derek. 'Newman, Froude and Pattison: Some Aspects of Their Relations', *Journal of Religious History,* iv (1966) 28–38. Holmes [1966a].

Holmes, J. Derek—*continued*.
'Newman's Reputation and *The Lives of the English Saints*', *Catholic Historical Review*, li (1966) 528–38. Holmes [1966b].
Review of *Newman on Tradition*, by Günter Biemer, *HJ* viii (1967) 462. Holmes [1967a].
and Robert Murray, eds. *On the Inspiration of Scripture*. By John Henry Newman. London 1967. Holmes [1967b].
'A Note on Newman's Historical Method', in Coulson [1967] 97–9.
'Cardinal Newman and the First Vatican Council', *Annuarium Historiae Conciliorum*. Ed W. Brandmüller and R. Bäumer. Jahrgang i, Heft 2 (1969), 374–98. Holmes [1969a].
'Newman and the Use of History'. Unpublished Dissertation, Cambridge 1969. Holmes [1969b].
'Cardinal Newman on the Philosophy of History', *Tijdschrift voor Filosofie*, xxxii (1970) 521–35. Holmes [1970a].
'Introduction' to *Newman's University Sermons*, 26–41. London 1970. Holmes [1970b].
'Newman's Attitude Towards Historical Criticism and Biblical Inspiration', *DR* lxxxix (1971) 22–37.

Hort, Arthur Fenton. *Life and Letters of Fenton John Anthony Hort*. 2 vols, London 1896.

Houghton, Esther Rhoads. '*The British Critic* and the Oxford Movement', *Studies in Bibliography: Papers of the Bibliographical Society of the University of Virginia*, xvi, 119–37. Ed Fredson Bowers. Charlotteville 1963.

Houghton, Walter E. *The Victorian Frame of Mind. 1830–1870*. London 1957.

House, Humphry. 'The Mood of Doubt', in *Id* [1966] 71–7. House [1966a].
'Qualities of George Eliot's Unbelief', in *Id* [1966] 157–63. House [1966b].

Hughes, Philip. 'The Coming Century', *English Catholics 1850–1950*. Ed George Andrew Beck. London 1950.

Hunt, William Coughlin. *Intuition: the Key to J. H. Newman's Theory of Doctrinal Development*. Washington 1967.

Hutton, R. H. *Cardinal Newman*. London 1891.

Huxley, Thomas H. 'Agnosticism and Christianity', *Nineteenth Century*, xxv (1889) 937–64.

Ideas and Beliefs of the Victorians. New York 1966. (First published 1949). *Id* [1966].

Infallibility in the Church: an Anglican-Catholic Dialogue. London 1968. *Inf* [1968].

Inge, William Ralph. *Outspoken Essays*. London 1919.
Outspoken Essays (Second Series). London 1922.

Irons, W. J. *Notes of the Church. A Sermon Preached at Brompton*. London 1845.
The Theory of Development Examined, with Reference Specially to

Irons, W. J.—*continued*.
Mr Newman's Essay, and to the Rule of St Vincent of Lerins. London 1846.

Irvine, A. *Romanism, as Represented by the Rev John Henry Newman, Briefly Considered; with Some Illustrations of its Necessary Tendency, from Personal Observations Made at Rome*. London 1846.

Jaki, Stanislaus. *Les Tendances Nouvelles de l'Ecclésiologie*. Rome 1957.

James, O. F. M. 'Newman as a Philosopher', in Tierney [1945] 232–45.

Jenson, Robert W. *The Knowledge of Things Hoped for: the Sense of Theological Discourse*. New York 1969.

John Henry Newman: Centenary Essays. London 1945. *JHN* [1945].

Jossua, Jean-Pierre. 'Immutabilité, Progrès ou Structurations Multiples des Doctrines Chrétiennes', *RSPT*, lii (1968) 173–200.
'Rule of Faith and Orthodoxy', *Concilium*, i, 6 (1970) 56–67.
'Signification des Confessions de Foi', *Istina*, xvii (1972) 48–56.

Kasper, Walter. 'Geschichtlichkeit der Dogmen?', *Stimmen der Zeit*, clxxix (1967) 401–16. Kasper [1967a].
'The Relationship Between Gospel and Dogma: an Historical Approach', *Concilium*, i, 3 (1967), 73–9. Kasper [1967b].

Kehm, George H. 'Translator's Preface' to *Basic Questions in Theology*. By Wolfhart Pannenberg. London 1970.

Kelly, E. E. 'Newman More Ecumenically Read', *JES* v (1968) 365–70.

Kenny, Terence. *The Political Thought of John Henry Newman*. London 1957.

Kent, John H. S. 'Models of the British Non-Conformist Ministry', *The Christian Priesthood*, 83–100. Ed Nicholas Lash and Joseph Rhymer. London 1970.

Keogh, C. B. 'Introduction to the Philosophy of Cardinal Newman,' Unpublished Dissertation, Louvain 1950.

Knox, Ronald Arbuthnott. 'Newman and Roman Catholicism', in *Id* [1966] 126–31.

Küng, Hans. *Justification. The Doctrine of Karl Barth and a Catholic Reflection*. Trans Thomas Collins, Edmund E. Tolk and David Grandskou. London 1964. (First published as *Rechtfertigung: Die Lehre Karl Barths und eine Katholische Besinnung*. Einsiedeln 1957).

Laframboise, J. C. 'Aux Sources de la Pensée Chrétienne: Newman Théologien', *Revue de l'Université d'Ottawa*, xvi (1946) 65*–89*, 129*–153*.

Landgraf, A. 'Scattered Remarks on the Development of Dogma and on Papal Infallibility in Early Scholastic Writings', *TS*, vii (1946) 577–82.

Laros, M. 'Kardinal Newmans Okumenische Sendung', *Festgabe Joseph Lortz*. I. *Reformation, Shicksal und Auftrag*, 469–80. Ed E. Iserloh and P. Manns. Baden-Baden 1958.

Lash, Nicholas L. A. 'Dogmas and Doctrinal Progress', *Doctrinal Development and Christian Unity*, 3–33. Ed Nicholas Lash. London 1967.

His Presence in the World. London 1968.

'Second Thoughts on Walgrave's "Newman" ', *DR*, lxxxvii (1969) 339–50.

'The Notions of "Implicit" and "Explicit" Reason in Newman's University Sermons: A Difficulty', *HJ*, ix (1970) 48–54.

'Can a Methodologist Keep the Faith?', *Irish Theological Quarterly*, xxxviii (1971) 91–102. Lash [1971a].

'Development of Doctrine: Smokescreen or Explanation?', *New Blackfriars*, lii (1971) 101–8. Lash [1971b].

'Faith and History: Some Reflections on Newman's "Essay on the Development of Christian Doctrine" ', *Irish Theological Quarterly*, xxxviii (1971) 224–41. Also published in French in *Istina*, xviii (1973) 6–24. Lash [1971c].

'De Ontwikkeling van het Geloofsdenken', *Tijdschrift voor Theologie*, xi (1971) 52–65. Lash [1971d].

Change in Focus: A Study of Doctrinal Change and Continuity. London, 1973.

Latourelle, René. 'Le Christ Signe de la Révélation Selon la Constitution "Dei Verbum" ', *Gregorianum*, xlvii (1966) 685–709. Latourelle [1966a].

'La Révélation et sa Transmission Selon la Constitution "Dei Verbum" ', *Gregorianum*, xlvii (1966) 5–40. Latourelle [1966b].

de Lavalette, H. 'Bulletin de Théologie Historique et Dogmatique. I Autour de Newman', *RSR*, li (1963) 463–8.

Layman, A. *Anglo-Romanism Unveiled: Or, Canon Oakeley and Dr Newman at Issue with the Catholic and Roman Church, and with One Another. A Letter Addressed to the Rev W. J. Irons*. London 1866.

Lebreton, Jules. 'Autour de Newman', *Revue Pratique d'Apologétique*, iii (1907), 488–504. Lebreton [1907a].

'Chronique Théologique', *Revue Pratique d'Apologétique*, v (1907) 279–89. Lebreton [1907b].

Lengsfeld, Peter. 'La Tradition dans le Temps Constitutif de la Révélation', in *MS* 2 [1969] 11–68. Lengsfeld [1969b].

'Tradition et Ecriture: Leur Rapport', *ibid* 270–305. Lengsfeld [1969b].

Leonard, Augustin. 'La Foi Principe Fondamental du Développement du Dogme', *RSPT*, xlii (1958) 276–86.

Le Roy, Edouard. *What is a Dogma?* Chicago 1918. (First published as 'Qu'est-ce qu'un Dogme?', *La Quinzaine*, 16 April 1905).

Leuba, Jean-Louis. 'La Tradition à Montréal et à Vatican II: Convergences et Questions', *Vatican II: La Révélation Divine*, ii, 475–97. Paris 1968.

Liddon, Henry Parry. *Life of Edward Bouverie Pusey*. 4 vols, London 1893.

Lilley, A. L. *Modernism: a Record and Review*. London 1908.

Lilly, William Samuel. *The Great Enigma*. London 1892.

Lindbeck, George A. 'The Problem of Doctrinal Development and Contemporary Protestant Theology', *Concilium*, i, 3 (1967) 64–72.
The Future of Roman Catholic Theology. London 1970.

Linnan, John E. 'The Search for Absolute Holiness: A Study of Newman's Evangelical Period', *Ampleforth Journal*, lxxxiii (1968) 161–74.

Loisy, Alfred Firmin. A. Firmin. 'Le Développement Chrétien d'après le Cardinal Newman', *Revue du Clergé Français*, xvii (1898) 5–20.
A. Firmin. 'La Théorie Individualiste de la Religion', *Revue du Clergé Français*, xvii (1899) 202–15. Loisy [1899a].
A. Firmin. 'La Définition de la Religion', *Revue du Clergé Français*, xviii (1899) 193–209. Loisy [1899b].
A. Firmin. 'L'Idée de la Révélation', *Revue du Clergé Français*, xxi (1900) 250–71. Loisy [1900a].
A. Firmin. 'Les Preuves et l'Economie de la Révélation', *Revue du Clergé Français*, xxii (1900) 126–53. Loisy [1900b].
A. Firmin. 'La Religion d'Israel', *Revue du Clergé Français*, xxiv (1900) 337–63. Loisy [1900c].
A. Firmin. *L'Evangile et l'Eglise*. Paris 1902.
Autour d'un Petit Livre. Paris 1903.
Simples Réflexions sur le Décret du Saint-Office 'Lamentabili Sane Exitu' et sur l'Encyclique 'Pascendi Dominici Gregis'. Privately printed 1908.

Lonergan, Bernard J. F. *Insight: A Study of Human Understanding*. London 1957.
Conceptio Analogica Divinarum Personarum. ²Rome 1959.
'The Dehellenization of Dogma', *TS*, xxviii (1967) 336–51. Lonergan [1967a].
'Dimensions of Meaning', *Collection*, 252–67. London 1967. Lonergan [1967b].
'Theology in its New Context', *Theology of Renewal*. I. *Renewal of Religious Thought*. 34–46. Ed L. K. Shook. New York 1968.
Doctrinal Pluralism. Milwaukee 1971.

Loome, Thomas Michael. 'The Enigma of Baron Friedrich Von Hügel—as Modernist', *DR*, xci (1973), 13–34, 123–40, 204–30.

de Lubac, Henri. 'Bulletin de Théologie Fondamentale. Le Problème du Développement du Dogme', *RSR*, xxxv (1948) 130–60.
'Commentaire du Préambule et du Chapitre I', *Vatican II: La Révélation Divine*, i, 157–302.
La Foi Chrétienne: Essai sur la Structure du Symbole des Apôtres. Paris 1969. de Lubac [1969a]
The Sources of Revelation. Trans Luke O'Neill. New York, 1969. (First published as *L'Ecriture dans la Tradition*. Paris 1967). de Lubac [1969b].

Lynch, T., ed. 'The Newman-Perrone Paper on Development', *Gregorianum*, xvi (1935) 402–47.

McCloy, S. T. *Gibbon's Antagonism to Christianity*. London 1933.

McCue, James F. 'The Roman Primacy in the Second Century and the Problem of the Development of Dogma', *TS*, xxv (1964) 161–96.

McDonald, Hugh Dermot. *Ideas of Revelation: an Historical Study, ad 1700 to ad 1860*. London 1959.
   Theories of Revelation: an Historical Study 1860–1960. London 1963.

MacDougall, Hugh A. *The Acton-Newman Relations: The Dilemma of Christian Liberalism*. New York 1962.
   'Newman—Historian or Apologist?', *Journal of the Canadian Historical Association*, (1968) 152–63.

McGrath, Fergal. 'The Conversion', in Tierney [1945] 57–83.
   Newman's University: Idea and Reality. London 1951.
   The Consecration of Learning. Dublin 1962.

McGrath, Mark G. *The Vatican Council's Teaching on the Evolution of Dogma*. Rome 1953.

MacKinnon, Donald M. *Borderlands of Theology, and Other Essays*. London 1968.
   'Introduction' to *Newman's University Sermons*, 9–23. London 1970.

MacLaughlin, P. J. 'Newman and Science', in Tierney [1945] 307–36.

Maguire, R. *The 'Oxford Movement': Strictures on the 'Personal Reminiscences' and Revelations of Dr Newman, Mr Oakeley, and Others*. London 1855.

Manning, Henry Edward. *Religio Viatoris*. ³London 1888.

Marin-Sola, F. *L'Evolution Homogène du Dogme Catholique*. 2 vols, Fribourg 1924. (First published as *La Evolucion del Dogma Catolico*. Valencia 1923).

Mathew, David. *Lord Acton and his Times*. London 1968.

Maurice, Frederick Denison. *The Epistle to the Hebrews; Being the Substance of Three Lectures with a Preface Containing a Review of Mr Newman's Theory of Development*. London 1846.

May, J. Lewis. 'Quis Desiderio—' in *JHN* [1945] 92–100.

Middleton, R. D. *Newman and Bloxam*. Oxford 1947.
   Newman at Oxford: His Religious Development. London 1950.

Milman, Henry Hart. 'Newman on the Development of Christian Doctrine', *Quarterly Review*, lxxvii (1846) 404–65.

Minon, A. 'L'Attitude de Jean-Adam Moehler (1786-1838) dans la Question du Développement du Dogme', *ETL*, xvi (1939) 328–82.

Misner, Paul. 'John Henry Newman on the Primacy of the Pope', Unpublished Dissertation, Munich 1968.
   'Newman's Concept of Revelation and the Development of Doctrine', *HJ*, xi (1970) 32–47.

Mivart, St. G. J. 'The Catholic Church and Biblical Criticism' *Nineteenth Century*, xxii (1887) 31–51.

Moberley, George. *The Sayings of the Great Forty Days Between the Resurrection and Ascension, Regarded as the Outlines of the Kingdom of God; in Five Discourses; with an Examination of Mr Newman's Theory of Developments.* ³London 1846.

Moberly, Robert Campbell. 'The Incarnation as the Basis of Dogma', *Lux Mundi*, 158–200. Ed Charles Gore. ¹⁵London 1904.

Moeller, Charles. 'Tradition et Oecuménisme', *Irénikon*, xxv (1952), 337–70.

Morley, John. *The Life of William Ewart Gladstone.* 2 vols, London 1908.

Mozley, Anne, ed. *Letters and Correspondence of John Henry Newman During his Life in the English Church.* 2 vols, London 1891. *Moz* i, ii.

Mozley, James Bowles. 'The Recent Schism', *Christian Remembrancer*, xi (1846) 167–218. Mozley, J. B. [1846a].
'The Church of England Cleared From the Charge of Schism', *Christian Remembrancer*, xii (1846) 377–97. Mozley, J. B. [1846b].
'Newman on Development', *Christian Remembrancer*, xiii (1847) 117–265.
'Dr Newman's Grammar of Assent', *Lectures and Other Theological Papers*, 275–300. London 1883. (First published in *Quarterly Review*, July 1870).
'The Roman Council', *Sermons Preached Before the University of Oxford and on Various Occasions*, 1–24. ⁶London 1886. (Sermon preached 7 November 1869).

Muirhead, John H. *The Platonic Tradition in Anglo-Saxon Philosophy.* London 1931.

Murphy, John L. 'The Influence of Bishop Butler on Religious Thought', *TS*, xxiv (1963) 361–401.

Murray, Placid, ed. *Newman the Oratorian. His Unpublished Oratory Papers.* Dublin 1969.

Murray, Robert, and J. Derek Holmes, eds. *On the Inspiration of Scripture.* By John Henry Newman. London 1967.

Murray, Robert. 'Who or What is Infallible?', in *Inf* [1968] 26–46.
'How Did the Church Determine the Canon of Scripture?', *HJ*, xi (1970) 115–26.

Mysterium Salutis: Dogmatique de l'Histoire du Salut. Paris 1969. I/1 *Histoire du Salut et Révélation*; I/2 *La Révélation dans l'Ecriture et la Tradition*; I/3 *L'Eglise et la Transmission de la Révélation.* *MS* 1, 2, 3, [1969].

Nédoncelle, Maurice. *Baron Friedrich von Hügel: a Study of his Life and Thought.* Trans Marjorie Vernon. London 1937.

Nédoncelle, Maurice—*continued*.

'Le Drame de la Foi et de la Raison dans les Sermons Universitaires de J. H. Newman', *Etudes*, ccxlvii (1945) 66–83.

La Philosophie Religieuse de John Henry Newman. Strasbourg 1946.

'L'Influence de Newman sur "Les Yeux de la Foi" de Rousselot', *Revue des Sciences Religieuses de l'Université de Strasbourg*, xxvii (1953) 321–32.

'Newman et le Développement Dogmatique', *ibid*, xxxii (1958) 197–213.

'La Suprématie Papale d'après L'*Essai sur le Développement* de Newman', *Parole de Dieu et Sacerdoce*, 139–52. Tournai 1962.

'Newman et Blondel: la Théologie des Développements Doctrinaux,' in *NS* [1964] 105–22.

'The Revival of Newman Studies—Some Reflections', *DR*, lxxxvi (1968) 385–94.

'Newman on the Development of Christian Doctrine'. Anon, *Dublin University Magazine*, xxvii (1846) 105–15.

Newman-Studien. Ed Heinrich Fries and Werner Becker. Vols 2,3,5,6,7. Nürnberg 1948–1970. *NS* [1954, 57, 62, 64, 67].

Newsome, David. *The Parting of Friends: a Study of the Wilberforces and Henry Manning*. London 1966.

'The Evangelical Sources of Newman's Power', in Coulson [1967] 11–30.

'Newman and the Oxford Movement', in Symondson [1970] 71–89.

Nicholls, David. 'Newman's Anglican Critics', *Anglican Theological Review*, xlvii (1965), 377–95.

'Developing Doctrines and Changing Beliefs', *Scottish Journal of Theology*, xix (1966) 280–92.

Nicolas, M.-J. 'Le Théologien et l'Histoire', *Revue Thomiste*, lx (1960) 485–508.

Northcote, J. Spencer. *The Fourfold Difficulty of Anglicanism: or, the Church of England Tested by the Nicene Creed. In a Series of Letters*. London 1846.

Novak, Michael. 'Newman on Nicaea', *TS*, xxi (1960).

Oakeley, Frederick. *The Claim to 'Hold, as Distinct From Teaching', Explained in a Letter to a Friend*. London 1845. Oakeley [1845a].

A Letter on Submitting to the Catholic Church. Addressed to a Friend. ²London 1845. Oakeley [1845b].

Popular Lectures. Lecture ii. *Personal Reminiscences of the 'Oxford Movement', With Illustrations From Dr Newman's 'Loss and Gain'*. London 1855.

Historical Notes on the Tractarian Movement (AD 1833–1845). London 1865.

O'Carroll, Michael. 'Our Lady in Newman and Vatican ii', *DR*, lxxxix (1971) 38–63.

O'Connell, Matthew J. 'The Development of Dogma', *Mission and Witness*, 261–72. Ed Patrick J. Burns. London 1965.

O'Foalain, Sean. *Newman's Way*. London 1952.

Ollard, S. L. *A Short History of the Oxford Movement*. London 1915.

Ong, Walter. 'Newman's Essay on Development in its Intellectual Milieu', *TS*, vii (1946) 2–45.

Orr, James. *The Progress of Dogma*. London 1901.

Pailin, David A. *The Way to Faith. An Examination of Newman's Grammar of Assent as a Response to the Search for Certainty in Faith.* London 1969.

Palmer, William (of Worcester College). *A Treatise on the Church of Christ: Designed Chiefly for the Use of Students in Theology.* 2 vols, London 1838.

  A Narrative of Events Connected With the Publication of the Tracts For the Times, With Reflections on Existing Tendencies to Romanism, and on the Present Duties and Prospects of Members of the Church. Oxford 1843.

  The Doctrine of Development and Conscience Considered in Relation to the Evidences of Christianity and of the Catholic System. London 1846.

Pannenberg, Wolfhart, ed. *Revelation as History*. Trans David Granskou and Edward Quinn. London 1969. (First published as *Offenbarung als Geschichte*. Göttingen 1961).

  'The Crisis of the Scripture Principle', *Basic Questions in Theology*, i, 1–14. Trans George H. Kehm. London 1970. (Original version first published as 'Die Fragwurdigkeit der Klassischen Universalwissenschaft [Evangelische Theologie]', *Die Krise des Zeitalters der Wissenschaften*, 173–88. Frankfurt 1963). Pannenberg [1970a]

  'Redemptive Event and History', *ibid* i, 15–80. (First published in *Kerygma und Dogma*, v [1959], 218–37, 259–88). Pannenberg [1970b].

  'What is a Dogmatic Statement?' *ibid* i, 182–210. (First published in *Kerygma und Dogma*, v [1962], 81–99). Pannenberg [1970c].

  'The Working of the Spirit in the Creation and in the People of God', in Pannenberg [1970e] 13–31. Pannenberg [1970d].

Pannenberg, Wolfhart, Avery Dulles and Carl E. Braaten eds. *Spirit, Faith and Church*. Philadelphia 1970. Pannenberg [1970e].

Parker, T. M. 'The Tractarians' Successors: the Influence of the Contemporary Mood', in *Id* [1966] 120–5.

  'The Rediscovery of the Fathers in the Seventeenth-Century Anglican Tradition', in Coulson [1967] 31–49.

Pattison, Mark. *Memoirs*. London 1885.

Pelikan, Jaroslav. *Development of Christian Doctrine: Some Historical Prolegomena.* London 1969.

  Historical Theology: Continuity and Change in Christian Doctrine. London 1971.

Philbin, William J. 'The Essay on Development', in Tierney [1945] 116–43.

Polanyi, Michael. *The Tacit Dimension*. London 1967.

Poschmann, Bernhard. *Penance and Anointing of the Sick*. Trans Francis Courtney. London 1963. (First published as *Busse und Letzte Olung*. Freiburg, 1951).

de la Potterie, I. 'La Vérité de la Sainte Ecriture et l'Histoire du Salut d'après la Constitution Dogmatique "Dei Verbum" ', *NRT*, lxxxviii (1966) 149–69.

Potts, Timothy C. 'What Then Does Dr Newman Mean?', in *NS* [1964] 55–81.

Poulat, Emil. *Histoire, Dogme et Critique dans la Crise Moderniste*. Tournai 1962.

Pozo, Candido. 'Development of Dogma', *Sacramentum Mundi*, ii, 98–102. New York 1968.

Price, H. H. *Belief*. London 1969.

Prickett, Stephen. 'Coleridge, Newman and F. D. Maurice: Development of Doctrine and Growth of the Mind', *Theology*, lxxvi (1973) 340–9.

Przywara, Erich. 'Newman—Möglicher Heiliger und Kirchenlehrer der Neuen Zeit?', in *NS* [1957] 28–36.

Purcell, Edmund Sheridan. *Life of Cardinal Manning, Archbishop of Westminster*. 2 vols, London 1895.

Quick, Oliver Chase. *Liberalism, Modernism and Tradition*. London 1922.

[Quondam Disciple, A]. *Mithridates: or, Mr Newman's Essay on Development its Own Confutation*. London 1846.

Rahner, Karl. 'The Development of Dogma', *Theological Investigations*, i, 39–77. Trans Cornelius Ernst. London 1961. (Trans of 'Zur Frage der Dogmenentwicklung', *Schriften zur Theologie*, i, 49–90. Einsiedeln 1954).

'Forgotten Truths Concerning the Sacrament of Penance', *ibid*, ii, 135–74. Trans Karl-H. Kruger. 1963. (Trans of 'Vergessene Wahrheiten Uber das Buss-Sakrament', *ibid*, ii, 143–83. 1955).

'Considerations on the Development of Dogma', *ibid*, iv, 3–35. Trans Kevin Smyth. 1966. (First published as 'Uberlegungen zur Dogmenentwicklung', *Zeitschrift für Katholische Theologie*, lxxx [1958] 1–16). Rahner [1966a].

'Virginitas in Partu', *ibid*, iv, 134–62. (First published as 'Virginitas in Partu: Ein Beitrag zum Problem der Dogmenentwicklung und Uberlieferung', *Kirche und Uberlieferung*, 52–80. Ed J. Betz and H. Fries. Freiburg 1960). Rahner [1966b].

'Theology in the New Testament', *ibid*, v, 23–41. Trans Karl-H. Kruger. 1966. (Trans of 'Theologie im Neuen Testament', *Schriften zur Theologie*, v, 33–53. Einsiedeln 1962). Rahner [1966c].

Rahner, Karl—*continued*.

'Exegesis and Dogmatic Theology', *ibid*, v, 67–93. (Trans of 'Exegese und Dogmatik', *ibid*, v, 82–111. 1962). Rahner [1966d].

'History of the World and Salvation-History', *ibid*, v, 97–114. (Trans of 'Weltgeschichte und Heilsgeschichte', *ibid*, v, 115–35. 1962). Rahner [1966e].

'What is a Dogmatic Statement?', *ibid*, v, 42–66. (Trans of 'Was ist Eine Dogmatische Aussage?', *ibid*, v, 54–81. 1962). Rahner [1966f].

'Observations on the Concept of Revelation', *Revelation and Tradition*, 9–25. By Karl Rahner and Joseph Ratzinger. Trans W. J. O'Hara. New York 1966. (First published in *Offenbarung und Uberlieferung*. Freiburg 1965). Rahner [1966g].

Rahner, Karl, and Lehmann, Karl. 'Les Modes de Transmission de la Révélation. II. Kérygme et Dogme', in *MS* 3, [1969] 183–280. (Partial English edition available as *Kerygma and Dogma*. Trans William Glen-Doepel. New York 1969). Rahner [1969a].

and Lehmann, Karl. 'L'Historicité de la Transmission', in *MS* 3 [1969] 317–82. Rahner [1969b].

Rahner, Karl. 'Pluralism in Theology and the Unity of the Church's Confession of Faith', *Concilium*, vi, 5 (1969) 49–58. Rahner [1969c].

'Schism in the Church?', *The Month*, xlii (1969) 242–56. Rahner [1969d].

Rambaldi, G. 'Immutabilita del Dogma e della Formole Dogmatiche', *Gregorianum*, xxxiii (1952) 58–84.

Rashdall, Hastings. *Doctrine and Development*. London 1898.

Ratzinger, Joseph. 'Revelation and Tradition', and 'On the Interpretation of the Tridentine Decree on Tradition', *Revelation and Tradition*, 26–49, 50–68. By Karl Rahner and Joseph Ratzinger. Trans W. J. O'Hara. New York 1966. (First published in *Offenbarung und Uberlieferung*. Freiburg 1965).

'Dogmatic Constitution on Divine Revelation', *Commentary on the Documents of Vatican* II, iii, 155–98, 262–72. Ed H. Vorgrimler. Fribourg 1969.

Reade, F. V. 'The Sentimental Myth', in *JHN* [1945] 139–54.

Reardon, Bernard M. G., ed. *Roman Catholic Modernism*. London 1970. *From Coleridge to Gore: a Century of Religious Thought in Britain*. London 1971. Reardon [1971a].

'Newman and the Catholic Modernist Movement', *Church Quarterly*, iv (1971) 50–60. Reardon [1971b].

Rich, Edward Charles. 'The Idea of Doctrinal Development', *Eastern Churches Quarterly*, xii (1958), 221–7.

Richard, R. L. 'Rahner's Theory of Doctrinal Development', *Proceedings of the Eighteenth Annual Convention, Catholic Theological Society of America*, 157–89. New York 1963.

'Contribution to a Theory of Doctrinal Development', *Spirit as Inquiry*.

Richard, R. L.—*continued*.
Studies in Honor of Bernard Lonergan, 205–27. Ed Frederick E. Crowe. *Continuum*, ii, 3 (1964).

Rivière, J. 'Newman Apologiste', *Revue des Sciences Religieuses*, vi (1926) 394–410.
Le Modernisme dans l'Eglise. Paris 1929.

Roberts, T. A. *History and Christian Apologetic*. London 1960.

Robinson, J. 'Newman's Use of Butler's Arguments', *DR*, lxxvi (1958) 161–80.

Rogers, Patrick. 'Anglican Background', in Tierney [1945] 1–26.

Rondet, Henri. *Les Dogmes Changent-ils?* Paris 1960.

Rose, Hugh James. *The State of the Protestant Religion in Germany*. Cambridge 1825.

Rousselot, Pierre. 'Petite Théorie du Développement du Dogme', *RSR*, liii (1965) 355–90.

Rupp, Gordon. 'Newman Through Nonconformist Eyes', in Coulson [1967] 195–212.

Sabatier, Auguste. *The Vitality of Christian Dogmas and Their Power of Evolution*. Trans Mrs Emmanuel Christen. London 1898.

Sabatier, Paul. *Les Modernistes*. Paris 1909.

Sanday, W. *England's Debt to Newman*. Oxford 1892.

Sanders, Joseph Newbould. 'The Meaning and Authority of the New Testament', in Vidler [1966] 125–42. (First published 1962).

Sarolea, Charles. *Cardinal Newman and his Influence on Religious Life and Thought*. Edinburgh 1908.

Sartory, Thomas. 'Reunion of Christians Despite Catholic Dogmas?', *JES* i (1964) 82–98.

Schillebeeckx, Edward. 'Revelation, Scripture, Tradition, and Teaching Authority', *Theological Soundings*. 1/1. *Revelation and Theology*, 3–26. Trans N. D. Smith. London 1967. (First published as 'Openbaring, Schriftuur, Traditie en Leergezag', *Kerk en Theologie*, xiv [1963] 85–99). Schillebeeckx [1967a].
'The Development of the Apostolic Faith into the Dogma of the Church', *ibid* 63–92 (First published as 'Dogma-ontwikkeling', *Theologisch Woordenboek*, i, cols. 1087–1106. Roermond 1952). Schillebeeckx [1967b].
'The Bible and Theology', *ibid*, 184–214. (First published as 'Exegese, Dogmatik und Dogmenentwicklung', *Exegese und Dogmatik*, 91–114. Ed H. Vorgrimler. Mainz 1962). Schillebeeckx [1967c].
'The Creed and Theology', *ibid* 223–39 (First published as 'Symbolum', *Theologisch Woordenboek*, iii, cols 4449–4460. Roermond 1952). Schillebeeckx [1967d].

Schlette, Heinz Robert. 'Dogmengeschichte und Geschichtlichkeit des Dogmas', *Münchener Theologische Zeitschrift*, xiv (1963) 243–52. *Epiphany as History*. Trans N. D. Smith. London 1969.

Schlink, Edmund. 'The Structure of Dogmatic Statements as an Ecumenical Problem', *The Coming Christ and the Coming Church*, 16–84. Trans G. Overlach and D. B. Simmonds. Edinburgh 1967. (First published as 'Die Struktur der Dogmatischen Aussage als Oekumenisches Problem', *Kerygma und Dogma*, iii [1957]).
'Ecriture, Tradition et Magistère selon la Constitution Dei Verbum', *Vatican* ii: *La Révélation Divine*, ii, 499–511. Paris 1968.

Schoof, Mark. *Breakthrough: Beginnings of the New Catholic Theology*. Trans N. D. Smith. Dublin 1970. (First published as *Aggiornamento*. Baarn 1970).

Schoonenberg, Piet. 'Historicity and the Interpretation of Dogma', *Theology Digest*, xviii (1970) 132–43. (English digest of 'Historiciteit en Interpretatie van het Dogma', *Tijdschrift voor Theologie*, viii [1968] 278–311).

Schultes, R. M. *Introductio in Historiam Dogmatum*. Paris 1922.

Schulz, Winfried. *Dogmenentwicklung als Problem der Geschichtlichkeit der Warheitserkenntnis*. Rome 1969.

Schutz, Roger and Max Thurian. *Revelation: a Protestant View*. Trans Kathryn Sullivan. Westminster, Maryland 1968. (First published as *La Parole Vivante au Concile*. Taizé 1966).

Scott, Thomas. *Essays on the Most Important Subjects in Religion*. London 1806. (First published 1793).
The Force of Truth: an Authentic Narrative. London 1824. (First published 1779).

Scott, William. 'The Notion of Tradition in Maurice Blondel', *TS*, xxvii (1966) 384–400.

Sewell, W. *The Plea of Conscience for Seceding from the Catholic Church to the Romish Schism in England. A Sermon Preached Before the University of Oxford, Nov 5, 1845*. Oxford 1845.

Seynaeve, Jaak. *Cardinal Newman's Doctrine on Holy Scripture*. Louvain 1953.

Sheets, John R. 'Teilhard de Chardin and the Development of Dogma', *TS*, xxx (1969) 445–62.

Sheridan, Thomas L. *Newman on Justification. A Theological Biography*. New York 1967.

Sillem, Edward A. 'Cardinal Newman's "Grammar of Assent" on Conscience as a Way to God', *HJ*, v (1964) 377–401.
The Philosophical Notebook of John Henry Newman Ed Edward Sillem. i. *General Introduction to the Study of Newman's Philosophy*. Louvain 1969.

Sillem, Edward A.—*continued*.
  ed. *The Philosophical Notebook of John Henry Newman*. Ed Edward Sillem and revised A. J. Boekraad. II *The Text*. Louvain 1970.

Simonin, H. D. 'La Théologie Thomiste de la Foi et le Développement du Dogme', *Revue Thomiste*, xviii (1935) 537–56.
  ' "Implicite" et "Explicite" dans le Développement du Dogme', *Angelicum*, xiv (1937) 126–45.

de Smet, W. 'L'Influence de Butler sur la Théorie de la Foi chez Newman', in *NS* [1964] 21–38.

Smith, B. A. *Dean Church. The Anglican Response to Newman*. London 1958.

Smith, William Robertson. 'The Fulfilment of Prophecy', *Lectures and Essays of William Robertson Smith*, 253–84. Ed John Sutherland Black and George Chrystal. London 1912.

Smyth, Charles. *Church and Parish*. London 1955.

Sontag, F. 'Continuity and Change in Theological Formulation', *HJ*, vii (1966) 43–51.

Sorel, G. *Reflections on Violence*. Trans T. E. Hulme. New York 1912. (First published as *Réflexions sur Violence*. 1906).

Spencer, Herbert. 'Progress: its Law and Cause', *Essays on Education and Kindred Subjects*, 153–97. London 1966. (First published in the *Westminster Review*, April 1857).

Spiazzi, R. 'Rivelazione Compiuta con la Morte degli Apostoli', *Gregorianum*, xxxiii (1952) 24–57.

Springer, H. 'Quelques Aspects des Rapports entre les Sciences et la Foi dans l'Oeuvre du Cardinal Newman', *NRT*, lxxxv (1963) 270–9.

Stark, Werner. 'The Social Philosopher: Essay on Development of Christian Doctrine', in Tierney [1945] 155–77.

Stephenson, Anthony A. 'The Development and Immutability of Christian Doctrine', *TS*, xix (1958) 481–532.
  'Cardinal Newman and the Development of Doctrine', *JES*, iii (1966) 463–85.
  'Cardinal Newman's Theory of Doctrinal Development: Reply', *JES*, v (1968), 370–7.

Stern, Jean. 'Traditions Apostoliques et Magistère selon J. H. Newman', *RSPT*, xlvii (1963) 35–57.
  'La Controverse de Newman avec l'Abbé Jager et la Théorie du Développement', in *NS* [1964] 123–42.
  Bible et Tradition chez Newman: aux Origines de la Théorie du Développement. Paris 1967.

Stewart, Dugald. *Elements of the Philosophy of the Human Mind*. 3 vols, London 1792, 1814, 1827. Stewart [1814].

Storr, Vernon F. *The Development of English Theology in the Nineteenth Century: 1800–1860*. London 1913.

Svaglic, Martin J., ed. *Apologia pro Vita Sua: being a History of his Religious Opinions*. By Cardinal John Henry Newman. Oxford 1967.

Symondson, Anthony, ed. *The Victorian Crisis of Faith*. London 1970.

Tardivel, Fernande. 'L'Art du Penseur, à propos de Newman', in *NS* [1957] 62–76.

Tavard, George H. *Holy Writ or Holy Church*. London 1959.
'Scripture and Tradition: Source or Sources?', *JES*, i (1964) 445–59.
'Commentary on *De Revelatione*', *JES*, iii (1966) 1–35.

Taymans, F. 'Le Progrès du Dogme', *NRT*, lxxi (1949) 687–700.

'The Theory of Doctrinal Development'. Anon, *Biblical Review and Congregational Magazine*, i (1846) 182–91.

Thils, Gustave. 'L'Evolution du Dogme dans la Théologie Catholique', *ETL*, xxviii (1952) 679–82.
'Le Décret "Lamentabili Sane Exitu" et la Convergence des Probabilités', *ETL*, xxxii (1956) 65–72.
'Autour de Newman', *ETL*, xxxiii (1957) 348–55.
L'Infaillibilité Pontificale: Sources—Conditions—Limites. Gembloux 1969.

Thompson, Edward Healy. *Remarks on Certain Anglican Theories of Unity*. London 1846.

Thureau-Dangin, Paul. *The English Catholic Revival in the 19th Century*. 2 vols, London 1914.

Thurian, Max. 'Renewal and the Scripture-Tradition Problem in the Light of Vatican ii and Montreal 1963', *Theology of Renewal. i. Renewal of Religious Thought*, 66–82. Ed L. K. Shook. New York 1968. Thurian [1968a].
and Roger Schutz. *Revelation: a Protestant View*. Trans Kathryn Sullivan. Westminster, Maryland 1968. Thurian [1968b].

Tierney, Michael ed *A Tribute to Newman: Essays on Aspects of his Life and Thought*, Dublin 1945. Tierney [1945].
'Catholic University' in Tierney [1945] 172–206. Tierney [1945a].

Tillotson, Geoffrey. 'Newman's Essay on Poetry', in *JHN* [1945] 178–200.

Toulmin, Stephen. *The Uses of Argument*. Cambridge 1964. (First published 1958).

Trethowan, Illtyd and Alexander Dru, eds; cf Dru [1964].

Trevor, Meriol. *Newman: The Pillar of the Cloud*. London 1962.
Newman: Light in Winter. London 1962.
Prophets and Guardians: Renewal and Tradition in the Church. London 1969.

Tristram, Henry. 'Two Leaders: Newman and Carlyle', *Cornhill Magazine*, lxv (1928) 367–82.
and Francis Bacchus. 'Newman (John-Henry)', *Dictionnaire de Théologie Catholique*, xi, cols 327–98. Paris 1931.

Tristram, Henry—*continued*.
'Cardinal Newman and the Dublin Review', *Du R*, cxcviii (1936) 221–34.
ed. 'Cardinal Newman's Theses de Fide and his Proposed Introduction to the French Translation of the University Sermons', *Gregorianum*, xviii (1937) 219–60.
'J. A. Moehler et J. H. Newman', *RSPT*, xxvii (1938) 184–204.
'The Classics', in Tierney [1945] 246–78. Tristram [1945a].
'With Newman at Prayer', in *JHN* [1945] 101–26. Tristram [1945b].
'In the Lists with Abbé Jager', *ibid* 201–22. Tristram [1945c].
'On Reading Newman', *ibid* 223–41. Tristram [1945d]
ed. *John Henry Newman. Autobiographical Writings*. London 1956.

Tyrrell, George. *Lex Orandi, or Prayer and Creed*. London 1903.
Through Scylla and Charybdis. London 1907.
Medievalism: a Reply to Cardinal Mercier. London 1909.
Christianity at the Cross-Roads. London 1913.

Van der Plancke, C. 'J. H. Newman, Révélation et Tradition. Etude sur les Rapports Doctrinaux entre la Théologie de Newman et la Constitution "Dei Verbum"'. Unpublished Dissertation, Louvain 1969.

Van Leeuwen, Peter. 'The Genesis of the Constitution on Divine Revelation', *Concilium*, i, 3 (1967) 4–10.

Van Ruler, A. A. 'The Evoluton of Dogma', *Christianity Divided* 89–105. Ed Daniel J. Callahan, Heiko A. Obermann, Daniel J. O'Hanlon. London 1961.

Vargish, Thomas. *Newman: The Contemplation of Mind*. Oxford 1970.

Vatican Council II. *Constitutio Dogmatica de Divina Revelatione*. Vatican City 1965. [*Dei Verbum*].
Constitutio Dogmatica de Ecclesia. Vatican City 1964. [*Lumen Gentium*].

Veiga Coutinho (da), L. *Tradition et Histoire dans la Controverse Moderniste. Analecta Gregoriana 73*. Rome 1954.

Venards, Louis. 'La Valeur Historique du Dogme', *Bulletin de Littérature Ecclésiastique de Toulouse*, v (1904) 338–57.

Vidler, Alec R. *The Modernist Movement in the Roman Church*. Cambridge 1934.
ed *Soundings: Essays Concerning Christian Understanding*, Cambridge 1966. Vidler [1966].
'Appended Note on "Authority" and "Liberty" in the Church', in Vidler [1966] 142–5. Vidler [1966a].
'The Tractarian Movement, Church Revival and Reform', in *Id* [1966] 113–19. Vidler [1966b].
A Variety of Catholic Modernists. Cambridge 1970.

Vollert, Cyril. 'Doctrinal Development: a Basic Theory', *Proceedings of the Catholic Theological Society of America*, (1957) 45–70.

Vorgrimler, Herbert, ed. *Commentary on the Documents of Vatican* II. 5 vols, Fribourg 1967–9. (First published as *Das Zweite Vatikanische Konzil: Dokumente und Kommentare*. Fribourg 1966–8).

Voss, G. 'Johannes Adam Möhler and the Development of Dogma', *TS*, iv (1943) 420–44.

Walgrave, Jan-H. *Newman the Theologian*. Trans A. V. Littledale. London 1960. (First published as *Newman: Le Développement du Dogme*. Tournai 1957).
'L'Originalité de l'Idée Newmanienne du Développement', in *NS* [1964] 83–96. Walgrave [1964a].
'Preface' to *J. H. Cardinal Newman: Essai sur le Développement de la Doctrine Chrétienne*, 7–48. Paris 1964. Walgrave [1964b].
Unfolding Revelation: The Nature of Doctrinal Development. London, 1972.

Ward, Josephine. 'Introductory Study', *Last Lectures by Wilfrid Ward*, vii–lxxi. London 1918.

Ward, Maisie. *The Wilfrid Wards and the Transition*. II. *Insurrection versus Resurrection*. London 1937.
Young Mr Newman. London 1948.

Ward, Wilfrid. *William George Ward and the Oxford Movement*. London 1889.
'New Wine in Old Bottles', *Witnesses to the Unseen, and Other Essays*, 68–96. London 1893. Ward, W. [1893a].
'Some Aspects of Newman's Influence', *ibid*, 97–118. (First published in *Nineteenth Century*, xxviii [1890], 563–74). Ward, W. [1893b].
'Philalethes: Some Words on a Misconception of Cardinal Newman', *ibid*, 119–55. (First published in *Contemporary Review*, lx [1891] 32–51). Ward, W. [1893c].
The Life and Times of Cardinal Wiseman. 2 vols, London 1897.
'Liberalism and Intransigeance', *Nineteenth Century*, xlvii (1900) 960–73.
'Newman and Sabatier', *Fortnightly Review*, lxxv (1901) 808–22.
'The Time-Spirit of the Nineteenth Century', *Problems and Persons*, 1–65. London 1903. (First published in *Edinburgh Review*, cxciv [1901] 92–131). Ward, W. [1903a].
'Unchanging Dogma and Changeful Man', *ibid* 99–132. (First published in *Fortnightly Review*, lxxiii [1900], 628–48). Ward, W. [1903b].
'Two Mottoes of Cardinal Newman', *ibid*, 260–82. (First published in *Fortnightly Review*, lxxiv [1900], 39–51). Ward, W. [1903c].
'Newman and Renan', *ibid*, 283–300. Ward, W. [1903d].
'Newman Through French Spectacles', *The Tablet*, cviii (1906) 86–9.
'Two Views of Cardinal Newman', *Du R*, cxli (1907) 1–15.
'John Henry Newman: an Address', *Ten Personal Studies*, 218–59. London 1908. Ward, W. [1908a].
'Newman and Manning', *ibid*, 260–98. (First published in *Quarterly Review*, ccvi [1907], 354–83). Ward, W. [1908b].

Ward, Wilfrid—*continued.*

The Life of John Henry Cardinal Newman. Based on his Private Journals and Correspondence. 2 vols, London 1912.

'Cardinal Newman's Sensitiveness', *Men and Matters*, 273–89. London 1914. (First published in *Du R*, cl [1912] 217–29). Ward, W. [1914a].

'The Conservative Genius of the Church: an Address to the Catholic Conference of 1900', *ibid*, 301–18. Ward, W. [1914b].

'Cardinal Newman on Constructive Religious Thought', *ibid*, 347–91. Ward, W. [1914c].

'The True Nature of Newman's Genius. A Criticism of Popular Misconception', *Last Lectures by Wilfrid Ward*, 1–149. London 1918. Ward, W. [1918a].

'On the Methods of Depicting Character in Fiction and Biography', *ibid*, 150–220. Ward, W. [1918b].

'Oxford Liberalism and Dogma', *ibid*, 276–90 (First published in *Fortnightly Review*, cii [1914], 29–40). Ward, W. [1918c].

Ward, William George. *The Ideal of a Christian Church Considered in Comparison With Existing Practice, Containing a Defence of Certain Articles in the British Critic in Reply to Remarks on Them in Mr Palmer's 'Narrative'.* London 1844.

'*Doctrinal Developments*', *Du R*, xxii (1847) 325–54. Ward, W. G. [1847a].

'Mr Brownson on Developments', *Du R*, xxiii (1847) 373–405. Ward, W. G. [1847b].

On Nature and Grace. London 1860.

'Theories on Developments of the Faith', *Du R*, NS xii (1869) 28–70.

'Catholic Devotion to Our Blessed Lady', *Essays on Devotional and Scriptural Subjects*, 1–104. London 1879. (First published 1866).

Essays on the Church's Doctrinal Authority. London 1880.

Webb, C. C. J. *Religious Thought in the Oxford Movement.* London 1928.

Weiler, Anton. 'Church History and the Reorientation of the Scientific Study of History', *Concilium*, vii, 6 (1970) 13–32.

Whately, Richard. *The Errors of Romanism Traced to Their Origin in Human Nature.* London 1830.

'Rhetoric', *Encyclopaedia Metropolitana: Or, System of Universal Knowledge: On a Methodical Plan Projected by Samuel Taylor Coleridge.* ²London 1849.

Wheeler, T. S. 'Newman and Science', *Studies*, xlii (1953) 179–96.

White, J. N. D. *John Henry Newman.* London 1925.

Whyte, Alexander. *Newman: an Appreciation in Two Lectures with the Choicest Passages of his Writings Selected and Arranged.* Edinburgh 1901.

Wicker, Brian. 'Newman and Logic', *NS* [1962] 251–68.

Widmer, G. P. 'Quelques Réflexions d'un Point de Vue Réformé sur la Constitution Conciliaire "Dei Verbum"' *Irénikon*, xlii (1969) 149–76.

Wiles, Maurice. *The Making of Christian Doctrine: a Study in the Principles of Early Doctrinal Development*. Cambridge 1967.

Willam, Franz Michel. 'Aristotelische Bausteine der Entwicklungstheorie Newmans', *NS* [1964] 193–226.
Vom Jungen Angelo Roncalli (1903–1907) zum Papst Johannes XXIII *(1958–1963)*. Innsbruck 1967.
Die Erkenntnislehre Kardinal Newmans: Systematische Darlegung und Dokumentation. Frankfurt 1969.

Willey, Basil. 'Origins and Development of the Idea of Progress', in *Id* [1966] 39–45.
Nineteenth-Century Studies. Coleridge to Matthew Arnold. London 1969. (First published 1949).

Williams, Isaac. *The Autobiography of Isaac Williams*. Ed Sir George Prevost. London 1892.

Williams, W. J. *Newman, Pascal, Loisy and the Catholic Church*. London 1906.

Wiseman, Nicholas. 'Anglican Claim of Apostolical Succession', *Du R*, v (1838) 285–309.
'Anglican Claim of Apostolical Succession', *Du R*, vii (1839) 139–80.

Wordsworth, Christopher. *Letters to M. Gondon, Author of 'Mouvement Religieux en Angleterre', 'Conversion de Soixante Ministres Anglicans', etc, on the Destructive Character of the Church of Rome, Both in Religion and Policy*. London 1847.

Young, G. M. *Daylight and Champaign*. London 1948. (First published 1937).

Indexes

Index of Newman References

With the exception of *1878*, to which reference is made by section and sub-section, the figures in the left-hand column indicate the page-number of the work in question.

1878

2.1.5–6	64
2.1.5	32, 84, 99, 100, 131, 135
2.1.6	88, 99
2.1.7	64
2.1.8–13	32
2.1.8–9	110, 162
2.1.8	29, 111, 119
2.1.9	84, 95, 99, 110, 177, 180, 190
2.1.10	111, 189
2.1.11	72
2.1.12	77, 78, 111
2.1.13	43, 162
2.1.14	58, 88, 94, 110, 190
2.1.15	89–90
2.1.16	74, 99, 143, 180, 200
2.1.17	32, 38, 119, 162
2.2	39, 76, 130
2.2.1–4	195
2.2.1–2	68
2.2.1	36, 118, 119, 134
2.2.2	43, 85, 99, 195
2.2.3	24, 99, 118, 123, 131, 166, 175
2.2.4	130, 195
2.2.5	12, 99, 119
2.2.8	99, 190
2.2.9–10	111
2.2.10	39, 161, 186, 207
2.2.11	99, 195
2.2.12	39, 88, 99
2.2.13	39, 85, 97, 130
2.2.14	20, 22, 23
2.3	16
2.3.1–2	99
2.3.1	99, 119, 167–8, 177, 180
2.3.2	40, 95, 99, 119, 177, 201
2.3.4	15, 143, 172
2.3.5	9, 43, 96, 120, 171
3	20, 30
3.1	83
3.1.1	16, 66, 86, 96, 119
3.1.2–3	160
3.1.2	36, 37, 119, 190
3.1.3	23, 84, 182
3.1.4	93, 109–10
3.1.5–6	110
3.1.6	93, 110, 185
3.1.7	82, 177

3.1.8–10	95
3.1.9	38, 73, 189
3.1.10	95
3.2.1–4	22, 25
3.2.1–2	36, 166
3.2.1	25, 31, 187–8
3.2.2	26, 99
3.2.3	26, 160
3.2.4	26, 73, 163
3.2.5	31, 36, 81, 83
3.2.11	31, 86
3.2.12	33, 178
4	20, 30, 39
4.0.1	30, 103, 106, 189
4.0.2	160, 189
4.1.3	84, 129, 187, 189
4.1.4	78, 101, 104, 189
4.1.5	189
4.1.6	189
4.1.7	78, 135, 189
4.1.8	87–8, 104, 189
4.1.10	168
4.1.11	23, 84, 159
4.2	66
4.2.1	66, 101
4.2.3	103–4
4.2.4	104
4.2.6	101
4.2.8	84
4.2.11	101
4.3	66
4.3.1–7	175
4.3.1–4	195
4.3.1–3	112
4.3.1	101, 112
4.3.2	207
4.3.3	112, 208
4.3.4	22, 189, 208
4.3.5	208
4.3.6	208
4.3.7	40, 113, 191
4.3.8	39–40, 74, 180, 208
4.3.9	84, 90, 112, 190
4.3.17	83, 84, 104
5.0.1–4	116
5.0.1–2	117
5.0.1	66, 96, 117, 119, 193
5.0.2–4	180
5.0.2	117, 193
5.0.3	68, 71
5.0.4	71
5.1.1–9	138–9
5.1.1	66, 177, 179, 180

Index of Names

DATE DUE

JUN 2 78			
4-11-97			
NOV 20 97			
GAYLORD			PRINTED IN U.S.A.